William Cornelius Reichel

Historical Sketch of Nazareth Hall from 1755 to 1869

With an Account of the Reunions of former Pupils and of the Inauguration of a

Monument at Nazareth on the 11th of June, 1868

William Cornelius Reichel

Historical Sketch of Nazareth Hall from 1755 to 1869
With an Account of the Reunions of former Pupils and of the Inauguration of a Monument at Nazareth on the 11th of June, 1868

ISBN/EAN: 9783337253592

Printed in Europe, USA, Canada, Australia, Japan

Cover: Foto ©Lupo / pixelio.de

More available books at **www.hansebooks.com**

Nazareth Hall.

NAZARETH HALL, NORTHAMPTON CO., PA.

HISTORICAL SKETCH

OF

NAZARETH HALL

FROM 1755 TO 1869;

WITH AN ACCOUNT OF THE

REUNIONS OF FORMER PUPILS

AND OF THE

INAUGURATION OF A MONUMENT AT NAZARETH
ON THE 11TH OF JUNE, 1868

ERECTED IN MEMORY OF ALUMNI WHO FELL IN
THE LATE REBELLION

BY WILLIAM C. REICHEL

CLASS OF 1834.

———————

PRINTED FOR THE
REUNION SOCIETY OF NAZARETH HALL
BY J. B. LIPPINCOTT & CO. PHILADELPHIA.
1869.

LIPPINCOTT'S PRESS,
PHILADELPHIA.

TO ITS FORMER PUPILS,

THIS

HISTORICAL SKETCH OF NAZARETH HALL,

WHICH HAS EXISTED DURING A PERIOD OF MORE THAN
ONE HUNDRED YEARS,

Is Affectionately Dedicated.

PREFACE.

A RESOLUTION adopted by the "Union Society of Nazareth Hall," at its second meeting, on the 8th of June, 1855, recommended the publication of a "Historical Sketch of Nazareth Hall, from 1755 to 1855," prepared by Rev. Levin T. Reichel, a former principal of that institution, then of Salem, N. C. It was suggested, furthermore, to incorporate the acts of the reunions of former pupils with this narrative. Mr. Ernest F. Bleck, of Bethlehem, Pa., undertook the arrangement of the materials, and in the summer of 1855 the first edition of "Nazareth Hall and its Reunions" appeared, at the expense of a member.

A desire expressed by its Alumni to possess an authentic account of the eight reunions held during the past twelve years, and of the proceedings of the 11th of June, 1868, which day witnessed the inauguration of a monument erected in memory of such former pupils of the institution as had fallen fighting for their country and its constitutional liberties during the late rebellion, was the occasion of this rewriting of "Nazareth Hall and its Reunions."

No funds having been provided for this purpose, and the balance remaining in the hands of the treasurer of the Monument Fund being sufficient only for the stereotype plates, the cost of printing this volume has been defrayed by the same member of the Society who issued the edition of 1855.

7

The writer has made a few additions to, but no material alterations in, Mr. Reichel's outline history. The facts bearing on the reunions have been reproduced as faithfully as possible from the Minute Book of the Society, and from the chronicles of its authorized historians. To the accounts of reporters of various public journals present on the occasion he is indebted for the data on which is based the narrative of the Reunion of June 11, 1868, and of the proceedings at the inauguration on that day of a memorial in honor of patriotic sons of Nazareth Hall.

The catalogue of pupils and teachers is brought down in full to December 31, 1868, and personal notices have been amended wherever such change was rendered necessary by the vicissitudes which time and life bring with them.

W. C. REICHEL.

BETHLEHEM, PENNA., *February* 1, 1869.

NAZARETH HALL.

A FRAGMENT.

By the late Right Rev. W. H. Van Vleck, its Fifth Principal.

'Tis morn.   Behold! with early radiance crowned,
The king of day ascends the eastern sky,
Gilding with roseate hue the mountain-tops,
The footstool of his high cerulean throne.
He comes, once more, to rule this lower world,
And usher in another checkered day
Of hopes and fears, of pleasure and of toil ;
Arousing from the arms of sweet repose
To sweeter rambles in the flowery path
Of knowledge, all her youthful votaries,
The inmates of this academic dome.
Arise, my soul ! obey the bright behest,
And early pay the morning sacrifice !
Refresh'd with balmy sleep, that renovates
Both mind and body worn with daily toils
(Thanks to that Power divine, whose angel-guards
Their nightly vigils round my pillow kept),
I wander forth to breathe the vernal air,
And list the woodland warblers' matin song.
Yon verdant hill, that rises in the west,
Whose brow full many a sacred tomb adorns,
Invites my steps.   I gain the steep ascent,
And there, with mute, ineffable delight,
I gaze upon the scene that smiles around,
So oft admired, and yet for ever new.
All hail ! thou ancient, venerable pile,
Sacred to Him, who fills the heav'n of heav'ns,
And yet delights with mortal man to dwell ;
Whose glittering spire the sixteenth vernal sun

9

Now gilds, since erst within thy hallowed walls
My tender youth a sweet asylum found.
All hail ! thou cradle of my infant mind !
Where childhood, happiest age, with golden dreams
Full many a swift-revolving day beguiled.
Thou sacred roof, beneath whose ample shade
Two heaven-born sisters, *Art* and *Science,* dwell,
Where, deeply smitten with celestial charms
I learned to glow, and vowed allegiance true.
There first with rapt'rous eye, the page sublime
Of classic Rome and Greece I wandered o'er ;
Now dared, with venturous pencil, to portray
Fair Nature's smiling face in mimic hues,
Or from my youthful lyre, with trembling hand,
Unpractis'd, rude, discordant accents flung.
But ah ! far greater debt than mortal skill
Or human knowledge do I owe to thee,
Thou hallowed temple of the living God.
'Twas here my tender mind was first imprest
With Revelation's awful truths divine ;
'Twas here that on the darkness of my soul
First dawn'd Religion's doubt-dispelling ray,
And my enfranchis'd heart, with rapture fired,
Was taught to pray, to praise, and to adore !
Such is the vast amount for which I stand
Eternally indebted.   This the soil
Where once with care was sown what now I reap.
Hither my grateful thoughts shall e'er return ;
Nor absence, lapse of time, or change efface
What Gratitude has written in my breast.

NAZARETH, 1815.

NAZARETH HALL.

THE spot now crowned by the stately structure of Nazareth Hall was, a century ago, still covered with primeval forest, and its immediate vicinity, the abode of Delawares or Fork Indians, as they were commonly called in those days of the Province. Just without the limits of the present borough of Nazareth there was in 1740 a populous village of these aborigines, under the jurisdiction of one " Captain John," who perversely disputed the right of Moravian occupancy until the verdict of the Iroquois, his liege lords, compelled him to relinquish his obstinate tenure. The discomfited chieftain now built him a hut some miles to the north, near the " Deep Hole," on Lehietan Creek, and, burying past differences, brought his venison statedly to Bethlehem to market, until death overtook him in his woodland cabin in August of 1747. A Moravian carpenter at the Gnadenthal settlement (now the site of the county almshouse) made the coffin of the shrewd old Ishmaelite, who, in accordance with his dying request, was buried after the Christian mode of burial.

The Delawares called the Nazareth tract " Welagamika," or Fat Lands. The abundance of flint arrowheads

and of other implements of stone found there, even at this
late day, testifies to the fact that the neighborhood was a
favorite resort or rendezvous of Indians from the earliest
times; for year after year these historical monuments of
an almost extinct race are ploughed up, and it would appear as if the hidden store were inexhaustible.

Whitefield, in 1740 (then in the zenith of his activity
in the British Provinces of North America), purchased of
Mr. William Allen, merchant of Philadelphia, five thousand acres of land in the Forks of Delaware, which he
called Nazareth. This purchase is now embraced within
Upper Nazareth township. Here the great champion of
Calvinistic Methodism undertook the erection of a school
for negro orphans, and here he designed settling such of
his followers in England as might be compelled to leave
their country for conscience' sake. His plans, however,
were never consummated. The school (now the Whitefield House) was only in course of erection when, in 1742,
the death of Mr. William Seward, Whitefield's zealous
coadjutor, compelled him to relinquish the noble enter-
prise. Financially embarrassed, he was glad to convey
the entire tract to the Moravians at the cost price, the
latter reimbursing him for whatever he had expended in
improvements. The transfer was made in London in
1743, for the consideration of £2200.

This domain was known as the Barony of Nazareth,
and was nominally the property of Erdmuth Dorothea,
Countess of Zinzendorf. It had the right of court baron,
the only manor sold by the Penns with that privilege, and
was, and indeed is yet held, on the condition of rendering
service to them and their heirs by paying, if demanded, a
red rose in June of each year for ever. An humble hos-
telry on the northern outskirts of the tract, erected about
1752 for the entertainment of occasional wayfarers (which

a few years later became an asylum for fugitives from Indian barbarities on the frontiers of the province), had
emblazoned on its swinging sign, yet within the memory
of living men, the beautiful floral emblem of fealty, and
as the " Rose Tavern" has passed into colonial history.

Settlements were gradually made by the Moravians at
Ephrata (1743) and Old Nazareth (1744), both within
the present borough ; at Gnadenthal (1745) and Christian
Spring (1748) to the west, and Friedensthal (1750) to
the east, which, in 1754, together numbered two hundred and seventy-nine souls. The estate, however, was
without a manor-house, and the scattered tenants without
a place of worship easily accessible to all. This serious
inconvenience suggested the speedy erection, at some
central point, of a spacious building, with arrangements
to meet these urgent wants, and which, at the same time,
might accommodate Count Zinzendorf and a corps of
assistants, who were positively expected from Europe.
The erection of such a *stately* structure as the Hall was
doubtless determined in view of the Count's prospective
sojourn. This, however, he was never permitted to make.
Financial troubles in the Church detained him abroad,
and in 1760 death ended his memorable career. Zinzendorf's personal labors in the establishment of the American branch of the Brethren's Church were confined to
the year 1742. It was left for Spangenberg to work out
into history the field-notes taken by that master spirit in
his brief but eventful reconnoissance in the wilds of North
America.

The corner-stone of Nazareth Hall was laid on the
3d of May, 1755, in the presence of the inhabitants of
the adjacent settlements, and brethren from Bethlehem
and elsewhere. The Delaware and Mohican converts of
the Gnadenhutten Mission, on the Mahoney (established

2

in 1747, near Lehighton, Carbon county), were represented respectively by their elders, Anthony and Jacob.
With these came the missionaries Schmick and Fabri-
cius, contributing each an ode, composed for the occasion
in Indian. John Samuel, a native of the Malabar coast,
and Andrew and Joseph, negroes from Africa, by their
presence characterized the gathering as an extraordinary
one. It was, in fact, an unpremeditated exposition of
Moravian missionary activity and success in the four quarters of the globe. The opening exercises of the festive
day were held on the green, before the stone house at
Ephrata, which the first handful of Moravian pioneers in
Pennsylvania had commenced to erect for Whitefield in the
summer of 1740, and were conducted by Bishop Augustus
G. Spangenberg, of Bethlehem. In the course of these, he
communicated the various papers which were to be deposited within the corner-stone. They comprised :

1. A document drawn up in Latin by Rev. F. C.
Lembke, pastor of the Moravians on the Nazareth Tract,
setting forth the design of the building in course of
erection, and such historical facts as had a bearing on
the occasion.

2. A catalogue of all Moravians belonging to the
" Bethlehem Economy" or communism, including those
resident at Bethlehem, Nazareth, Christian Spring, Gnadenthal, Friedensthal, and Gnadenhutten on the Mahoney ; and also such as were engaged as home missionaries in the colonies or on the foreign mission in the
West Indies and South America (both of which fields
were at this time under the immediate jurisdiction of, and
supplied with laborers by, the presiding Board at Bethlehem), showing a sum-total of one thousand and thirty-
four souls.

3. The act of the English Parliament of 1749, which

acknowledged the episcopacy of the Unitas Fratrum, or Ancient Church of the United Brethren.

4. Two German hymn-books.

5. An ode, written in German for the occasion, by Bishop Matthew Hehl.

These introductory services having been concluded, the congregation, headed by a corps of musicians and the clergy, moved in procession to the site of the proposed building. The ceremony of laying the corner-stone was conducted by the pastor and Bishop Spangenberg, assisted by Mr. C. Schulze, the master mason. The stone is a limestone of the neighborhood, four and a half feet long, eighteen inches broad, and fourteen inches thick, and lies two feet underground in the north-east angle of the building. In the afternoon, a love-feast was celebrated on the lawn before the Whitefield House, on which occasion Rev. Peter Boehler narrated his personal recollections of the commencement of Nazareth in 1740. He had led the first Moravians into Pennsylvania from Georgia ; had contracted in their behalf with Whitefield for the erection of his proposed school ; had prospected the tract with Mr. Henry Antes, of Frederic township (now Montgomery county), in May of the year ; and on the 30th of the same month had for the first time held divine service for his little flock under an oak, which he pointed out, not far off, to his interested audience.

The solemnities of this memorable day were closed by an evening service, in which the inhabitants of Nazareth and its dependencies participated.

The building, thus auspiciously begun, was brought under roof within five months ; and it was a matter of special thankfulness to Providence, on the part of the Moravians, that the work suffered from no serious interruptions, and was attended by no accident. Those who have remarked the solidity of its masonry and the compact joining of its staunch timbers, (both of which promise to outlive many generations of men to come) express surprise at the industry and skill of the workmen, who amid the multifarious labors of a self-dependent settlement, so speedily erected this noble old structure on the outskirts of Pennsylvania civilization.

A portentous time was now at hand; and a cloud rose on the north-western horizon, which soon burst in fury over the devoted province, bringing ruin and death to hundreds of its isolated and unprotected settlers. The French and Indian war was inaugurated in the summer of 1755, and in the autumn of the year Eastern Pennsylvania became the theatre of its atrocities. Along the whole extent of its western frontier, in the valley on this side of the Kittatinny or "Endless Mountains," from the Maryland line to the Delaware, (where hardy Scotch-Irish and Germans had wielded the axe and guided the plough since 1730,) the horrors of Indian warfare were transforming the homes of rural peace into universal desolation. Burning tenements and smouldering ruins, the scalped corpses of defenceless women and children, and the mutilated carcasses of dumb animals marked the path of the bloody marauders. In the night of the 24th of November the mission-house on the Mahoney was surprised by a party of Shawnese, eleven of its inmates butchered, and the entire settlement laid in ashes. Words are inadequate to convey the panic which now seized the frontier population. Their only safety lay in flight; and in this dark day in the history of the province, the well-ordered Moravian settlements on the Nazareth Tract and at Bethlehem proved her bulwark, and hundreds of her defenceless inhabitants fled to them as to cities of refuge. Bethlehem was palisaded, and the Rose and the Fried-

ensthal mill. garrisoned as for a siege. It was a time of harrowing uncertainty, and for almost a year the Brethren were disconcerted in their secular and ecclesiastical enterprises. Thus it happened that the manor-house on the Nazareth Tract was not completed until in November of 1756. on the 13th day of which month the chapel on the first floor was solemnly dedicated to the worship of God by Bishops Spangenberg and Hehl. Here the Nazareth congregation worshiped until the completion of the church erected in 1841 (now the parochial school), during the pastorate of the Rev. Samuel Reinke.

During the century of its existence, the Hall has at different times undergone changes in the details of its interior arrangements, as well as externally. In June of 1785 it was surmounted with a belfry, ball and vane. The hollow ball contains a document giving a short historical account of the origin of the neighboring settlements. In 1796 a terrace constructed on the roof enabled the eye for the first time to take in the lovely landscape which stretches around the old manor-house with never-tiring charms. In December of the same year the belfry was furnished with a clock, the workmanship of Mr. Joseph Eberman, of Lancaster, Penna., which, until 1841, notified the inhabitants of the village, as well as the inmates of the house, of the hours of the day and their quarters. The old bell, with its devout inscription, " *Deo soli gloria*," still rings where it rang at first. The clock does duty on the Nazareth Church.

On the purchase of Nazareth Hall by its Board of Trustees in 1841, the building was entirely renovated. Since 1785 it had been used as a boarding-school for boys, and the wear and tear of more than half a century in such service told fearfully on the interior woodwork. Those who were inmates of the institution at that period

doubtless remember the polished slide down the stairways ;
the steps and floors. heart-of-oak as they were, worn hollow by the incessant fall of feet, and like indications elsewhere of a long-sustained and nobly-contested siege against
tide and time.   The improvements made in the above-
mentioned year, both within and without, (for a coat of
cream-colored cement was given to the gray limestone
masonry, and a belfry of more recent model supplanted
the one of 1785), modernized the Hall completely.   From
time to time lesser changes have been made in the internal
arrangements of the old manor-house, which deserve no
especial notice here.   Some of these may be remembered
by its whilom denizens, others forgotten ; and yet the
character of the entire building, its beautiful symmetry
of outline and sterling solidity of structure, will doubtless
be ever present in the memories of its alumni, involun-
tarily suggestive of the character of the education given .
within its walls, whose intrinsic worth and salutary influences were first appreciated when in later years they
engaged in the battle of life.

Transcript of the Latin Document Deposited in the Corner-stone.

Quod Deus Triunus
in Christo Jesu, Universi Conditore
Mundique per Sanguinem secum Salvatore
pie colendus,
foveat, juvet ac felix omnino esse jubeat !
Anno post nativitatem Christi
M D C C L V.,
quo uterque terrarum Orbis Illius patuit Evangelio
et quoad magnam satis partem Optimi ejusdemque grandævi
præ ceteris Principis *Georgii II.* paret Imperio
primo *Roberti Hunteri Morris*, Equitis,
Præfectura in Pennsylvania Anno
his in Baronia Nazareth ponendis Fundamentis operam adhibuere
Fratres.

Lapidemque collocaverunt Angularem
Viris—ex celebri Bethlehem Municipe ex quo ceu
Columbario in omnes Americæ evolant Regiones redeuntque
Evangelistæ Fratres,
admodum Reverendis *Josepho*, Ordinarii Unitatis
Fratrum vicario generali per Americam,
Petro et *Matthæo*, Episcopis,
Andr. Ant. Lawatsch et Gottlieb Bezold, Presbyteris, et
Martino Mack, Indorum Evangelista,
acclamante omni fere, qui Bethlehem, Nazareth,
Gnadenthal, Christiansbrunn et Friedensthal
inhabitant Fratrum et Sororum grege,
Indis etiam non nullis, immo pueris et puellis,
simul orantibus, et Fratribus præterea non solum in
Europa et America, sed et in Asia et Africa natis,
præsentibus ;
solemnique huic Actui *Tertium Mensis Maji*
condixere Diem, Charactero Domini :
" Ancipitem habet, quo omnia penetrat, gladium ;"
Verbis Magistri :
" Cui, futuri seculi ut consors sit, continget ;
post omnes in Cœlitum Familia superstes erit acomes ;"
Ecclesiæ Symbolo :
" In Te omnes Terrarum benedicentur Gentes ;"
insignum felicia quavis præsagientem Fata
superstruendæ hisce Fundamentis Domus, quæ
Cultui Concionibusque dicata est sacris,
destinata simul
(utinam cito nobis advolaret !)
Usibus
Unitatis Fratrum Ordinarii,
immo Philadelphiæ Ecclesiæ, quæ hoc præsertim tempore floret, et in
Cruce Christi gloriatur, Angeli, quem cum lectissima Conjuge
Erdmuth Dorothea,
ex Illustrissima Ruthenorum Comitum Prosapia, exoptatissimo Ge-
nero, *Johanne*, Congregationum ex Gentilibus Ordinarii vices gerente,
Filiabus, Nepote ac nepte omni veneratione prosequitur ac pietate
Totus Unitatis Populus,
cujus de Jesu Christo, Testimonio ita adfuit Dominus, ut non solum
Europa Doctrina salutari gaudeat, et Ecclesiolis in Morte Christi glori-

antibus redundet, sed et America, tam quod Insulas quam quod Contin-
entem adtinet, repleta sit Gregibus, in Christo Pastore exultantibus,
Indis etiam, qui in servitute atrocissima gemunt,
nunc Evangelio imbutis,
Facit Universi Deus,
Dominus Jesus Christus, Paterque familias noster alme nobis prospi-
ciens, ut in quovis hujus Domus sibi sacræ
Angulo exoptatissima Ipsius Præsentia,
Patris Christi et nostri mirifica pro familia Filii sui cura,
Spiritus Sancti, Almæ Matris nostræ, in
formandis, præparandis, ornandisque.
Virginibus, Sponsisque cœlestis et æterni Sponsi,
Labor indefatigabilis
Sentiatur et percipiatur,
Utque hoc ratione Doctrina σωτηριας
Sacramentis divini fœderis
Ordinibus sanctissimis
Precibus ardentissimis
Theocratia augustissima
et Ecclesiæ Dei, et permultorum hominum
prospiciatur Saluti ;
indique Evangelistarum catervæ in quascunque
Orbis exeant Regiones !
Hocce Votum
Votis jam multorum Christi Fratrum
Sororumque addit et
Inscriptioni
monumentis hujus
(sit ære perennius !)
inscrit
Franciscus Chr. Lembke
p. t. in Nazareth.
Ordinarius.

Previous to 1759, up to which time the authorities of
the Church had not fully decided to what permanent use
to convert the large building intended for the seat of Zinzendorf and his collaborators, apartments in the Hall
were let to families, or reserved for the entertainment of
home missionaries returned from their stations, either to

report on their labors or to recuperate for a season in the society of friends.

In May of 1757 a synod of the Church held its sessions in the chapel on the first floor, and another in August of the same year. Such religious convocations were of frequent occurrence in those days; and their speedy repetition not calculated to derange or embarrass by multifarious legislation, as they were mainly intended for mutual encouragement in the work which the Church almost instinctively recognized as its allotted sphere. "We meet," said Spangenberg, "to cheer and strengthen each other in our communion with the Lord." The synod of May was numerously attended. There were one hundred and twelve members from Bethlehem alone; among these the wives of clerical brethren, whose personal labors in the Church constituted an interesting feature of the time, entitling them to participate to a certain extent in the deliberations of such assemblies. On the morning of the 5th of May this large delegation set out from Bethlehem in wagons, on horseback and on foot, convoyed by a party of convert Indians, and, as a pious chronicler of that day informs us, "under the escort of numerous holy angels." This was a necessary precaution, as but a few days before the French Indians had made inroads on the south side of the mountain, and the Friedensthal Mill and the Rose were again filled with panic-stricken fugitives. Bishop Spangenberg, who at this time had temporarily taken up his residence in the Hall, presided at this synod, as well as at the one convened in August. The uses to which the upper floors of the building could best be applied came up as a subject of deliberation in the sessions of the latter; and its conversion into a mission-house or rendezvous for such of the brethren and sisters as were laboring in neighborhoods destitute of the means of grace, (a home-mission

work of considerable magnitude, and which was conducted almost exclusively by the Moravians) was finally
adopted as a measure entirely in consonance with the design of its projectors. The tenor of this resolution was
however never carried into effect, for in 1759 Nazareth
Hall became the seat of a Moravian school, and has ever
since been an educational institution.

The Moravians, mostly of German origin, are a musical people ; and music, both vocal and instrumental, has
always been an element in their divine worship. The
Chapel in Bethlehem was provided with an organ and
stringed instruments for use on festive occasions. It was
only proper that the place of worship for Nazareth and
its dependencies should be supplied with the same aids to
devotion. Accordingly John G. Klemm,* an expert
organ-builder, originally from Dresden, was despatched
to the Hall, where, in the course of the year 1758, assisted by Mr. David Tanneberger, he completed an excellent instrument. The wood used in its erection was pro-
cured from Philadelphia. Valentine Haidt was likewise
an inmate of the Hall in the same year, engaged in embel-

---

* John Gottlob Klemm, born near Dresden in 1690, in which city he
learned organ-building, immigrated to this country in 1736, and first
settled in Philadelphia. In 1745 he removed to New York, and there
renewed his connection with the Brethren, whose infant association at
Herrnhut he joined in 1726. In 1757 he was admitted into the society
at Bethlehem, where, until his death in May of 1762, he was employed
in the construction of organs for several of their churches, as well as
smaller instruments for the chapels in the different "choir-houses."
Organs of his make are still in existence and known among Moravians
as " Tanneberger's ;" from the fact that Tanneberger, after Klemm's
decease, continued the business, the artistic details of which he had
learned from the old Dresden organ-builder. The instruments in the
churches at Nazareth and Litiz, Pa., are the workmanship of Tanneberger. The former was put up in Nazareth Chapel in 1792, and
dedicated on the 16th of December of that year.

lishing the prayer-hall on the second floor with scenes in the Redeemer's life, which are doubtless yet remembered by some of the pupils of the Hall, whom these mysterious relics of a "picture age" never failed to inspire with awe, as often as they were permitted to look upon the conceptions of the Moravian painter, in their dimly-lighted repository.*

The attention paid to the education of their children in well-conducted schools by the early Moravians of Pennsylvania (which led to the erection of boarding-schools in order to gratify a desire expressed by the public at large to participate in the advantages afforded by them to the young) was a consequence of the social system they had adopted for the successful extension of Christ's kingdom. They had come to Pennsylvania, taken up large tracts of land, laid out farms, and made settlements and built villages, approving themselves a peaceful and loyal population,

---

* Valentine Haidt, the painter, was born in 1700 in Dantzig, and educated in Berlin, where his father was goldsmith to the court. In 1714 young Haidt went to Dresden to enter upon the study of the art he purposed making his profession. After a sojourn in Venice and Rome he repaired to Paris, and thence to London, where in 1724 he married Catherine Compigni. His acquaintance here with the Moravians in Fetter Lane led to his joining their society. In 1740 he went to Herrnhaag, in Western Germany, where, during the prevalence of the almost sensuous spirit of devotional excess which characterized that settlement, he was engaged to execute a series of historical paintings on New Testament subjects relating to the sufferings of Christ. Haidt made similar contributions to the chapels in Herrnhut, London and Bethlehem. Portraits by him of clergymen and missionaries, prominent in the American Brethren's Church in the middle of the last century, are preserved in the archive-rooms at Bethlehem. In 1754 Haidt was called to Pennsylvania. For fourteen months he preached for the Moravians in Philadelphia, was also employed as a home missionary. and passed his remaining years between the pulpit and the easel. On the 11th of June, 1774, he celebrated his golden wedding at Bethlehem. Here he died on the 18th of January, 1780.

whose industry contributed in fair proportion to the prosperity of the province. But they had not come for self-
aggrandizement ; nor were they adventurers nor refugees
from religious persecution. It was a noble idea, and a
holy wish, which impelled the tide of Moravian immigra-
tion to the Western world. Word had been brought
them of the degraded condition of the Indians and of the
religious destitution of hundreds of the immigrants from
abroad ; and this was sufficient to stimulate the smallest
of the churches of Protestant Christendom to immediate
and strenuous efforts in behalf of a two-fold mission,
which enlisted its deepest sympathies. They entered
the field opened to them in Pennsylvania in 1741 ; and
the history of their activity in the cause of Christian phi-
lanthropy here, from that time till 1760, is the history, not
of a Missionary Church, but of a Church of missionaries ;
in perusing which, the reader's attention is arrested by the
singular phenomenon of an entire society of men and
women engaged in preaching or teaching Christ to Indians in the wilderness, and to white men almost without
the pale of civilization.

The better to divest themselves of all secular embar-
rassments, the Brethren, on their firm establishment in
Pennsylvania, instituted a social system, which might not
incorrectly be called a communism of labor. The lands
were the property of the Church, and the farms and various departments of mechanical industry stocked by it and
worked for its benefit. Pecuniary compensation was unknown. On admission into this society, the candidate
pledged himself to devote his time and powers in whatever
direction they could be most advantageously applied for
the spread of the Gospel ; while the Church pledged her-
self in turn to provide him and those dependent on him
with the necessaries of life. These conditions exhausted

the contract. Whoever had means retained them; for there was no common treasury, as was the case among the primitive Christians. For upward of twenty years Bethlehem was the center of this "Economy," and the seat of the Board which controlled all its operations in North America, except on the missions in Greenland and Labrador.

It was this surrender of the means of individual support on the part of all its members which necessitated the Church to provide for the education of their children. As the life of the little commonwealth depended upon the harmonious co-operation of both clergy and laymen, the sons and daughters of both were alike cared for. Hence there was gradually developed a perfect system of educational institutions, graduated for children of all ages, both male and female. Provision was made even for infants; and the Whitefield House was the seat of a nursery in the interval between 1750 and 1764. No other testimony in support of the sincerity of a patriotism which made a sacrifice of feeling, such as this unnatural separation of parent and offspring involved, need be adduced.

The first Moravian school in Pennsylvania was opened in Germantown in 1742, in which the young Countess Benigna von Zinzendorf gave instruction during her father's sojourn in the country. Others well known were at Bethlehem and Nazareth, in Frederic (Montgomery county), in Oley, Tulpehocken and Heidelberg (Berks), in Warwick (Lancaster), in Maguntsche and Allemængel (Lehigh), and in York on the Codorus. Thus, it will be seen, ample provision was made for the children of the far-extended "Economy," and the Moravians unconsciously entered upon a new career of usefulness, which is now identified with their life and activity as a Church.

On the 6th of June, 1759, Nazareth Hall was opened as

3

a boarding-school for sons of Moravian parents, with ninety-two pupils, by a transfer thither of the Boys' Institute which had been in existence for upward of fifteen years in Bethlehem. Mr. J. C. Ekesparre and next Mr. T. Michael Graff, with nineteen assistants, managed its details. The abrogation of the Economy, initiatory steps to which were taken in the following year, rendering the existence of such an institution no longer a necessity, it now assumed the character of a more select school, and opportunities were even afforded for the training of assistants in the work of the ministry, who up to this time had been supplied by the European Church. Liberally educated tutors from abroad were accordingly provided, and in 1763 the Rev. F. C. Lembke, an able schoolman, appointed inspector or principal. In December of 1764 there were one hundred and six pupils, (in charge of sixteen teachers,) under his care, and one hundred and thirty-four persons resided in the building. From this time the number of pupils gradually diminished, owing in part to the establishment of day-schools in the different Moravian villages, and in part to the inability of the Church to meet the heavy expense of educating so many children and youth almost gratuitously. The pecuniary embarrassment furthermore in which she was involved, in consequence of her numerous and costly mission enterprises, rendered a system of rigid retrenchment in America, as well as in Great Britain and on the Continent, imperatively necessary. In 1769 the number of pupils in the Hall had diminished to sixty-seven, in 1770 to forty-five, and in 1779, on the transfer of the remaining eleven to Bethlehem, the first boarding-school at Nazareth Hall was closed.

During the next six years, the upper floors of the building were occupied as dwellings by Brethren employed in the service of the Church, or let to families.

On the opening of hostilities between Great Britain and France in their North American Colonies, the Moravians in Pennsylvania were gradually drawn out of the seclusion in which they had lived for upward of twenty years. Preferring at all times to prosecute their Christian labors unostentatiously in the spirit of their heavenly Master, it proved a sore trial when, on the outbreak of the Indian war, they suddenly found themselves objects of public interest. This was owing to the situation of their establishments on the confines of what was then the Indian country and to their reliable knowledge of, and experience in, Indian life and character, both of which circumstances they rendered subservient to the welfare of the province in those times of alarm and danger. The pacifying influence exerted by the Moravians over the exasperated Indians, the services rendered to the Crown both by themselves and their converts as scouts and on embassies, as well as the respect with which their well-ordered settlements had inspired even distant tribes of Indians, were recognized by the proprietaries' agents in letters to their employers abroad as bearing most favorably on the integrity of their interests.

Bethlehem and Nazareth, and its dependencies, were repeatedly converted into asylums for refugees from the "back country;" and through them lay the thoroughfare to the seat of war. Moravian institutions and Moravian manners and customs thus became generally known, and the public learned to appreciate what it had before misapprehended. The same thing occurred during the Revolutionary war; and so favorably were visitors impressed with the systematic details of Moravian education that they urged the Brethren to open their schools for the admission of the youth of the colonies generally.

This suggestion was favorably entertained, and laid

before the General Synod of the Church convened at Herrnhut, Saxony, in 1782, which body entrusted its development to Rt. Rev. John de Watteville, on his official visitation to the Moravian churches in North America, in the interval between 1784 and 1787. The result was the establishment of a boarding-school for boys in Nazareth Hall, in the autumn of 1785. The following prospectus was its announcement to the public:

" *Regulations adopted for the Pædagogium or Board- ing-school, about to be established by the United Brethren at Nazareth, in the County of Northamp- ton, in Pennsylvania.*

" 1. The principal intention of this Institution is to educate youth for the service of the Brethren's congregations. But since various persons of other denominations have repeatedly signified a wish to have their children educated by the Brethren, it has been resolved to admit also children of such parents, who, though not members of the Brethren's congregations, approve of their manner of instructing and educating youth, and are desirous to have them brought up in the nurture and admonition of the Lord, preserved from seduction and the prevailing vices of the age, and at the same time to become useful members of society.

" 2. The general direction of this Institution is lodged in the hands of the Elders and Teachers, who have the superintendence of all the congregations of the Brethren in Pennsylvania.

" 3. But the special care and management of this school is committed to the minister of the congregation at Nazareth, the Rev. Charles Gott- hold Reichel, as Inspector of said school. To him all those parents or guardians who desire to place their children or wards in the said school will make application in writing, giving notice at the same time of the age and capacity of the boy, what proficiency in learning he has already made, and (if he is above the age of ten years) what their intention with him may be relative to his future life ; also how many years they propose to leave him at this school. Such application will be con- sidered by the Directors of the Institution, and as soon as possible an answer will be given whether the request can be complied with or not.

"4. No boy under the age of seven years, and above the age of twelve years, can be admitted, some particular cases excepted.

"5. The usual time for admittance is in the beginning of the months of April and October.

"6. Boys who have already been seduced into sinful practices and irregularities cannot be admitted, and it is requested, where this is known, that no application may be made in their behalf. In like manner it is unavoidably necessary to reserve the liberty to return to their parents or guardians such scholars as shall be so unhappy as to come into and persevere in evil courses, and seduce others into sinful things. But in such cases previous notice will be given.

"7. Instruction will be given in this school in Reading, Writing, Arithmetic ; the English, German, Latin, French and Greek languages ; History, Geography, Mathematics, Music and Drawing.

"8. If it is desired that any scholar, besides the public lessons, shall have private instruction in any particular language or science, a separate consideration will be paid for the same, which, in every such case, will be settled beforehand with the parents or guardians.

"9. A particular attention will be paid that the scholars are constantly under inspection, not only in school hours, but also at all other times.

"10. A like regard will also be paid as well to their morals as to their health, by proper exercises, cleanliness and gentleness of deportment, etc.

"11. It is earnestly wished that the visits of the scholars to their parents, relations and friends, especially if they live at a considerable distance, may occur as seldom as possible, because they frequently dissipate the mind of youth and cause more damage than pleasure.

"12. Every scholar from six to twelve years of age pays for tuition, board, lodging, wood, etc., $66.66 per annum, and every scholar above twelve years $80. The payment to be made quarterly, the first quarter to be paid at the admittance of a boy, and so every quarter following.

"13. Besides the above, every scholar who comes to this school pays at his entrance one guinea, for the use of the library, procuring musical instruments, etc. If parents of property should find themselves inclined to add to this entrance money, it will be thankfully acknowledged.

"14. The diet of the boys is plain and wholesome. For breakfast, bread and butter and milk, now and then tea or coffee ; at dinner, boiled or roasted meat, with suitable vegetables ; for supper, bread and butter, milk, salad, etc.

3 *

" 15. Clothing, linen, bedding, books, medicine, etc., will be provided by the parents or guardians, or, if desired, by the Inspector of the school. An account of these extraordinary expenses will be sent in every quarter of a year, and it is expected that the payment will be made punctually and without delay.

" 16. All parents and guardians are requested to provide decent but plain clothes for the scholars, and to avoid all excess and vanity therein."

Nazareth Hall entered the ranks of American boarding-schools, under Moravian control, on the 3d of October, 1785. During a period of more than three-fourths of a century it has sustained its reputation for salutary discipline and well-grounded instruction; enjoying a fair proportion of the public confidence, as may be inferred from an inspection of its catalogue of pupils entered from the States, the Canadas, the West Indies and from abroad. Its concerns are managed by a Principal selected from the clergymen of the Church by a Board of Trustees, and its revenues are applied to Church purposes, to the maintenance of disabled clergymen or their widows, and to the education of their children. Thirteen principals have thus far presided over the Institution. The present incumbent is the fourteenth.

· Many of its former pupils doubtless at times, even amid the engrossing cares of business and the duties of life, revert to the years spent in the venerable Hall; or uncalled shadow-pictures of school-boy days move their memories to recall what to them is in the distant past. To aid all such in the interpretation of this hand-writing on the wall, the following sketch of the history of the school during its successive administration is here appended :

Plan of tl

laid out on a parcel of 600 ACI
and X
Surveyed ar

Spring

1736

Plan of the Moravian settlement,
NAZARETH,

laid out on a parcel of 600 ACRES of the Whitefield tract, between Old Nazareth and Nazareth Hall in Jan.ry of 1771

Surveyed and drawn September 30.th 1774.

N
W — E
S

Spring

Explanations
a Nazareth Hall 1755
b Brethren house 1773
c Store 1772
d House for the young men entered May 1774
e Spring supplying the aqueduct, constructed in 1772
f Graveyard, laid out 1756 for the use of Nazareth, Old Nazareth, Gnadenthal, Christansspring, Friedensthal & ... Settlements on the Upper Moravian tract in Northern Delaware. First buried Peter Lehnert Febr.y 14.th 1756.
g First house 1771

Old Nazareth Farm 1740

Road to Nazareth 1771

THE FOURTEEN PRINCIPALS OF NAZARETH HALL.

I.—REV. CHARLES G. REICHEL, 1785–1802.

Rev. C. G. Reichel, who had been appointed to superintend the projected boarding-school at Nazareth Hall, was graduated at the Moravian Theological Seminary in Barby, Saxony. He came to America in the autumn of 1784, and entered upon his duties as Inspector or Principal on the 3d of October, 1785. On this day eleven pupils from Bethlehem were admitted and given in charge of Mr. George G. Mueller* and Mr. Ludwig Huebner for tuition. The room in the north-west corner of the third floor was assigned them for a dwelling and for recitations, and the attic was their dormitory. Three families continued to reside in the Hall for some years, until an increase in the number of pupils necessitated their removal, and the entire building was appropriated to school purposes. The first boarder not of Moravian parentage was Joseph Shaw, of Philadelphia; one of the next was John Konkaput, a Housatonic Indian from Stockbridge, Mass., who was placed at the Institution by Government. Accessions from those of the West Indies, on which Moravian missions were located, now became frequent; and ever afterward sons of English and Danish planters from those islands were among the number of the inmates of the Hall. In 1791 there were three divisions or room-companies of pupils. In 1798 the number of boarders was forty-five. During Mr. Reichel's administration, of seventeen years, one hundred and sixty-three pupils were entered.

* Mr. Mueller, who accompanied Mr. Reichel to this country, was an able scholar, and father of Rev. G. Benjamin Miller, Professor of Theology in Hartwick Lutheran Seminary, N. Y. He died March 19, 1821, at Lititz, Pa.

The following was the day's order of recitations at this period :

From 7½ to 8½ A. M.—German and English Reading ; Grammar and History.

From 8½ to 9 A. M.—Children's meeting, a short devotional exercise, in English and German.

From 9 to 10 A. M.—Latin, Corn. Nepos and Gedike's Reader, Geography (Reichel's or Morse's United States), Natural History, with Seman's Text-Books.

From 10 to 11 A. M.—Arithmetic, Geometry, Book-keeping and Mathematical Geography.

From 2 to 3 P. M.—Writing and Drawing.

From 3 to 4 P. M.—French.

Strict attention was paid to the practical acquisition of both English and German, pupils being required to use one or other of the languages exclusively in their daily intercourse, as specified by their tutors. The first examination of classes open to the public was held in October of 1789.

On the 28th of August, 1786, a small park of fifty-five and a half perches was laid out to the left of the building, which has been gradually enlarged, planted with a variety of forest trees, shrubbery and wild flowers, and has been the favorite " shades of the Academy" for successive generations of its disciples.

The project of making the Hall exclusively a *boarding*-school, and of erecting a building for the use of the day scholars who frequented it, was entertained by the Principal, but not carried out.

In May of 1802 Mr. Reichel, after having been consecrated a Bishop, was called to Salem, N. C. (in which State the Moravians erected their first settlement in 1753), to the pastorate of that church, and chosen President of the Executive Board in the Southern Province. In April of 1811 he removed to Bethlehem, attended the General

Synod of the Church at Herrnhut in 1818, and thus closed his career in office. The remaining years of his life were spent in retirement in Nisky, in Lower Silesia, where he died April 18, 1825.

II.—REV. JACOB VAN VLECK, 1802–1809.

Mr. Van Vleck was a descendant of an old Dutch family in New York—one of a small circle of friends and admirers in that city which the first Moravians in this country drew around them. His father, Mr. Henry Van Vleck, a well-to-do merchant and partner in business of Mr. Thomas Noble, joined their Society in 1748, and placed his children in Moravian schools. Jacob was educated at Nazareth Hall with a view to the ministry, while Mr. Lembke was its Principal, and after completing a collegiate course went abroad to study theology in the Barby Seminary. He returned to America, after a seven-year's absence, in 1779, and soon after entered the ministry. Between 1790 and 1800 he conducted the Seminary for Young Ladies, at Bethlehem, opened there in October of 1785, by Rev. J. Andrew Huebner, and in 1802 was appointed Mr. Reichel's successor.

During his administration, one hundred and nine pupils were admitted, eighteen of whom only were Moravians. In consequence of this numerical preponderance, the English language entered more largely into the course of instruction pursued, and the scholastic arrangements were modified so as to accord more nearly with those in vogue at American schools of the day.

The heavy expense incurred in procuring classically-educated tutors from Germany now suggested the idea · of founding a Theological Seminary, in connection with the Hall, in which young men of the Church could be trained as instructors while pursuing their studies for the

c

ministry. This was carried into effect in 1807; and ever since the majority of teachers in the boarding-school at Nazareth have been candidates for the ministry and graduates of the Seminary. The three young men, Peter Wolle, Samuel Reinke and Wm. H. Van Vleck, thus educated, entered the Hall as tutors in 1809. The first two are at present living in retirement at Bethlehem, venerable bishops of the Church; the third, also a bishop, entered into the joy of his Lord in January of 1853.

In July of 1809 Mr. Van Vleck resigned his office, entering upon the pastorate of the Nazareth congregation. In 1811 he removed to Litiz, and in 1812 to Salem, N. C. He was consecrated bishop, at Bethlehem, in 1815; soon after retired from active service, and died July 3, 1831.

III.—Rev. Charles F. Seidel, 1809–1817.

Mr. Seidel, a graduate of the Moravian Theological Seminary at Nisky, Lower Silesia, came to Pennsylvania in 1806, and was at first engaged in the service of the Church in Salem, N. C. Here he married the daughter of Rev. C. G. Reichel, and in 1809 took charge of Nazareth Hall, whose concerns he conducted for eight years. A memorable day in his administration was the 3d of October, 1810, it being the twenty-fifth anniversary of the existence of the boarding-school, into which up to that time two hundred and ninety-five pupils had been admitted, and forty-four teachers employed. The occasion was observed with impressive festivities. The pupils ate for the first time in a common refectory in the basement, (meals having till then been served in the apartments of the several divisions): the Chapel was decorated (a pyramid, hung with twenty-five lamps, emblematic of the age of the institution, being a prominent feature); and a musical soirée enlivened the closing hours of the day.

On commencement or "public examination," in 1815, the Chapel (which since that time has witnessed the annual return of its festive paraphernalia) was trimmed with hemlock and spruce, and an obelisk in the centre of the hall, adorned with flowers and evergreens, set forth in ornamental characters the branches of education pursued. Among the audience on this occasion were the two former Principals of the Institution.

In 1817 Mr. Seidel was called to the pastorate of the Bethlehem congregation. As Principal of the Seminary for Young Ladies, at that place, he spent thirteen years of his active life. Until his seventy-eighth year he continued in the service of the Church, chiefly at Bethlehem, and latterly as a member of the Executive Board of the Province North. In 1855 he retired from official life, and died at Bethlehem April 26, 1861.

IV.—Rev. John C. Beckler, 1817–1822.

Mr. Beckler was of European birth and a graduate of the Moravian Theological Seminary at Nisky. He came to Pennsylvania in 1806, and from that year to 1812 was tutor at the Hall, and assistant Professor in the Theological Seminary. His first appointments in the ministry, for which he had studied, were in Philadelphia and on Staten Island. In the fall of 1817 he entered upon his duties as Principal of Nazareth Hall. During his administration, the present Principal's residence was built, his predecessors and their families having occupied apartments in the Hall. In 1820 the Theological Seminary was revived, with a class of three students of divinity.

In November of 1822 Mr. Beckler closed his connection with the school, having been called to the service of the Church at Litiz. From 1829 to 1836 he labored in

the ministry at Salem, N. C., having been consecrated a
bishop in that interval.

After the General Synod of the Church at Herrnhut in
1836, which he attended, a distant appointment to Sa-
repta, on the banks of the Wolga, in the Government of
Astracan, was allotted him. For ten years he was pastor
of the Moravian settlement there, established in 1765 as
the seat of a mission among the Calmuc Tartars.

After a brief term of service at Zeyst, near Utrecht.
Mr. Beckler went to Herrnhut into retirement, and deceased April 18, 1857.

V.—Rev. Wm. II. Van Vleck, 1822–1829.

Mr. Van Vleck was a son of the second Principal of
Nazareth Hall, in which Institution he had been educated
and been tutor, previous to his entrance into the ministry
in 1817. From the pastorate of the Moravian Church in
Philadelphia, his first charge, he was called to his Alma
Mater in December of 1822. Here he found his aged
father superintending the affairs of the school for a short
interim period, and only twenty-five pupils. There was,
however, a rapid increase in the number, owing largely to
his judicious management and personal address, and it
eventually rose to sixty-one. Want of suitable accommodations in the Hall compelled the Principal to vacate
apartments in his residence for the use of students of the
Theological Seminary.

In 1826 a love-feast *for the last time* closed the exercises
of the public examination.

In 1829 Mr. Van Vleck was appointed to New York
city, and was pastor of the Fulton street Moravian Church
until 1836. After his consecration to the episcopacy in
that year he removed to Salem, N. C., where he presided
over the deliberations of the Executive Board of the

Southern Province, and also labored in the ministry. In 1849 he was called to Bethlehem, and was senior pastor of the congregation until the day of his decease, January 29, 1853.

VI.—REV. JOHN G. HERMAN, 1829–1837.

The sixth Principal of Nazareth Hall was a native of Germany and graduate of the Moravian Theological Seminary at Nisky; came to this country in 1817, and after twelve years' service, in the ministry, both at Newport, in Philadelphia, and at Lancaster, entered upon his administration of that Institution. In 1833 he had seventy-three pupils, divided into five room-companies and in charge of nine teachers, under his care. Eight students of theology with their Professor occupied a small building near by (now known as " The Cottage"), which had been purchased by the school in 1830.

The fiftieth anniversary of the Hall, on the 3d of October, 1835, was impressively observed. In the afternoon the pupils, together with the inhabitants of the village, partook of a common love-feast in the Chapel; and after divine service the evening hours of that lovely October day were spent in the park, which was brilliantly illuminated with hundreds of colored lanterns suspended from the trees. At the upper end of the first walk stood an obelisk with the words of Scripture, " Hitherto the Lord hath helped us" and " Jesus Christ, the same to-day, yesterday and for ever," in transparency. On the following day, Rev. Wm. H. Van Vleck delivered a feeling discourse on the words of the Psalmist, " I have considered the days of old, the years of ancient times," in the course of which he referred to his past connection with the school as pupil, tutor and principal.

4

The number of pupils entered since 1785 amounted to *eight hundred and seventeen*, of whom

204 were from Philadelphia.
117   do.   the State of Pennsylvania.
159   do.   the City and State of New York.
53   do.   Baltimore.
82   do.   the West India Islands.
49   do.   Bethlehem.
18   do.   Nazareth.
14   do.   Litiz.
12   do.   Salem, N. C.
109   do.   other States of the Union, from Canada, the West Indies and from abroad.

In 1836, in a frame addition erected at the east end of the Hall, a commodious refectory was opened for the use of the household.

In January of 1837 Mr. Herman removed to Bethlehem, and was pastor of the congregation there till 1844. In this year he went to Europe, having been elected a member of the Unity's Executive Board, which has its seat near Herrnhut in Saxony. After his consecration to the episcopacy in 1846, he held an official visitation to several of the Missions in the West Indies, presided at the General Synod of 1848, and in the following year returned to America. The field of his labors was now in the Southern Province, having been appointed President of its Executive Board, located at Salem. In 1854 he undertook a visit to the mission among the Cherokees in the Indian Territory, on his return from which, while in Green co., Missouri, he was taken with malignant fever, and died on the 20th of July, in the sixty-sixth year of his age.

Mrs. Herman, the well-remembered mother of the large household, deceased Jan. 30th last, at Salem, N. C.

VII.—Rev. Charles A. Van Vleck, 1837–1839,

son of the second, and brother of the fifth Principal, received his classical and theological education at Nazareth Hall, and labored in the ministry successively at Bethania (near Salem), N. C., Newport, R. I., Lancaster and York, Penna.

In 1838 the Theological Seminary was translocated to Bethlehem, and Mr. Van Vleck appointed one of its professors in the following year.

In 1844 he accepted an invitation to take charge of a Female College in Greenville, Tenn., at which place he died December 21, 1845. His remains were taken to Salem, N. C., for interment.

VIII.—Rev. Charles F. Kluge, 1839–1844,

the eighth Principal of Nazareth Hall, is a graduate of the American Theological Seminary of his church. Having been engaged as tutor from 1821 to 1828, he was appointed Principal of the Seminary for Young Ladies at Litiz, and was subsequently pastor of the New York church, and warden of the Nazareth congregation.

During his administration several important changes bearing on the prosperity of the Hall, and conducive to the comfort of its pupils, were happily consummated. Board had up to this time been furnished from the Sisters' House near by, an arrangement which was attended with serious inconvenience, and not satisfactory. On the abrogation of that "Economy," a building adapted for kitchen purposes was built in the rear of the Hall in 1839, and board provided for the pupils under the direction of the wife of the Principal. About this time the Nazareth congregation engaged in the erection of a church, as the chapel in the Hall, which, as was stated, had been their place of worship since November of 1756, was no longer desirable as such. This induced its Board of Trustees to purchase Nazareth Hall building, and to subject it to thorough renovation, a work which was completed in 1841. Besides a more cheerful disposition of the interior arrangements, part of the Chapel was converted into a refectory, leaving a hall sufficiently large for the purposes of worship for the inmates of the Institution, and for their annual commencements. The former refectory at the east end was converted into an infirmary.

Eighty-eight pupils were entered by Mr. Kluge during his administration; twenty-two of which were sons of Moravian clergymen, a larger number of that class than had been admitted by any of his predecessors.

In 1844, pursuant to an appointment as Unity's financial agent in the Southern Province, Mr. Kluge removed to Salem, N. C. In 1853 he was elected a member of the warden's department of the Unity's Executive Board at Herrnhut, Saxony, and sailed for Europe in 1854. Since his return from abroad in 1857, Mr. Kluge has resided in retirement, and at present lives in the borough of Nazareth.

IX.—Rev. John C. Jacobson, 1844–1849.

Mr. Jacobson was educated for the ministry in the Moravian Theological Seminary at Nisky; came to America in 1816, and for ten years was tutor in Nazareth Hall. His first pastoral charge was the church at Bethania, near Salem, N. C. Here he was stationed from 1826 to 1833. In the following year he was appointed principal of the Salem Female Academy, and in June of 1844 entered upon his duties as Inspector of Nazareth Hall. One hundred and thirty-two pupils were entered during his administration of five years. The highest number, which was *seventy*, was reached in 1847.

In 1848, Mr. Jacobson attended the General Synod of the Church convened at Herrnhut. Rev. Robert de Schweinitz superintended the school during his absence abroad, from April to October of the year.

Having been elected a member of the Executive Board of the Province North, newly organized in 1849, he removed to Bethlehem, the seat of that body. He was its presiding officer for eighteen years, and since his retirement from public life in 1867, resides at Bethlehem.

X.—Rev. Levin T. Reichel, 1849–1853.

Mr. Reichel, a son of the first Principal, was born at Bethlehem and educated in Germany. He entered the Hall as tutor in 1834, and in 1837 was appointed pastor of the congregation at Schœneck, and subsequently of those at Emmaus and Nazareth.

During his administration, the school for day-scholars, hitherto conducted in the Hall, was transferred to a newly-erected school-house; the students of the Theological Seminary at Bethlehem furnished with apartments in the Hall; its interior arrangements altered, and the course of study materially modified; and the charges for board and tuition advanced. The number of pupils, however, decreased, and at one time there were but twenty-three boarders.

In 1853, Mr. Reichel was called to the pastorate of the church in Litiz, Pa.; and in 1854 to Salem, N. C., where he was the presiding officer of the Executive Board of the Southern Province until his election to a seat in the Missions' Department of the Unity's Board in Berthelsdorf, near Herrnhut. After having attended the General Synod of 1857, Mr. Reichel, in the autumn of that year, left for Europe to enter upon the duties of his new appointment, in which he is still active.

4 *

XI.—Rev. Edward Rondthaler, 1853–1854,

was born at Nazareth and educated for the ministry in
the Theological Seminary located there. Having taught
in the Hall for six years, he, in 1841, was called to his
first pastoral charge, the congregation of Schœneck, near
by. Subsequently, he was stationed at Graceham, Frederic co., Md., and next in Philadelphia. In July of 1853
he entered upon his duties as Principal of Nazareth Hall,
and had already given evidence of his administrative
abilities in the growing accession to the number of pupils,
when the death of his wife, in January of 1854, and his
own failing health, led him to resign his office in July following.

On the 10th of June of this year the first reunion of
former pupils of Nazareth Hall transpired.

Mr. Rondthaler was now appointed Professor in the
Theological Seminary, in which he served acceptably until
his decease, which occurred on the 5th of March, 1865.
His remains were taken to Bethlehem for interment.

XII.—Rev. Edward H. Reichel, 1854–1866.

Mr. Reichel, a grandson of the first Principal of Nazareth Hall, was graduated at the Theological Seminary
while at Bethlehem, and after serving as tutor in the first-
named Institution, was in 1849 appointed pastor of the
Moravian Church in Camden Valley, Washington co.,
N. Y. In 1854 he was recalled to Nazareth Hall, as its
Principal.

The number of pupils continuing to increase, the
students of the Theological Seminary vacated their apartments (removing to the Ephrata House in 1856) ; the
" Cottage" near by, as well as a second on Cemetery Hill,
was fitted up for the reception of " room-companies ;" and
in the autumn of 1865 a three-story brick building was

attached to the east end of the Hall. Thus permanent accommodations for one hundred and twenty-five pupils were secured. The chapel was also restored to its original dimensions, the refectory being transferred into the addition.

In the winter of 1864–1865 the number of pupils was at one time *one hundred and twenty-eight.* The entire number entered during this administration of twelve years was not far from *seven hundred.*

In 1862, Mr. Reichel organized his pupils into a uniformed cadet company, and introduced military drill as part of the routine of physical culture. Valuable additions to the library and the philosophical apparatus of the Institution were also made; and the former, which now numbered some four thousand volumes, advantageously arranged in the enlarged chapel.

Reunions were held annually as late as 1859. On the occasion of the one of June 11, 1858, a mural tablet, bearing the names of the twelve Principals of Nazareth Hall (a tribute from their pupils), was inserted in the east wall of the Chapel. The reunion of 1866 was one of more than ordinary interest, calling forth the rehearsal of services rendered to their country in the time of her danger, by patriotic Alumni of the Hall.

In July of 1866, Mr. Reichel, in view of failing health, was induced to resign his charge, and now lives in retirement at Nazareth.

XIII.—Rev. Robert de Schweinitz, 1866–1867,

a graduate of the Theological Seminary while located at Bethlehem, and tutor in Nazareth Hall between 1839 and 1845. Mr. de Schweinitz received his first appointment in the ministry in 1848, being stationed at Graceham, Frederic co., Md. His next charge was the Moravian

Church in Lancaster.   In January of 1853 he was called
to Salem, N. C., and there conducted the well-known
Female Academy until the summer of 1866.   In July of
that year he became Principal of Nazareth Hall.

Having been elected member of the Executive Board
of the Moravian Province North, in May of 1867, he removed to Bethlehem in July following, and is now the
presiding officer of that Board.

XIV.—Rev. Eugene Leibert, 1867,

the present Principal of Nazareth Hall, is a graduate of
the Theological Seminary while located at Nazareth.
In 1858 he entered the ministry, having been called to the
pastorate of the Moravian Church at Sharon, Tuscarawas
co., Ohio.   In 1862 he was stationed on Staten Island, and
in July, 1867, recalled to Nazareth Hall.

The number of pupils in the Institution under his care,
at the close of last year (December 31, 1868), was one
hundred, in charge of nine tutors.

An account of the proceedings of the Reunion and
Memorial Day, June 11, 1868, is found in full elsewhere
in this history.

It is deserving of special notice, in conclusion, that of
the two thousand and fifty pupils, entered during the last
eighty-three years, only thirteen died while inmates of
the Hall.   Their names are as follows:

Christian L. Schnepf, of St. Thomas. W. I., died August 4, 1789.

John G. Meyer, of St. Croix, W. I., died March 10,
1798.

George T. Graeff, of Lancaster, Pa., died May 11, 1808.

Thomas Singer, of Lancaster, Pa., died March 10, 1809.

Benjamin R. Reinke, of Hope, N. J., died January 9, 1810.

John Hooper, Jr., of Philadelphia, died April 4, 1837.

Jacob Bininger, Jr., of New York, died April 11, 1837.

Thaddeus McAlpin, of Mobile, Ala., January 17, 1841.

Martin Klosé, of Barbadoes, W. I., died July 21, 1842.

William C. Kluge, of Bethlehem, died June 27, 1845.

Samuel F. Reinke, of Bethlehem, died August 16, 1846.

William Cummins, of New York, died March 23, 1852.

Charles F. Vogler, of Fairfield, C. W., March 19, 1865.

The mortal remains of most of these, whose sad lot it was to die away from home and friends, were deposited in the beautiful cemetery on the hill—within the gate, whose superscription tells of hope and a better life to come—there to await the resurrection from the dead.

IN MEMORIAM.

"Ich lebe, und ihr sollt auch leben."
"The body rests in hope."

CHRISTIAN LUDWIG SCHNEPF,
born March 17, 1785, on the Island of St. John,
departed August 4, 1789.

JOHN GODFREY MEYER,
born December 22, 1786, on St. Croix,
departed March 10, 1798.

In memory of
GEORGE THOMAS GRAEFF,
son of George and Eve Graeff,
born May 14, 1794,
at Lancaster, Pa.,
a pupil in the Boarding-school,
departed May 11, 1808,
aged 14 years.

THOMAS TRESSE SINGER,
son of Abraham and Ann Singer,
of the
City of Philadelphia, who, after a residence
of 2 years and 9 mos.
at the Nazareth Seminary,
died of a short illness of twelve hours,
on March 10, 1809,
aged 12 years, 5 mos. and 8 days.

Fathers alone, a father's heart can know,
To the Almighty's will 'tis ours to bow.

BENJAMIN RUDOLPH REINKE,
born March 20, 1800, at Hope, in Jersey,
departed January 9, 1810.

JACOB BININGER, of New York,
son of Jacob and Harriet Bininger,
born N. York, Feb. 2, 1822,
died, Nazareth, April 11, 1837,
aged 15 years, 2 mos. and 9 days.

The spirit is gone
  In peace to God's throne
To praise God our Saviour, where we shall be soon.

He rests now in peace,
  Beholds the Lord's face,
Hath happily finished thus early his race.

In memory of
THADDEUS McALPIN,
a pupil of Nazareth school,
born Nov. 17, 1824, at
Tuscaloosa, Ala.,
departed January 17, 1841,
aged 16 years and 2 mos.

MARTIN KLOSE,
born June 29, 1833, at Sharon,
Barbadoes, departed July 21, 1842.

WILLIAM C. KLUGE,
born Oct. 16, 1835,
in Bethlehem,
departed June 27, 1845.

SAMUEL F. REINKE,
born Oct. 14, 1836, at Lancaster, Pa.,
departed Aug. 16, 1846,
aged 9 years, 10 mos. and 2 days.

"His soul pleased the Lord; therefore hasted he to take him away."—Wisdom iv. 14.

CHARLES FREDERIC,
son of the late Rev. Jesse Vogler,
of New Fairfield, Canada West,
born Sept. 14, 1852,
died March 19, 1865,
while a pupil in Nazareth Hall.

"Those that seek me early shall find me."—Prov. viii., 17

CATALOGUES.

D

PRINCIPALS OF NAZARETH HALL,

FROM 1785 TO 1869.

The names marked * are of persons DECEASED.

1. **Rev. Charles G. Reichel*** (1785 to 1802), deceased at Nisky, Lower Silesia, April 18, 1825.

2. **Rev. Jacob Van Vleck*** (1802 to 1809), deceased at Bethlehem, Pa., July 3, 1831.

3. **Rev. Charles F. Seidel*** (1809 to 1817), deceased at Bethlehem, April 26, 1861.

4. **Rev. John C. Beckler*** (1817 to 1822), deceased at Herrnhut, Saxony, April 18, 1857.

5. **Rev. William H. Van Vleck*** (1822 to 1829), deceased at Bethlehem, Pa., January 19, 1853.

6. **Rev. John G. Herman*** (1829 to 1837), deceased in the State of Missouri, July 20, 1854.

7. **Rev. Charles A. Van Vleck*** (1837 to 1839), deceased at Greenville, Tenn., December 21, 1845.

8. REV. CHARLES F. KLUGE (1839 to 1844), resides at Nazareth, Pa.

9. REV. JOHN C. JACOBSON (1844 to 1849), resides at Bethlehem, Pa.

10. REV. LEVIN T. REICHEL (1849 to 1853), member of the Unity's Board, Berthelsdorf, Saxony.

11. **Rev. Edward Rondthaler*** (1853 to 1854), deceased at Nazareth, March 5, 1855.

12. REV. EDWARD H. REICHEL (1854 to 1866), resides at Nazareth.

13. REV. ROBERT DE SCHWEINITZ (1866 to 1867), President of Provincial Board of the Northern Province, Bethlehem, Pa.

14. REV. EUGENE LEIBERT, 1867.

CATALOGUE

OF

TEACHERS

EMPLOYED IN NAZARETH HALL

Between 1785 *and* 1869.

———

The names marked thus * are of persons DECEASED.

———

George G. Miller* (1785 to 1788), pastor of Moravian Church in Philadelphia (1814 to 1817), deceased at Litiz, Pa., March 19, 1821.

Ludwig Huebner* (1785 to 1786), deceased December 6, 1813, at Bethlehem, Pa.

Matthew Eggert* (1786 to 1791), deceased September 22, 1831, at Bethlehem, Pa.

Nathaniel Michler* (1786 to 1790), deceased at Easton, Pa.

Samuel Kramsch* (1786 to 1788), first Principal of Salem Female Academy, founded in 1804, deceased February 2, 1824.

John F. Frueauff* (1788 to 1791), Principal Bethlehem Boarding-school (1819 to 1821), deceased November 14, 1839, near Bethlehem, Pa.

Abraham Levering* (1789 to 1790), deceased March 16, 1835, at Bethlehem, Pa.

John L. Strohle* (1790 to 1793), deceased 1827, while pastor of Moravian congregation at Bethabara, N. C.

52

Samuel F. Bader,* 1790 to 1791.

David Peter,* 1790 to 1792.

Thomas Schuall,* 1791 to 1795.

Joseph Schweishaupt* (1791 to 1796), deceased September 30, 1842, at Nazareth, Pa.

Benjamin Mortimer* (1791 to 1798), deceased while pastor of Fulton Street Moravian Church, in New York, 1832.

Nathaniel Brown* (1792 to 1797), deceased July 11, 1813, while pastor of Moravian Church on Staten Island, N. Y.

William Lembke* (1792), deceased at Graceham, Frederic co., Md.

Thomas Horsfield* (1791 to 1794), librarian of East India House, London, deceased July 24, 1859.

John B. Anders,* 1793.

J. Sebastian Oppelt* (1793 to 1799), deceased August 9, 1832, at Nazareth, Pa.

Henry Christian Mueller,* 1794 to 1795.

F. Balthazar Vognitz* (1795), deceased December 13. 1837, at Bethlehem, Pa.

Andrew Benade* (1795 to 1800), Principal Bethlehem Female Seminary (1800 to 1813), deceased October 31. 1859, at Bethlehem, Pa. (Bishop).

David Moritz Michael* (1795 to 1804), returned to Europe.

Christian Francis Denke* (1796 to 1800), deceased January 12, 1838, at Salem, N. C.

Paul Weiss* (1797 to 1803), deceased October 31, 1840. at Bethlehem, Pa.

Abraham Luckenbach* (1798 to 1800), missionary among the Delawares, deceased March 8, 1854, at Bethlehem, Pa.

Jacob Rauschenberger,* 1799 to 1808.

5 *

George Fetter* (1800 to 1808).

John Jacob Schmidt* (1800 to 1805), deceased August, 1821, on St. Thomas, W. I.

Joseph Zaeslein* (1800 to 1803), pastor of Moravian Church in Philadelphia (1803 to 1812), united with the Lutherans.

Ernst Ludwig Hazelius* (1800 to 1809), Lutheran clergyman, deceased February 20, 1853, at Lexington, S. C.

John Jacob Kummer* (1803 to 1808), deceased May 5, 1857, at Bethlehem, Pa.

John Henry Von Hof* (1804 to 1806), Lutheran clergyman, deceased 1861, near Mechanicsburg, Pa.

Frederic Felgentreff,* 1805 to 1806.

ABRAHAM VAN VLECK (1805 to 1806), resides at Litiz, Penna.

John Nicholas Hemping* (1806 to 1810), Lutheran clergyman, deceased March, 1855, in Halifax township, Dauphin co., Pa.

John C. Beckler* (1806 to 1812), deceased April 18, 1857, at Hermnhut, Saxony (Bishop).

Abraham Reinke,* 1806 to 1807.

George Adolphus Hartman* (1807 to 1817), deceased May 7, 1839, at Bethlehem, Pa.

G. Renatus Schmidt* (1807 to 1815), missionary among Cherokees, deceased December 16, 1852, at Salem, N. C.

John S. Haman* (1808), deceased February 18, 1866, at Nazareth, Pa.

William H. Van Vleck* (1809 to 1816), deceased January 29, 1853, at Bethlehem, Pa. (Bishop).

SAMUEL REINKE (1810 to 1816), resides at Bethlehem (Bishop).

Peter Wolle (1810 to 1814). resides at Bethlehem (Bishop).

Peter Ricksecker (1811 to 1821), resides at Bethlehem, Pa.

Charles A. Van Vleck* (1813 to 1823), deceased December 21, 1845, at Greenville, Tenn.

Adam Haman* (1815 to 1820), deceased January 13, 1857, at Salem, N. C.

John G. Kummer* (1815 to 1817), deceased August 6, 1846, at Litiz, Pa.

Charles Levering (1816), resides at Hope, Ind.

John C. Jacobson (1816 to 1826), resides at Bethlehem, Pa. (Bishop).

Samuel Huebner* (1817 to 1823), deceased June 7, 1849, at Salem, N. C.

James Sandiford, 1817 to 1818.

William Phillips, 1817.

Benjamin Lockwood,* 1817 to 1818.

William L. Benzien* (1818 to 1821). deceased while warden of the Moravian congregation at Salem, N. C., December 1, 1832.

Matthew Christ (1819 to 1822), resides at Bethlehem, Pa.

Christian Rusmeyer Schropp* (1819 to 1821), deceased June 23, 1821, at Nazareth, Pa.

Charles F. Kluge (1821 to 1828), resides at Nazareth, Pa.

Samuel Thomas Pfohl (1821 to 1823), warden of congregation at Salem, N. C.

George H. Bute (1822 to 1825), physician at Nazareth, Pa.

Jacob Zorn* (1823 to 1826), superintendent of Jamaica mission, deceased May 27, 1843, at Fairfield Station.

Charles A. Bleck* (1823 to 1831), deceased January 17, 1850, at Gnadenhutten, Ohio.

DAVID BIGLER (1824 to 1831), pastor of Moravian Church at Lancaster, Pa. (Bishop).

JOHN C. BRICKENSTEIN (1824 to 1830), resides at Nazareth, Pa.

JOHN HENRY KLUGE (1825 to 1826), teacher, Hope, Ind.

ABRAHAM L. HUEBNER (1825 to 1827), physician and professor in Female Boarding-school, Bethlehem, Pa.

ERNEST F. BLECK (1825 to 1831), treasurer of Moravian congregation, Bethlehem, Pa.

HENRY I. SCHMIDT (1825 to 1829), professor in Columbia College, N. Y.

John Rickert* (1825 to 1832), teacher, deceased December 3, 1849, at Litiz, Pa.

H. William Hall* (1827 to 1829), deceased May 19, 1868, at Litiz, Pa.

EUGENE A. FRUEAUFF (1828 to 1830), principal Linden Hall, Litiz, Pa.

LAWRENCE F. OERTER (1828 to 1835), resides at Bethlehem, Pa.

FRANCIS LENNERT (1828 to 1829), watchmaker, Litiz, Pa.

William L. Meinung* (1829 to 1833), teacher, deceased October 14, 1863, at Salem, N. C.

JAMES HENRY (1829 to 1831), manufacturer, Bolton, near Nazareth, Pa.

GEORGE F. BAHNSON (1829 to 1834), president of Executive Board of American Province South, Salem, N. C. (Bishop).

JOSEPH H. SIEWERS (1830 to 1832), attorney-at-law, Mauch Chunk, Pa.

JOSEPH F. BERG (1830 to 1835), professor of Theology, Rutgers College, New Brunswick.

Jesse Vogler* (1831 to 1833), missionary, deceased January 22, 1865, at Fairfield, C. W.

HERMAN J. TITZE (1832 to 1837), pastor of Moravian Church at West Salem, Ill.

WILLIAM L. LENNERT (1832 to 1836), pastor of Moravian Church at Hope, Ind.

Charles C. Dober* (1831 to 1832), professor in Theological Seminary, deceased January 21, 1840, at Bethlehem, Pa.

AMBROSE RONDTHALER (1832 to 1835), Principal Moravian Day School, Bethlehem, Pa.

Emanuel Rondthaler* (1832 to 1839), deceased November 30, 1848, while pastor of Moravian Church on Race street, Philadelphia, Pa.

JULIUS T. BECKLER (1832 to 1838), resides at Litiz, Pa.

PHILIP A. CREGAR (1833 to 1835), Principal Hamilton Institute, West Philadelphia.

LEVIN T. REICHEL (1834 to 1837), member of mission department of Unity's Executive Board, Hermnhut, Saxony.

Daniel Steinhauer* (1834 to 1835), deceased September 1, 1852, at Bethlehem, Pa.

SYLVESTER WOLLE (1835 to 1839), member of Executive Board of American Province North, Bethlehem, Pa.

WILLIAM H. BENADE (1835 to 1841), Swedenborgian clergyman, Pittsburg.

Edward Rondthaler* (1835 to 1841), deceased March 5, 1855, at Nazareth, Pa.

LEWIS F. KAMPMAN (1835 to 1840), member of Executive Board of American Province North, Bethlehem, Pa.

C. David Senseman* (1835 to 1842), professor of music, deceased August 10, 1861, near Philadelphia.

LAWRENCE DEMUTH (1837 to 1839), manufacturer, Philadelphia.

EMILE A. DE SCHWEINITZ (1837 to 1841), member of Executive Board of American Province South, Salem, N. C.

FRANCIS F. HAGEN (1837 to 1841), pastor of Moravian Church on Staten Island.

Henry A. Seidel* (1839 to 1840), deceased June 10, 1844, at Hopedale, Wayne co., Pa.

ROBERT DE SCHWEINITZ (1839 to 1845), president of Executive Board of American Province North, Bethlehem, Pa.

REUBEN A. HENRY (1839 to 1841), general ticket and freight agent Lackawana and Delaware and Western Railroads, Scranton, Pa.

FRANCIS WOLLE (1839 to 1846), principal Female Boarding-school, Bethlehem.

GEORGE W. PERKIN (1840 to 1842), bookseller, Bethlehem, Pa.

EDWARD H. REICHEL (1841 to 1848), resides at Nazareth, Pa.

HENRY J. VAN VLECK (1841 to 1845), pastor of German Mission Church, South Bethlehem.

AMADEUS A. REINKE (1842 to 1844), pastor of Moravian Church in New York.

Andrew G. Kern* (1842 to 1847), professor of music, deceased January 26, 1861, at Lake City, Florida.

EDWIN E. REINKE (1844), pastor of Indian congregation, Fairfield, C. W.

WILLIAM C. REICHEL (1844 to 1851), now at Bethlehem, Pa.

CHAS. GOEPP (1845 to 1846), attorney-at-law, New York.

FRANKLIN MILLER (1845 to 1847), druggist, New Philadelphia, Ohio.

SAMUEL C. WOLLE (1845 to 1848), cashier Thomas' iron works, Hockendaqua, Pa.

Joseph Hark (1845 to 1847), physician, Nazareth.

Julius Kern* (1845 to 1848), deceased July 9, 1860. at Salem, N. C.

Edmund A. de Schweinitz (1847 to 1850), pastor Moravian Church, Bethlehem, Pa.

Joseph Fahs (1847 to 1848), pastor of St. John's (Lutheran) Church, Allentown, Pa.

Eugene Grider (1847 to 1848), resides at Litiz, Pa.

Lewis Harbaugh, 1848.

Charles Klose (1848), merchant, Philadelphia.

Bernard de Schweinitz* (1848 to 1852), pastor of Moravian Church on Staten Island, deceased July 20, 1854. at Salem, N. C.

James N. Beck (1848 to 1850), professor of music, Philadelphia.

Maximilian Goepp (1848 to 1849), attorney-at-law, New York.

Theophilus Wunderling* (1848 to 1851), deceased while pastor of Moravian Church at Nazareth, April 8. 1864.

Theophilus Kramer (1848 to 1849), druggist, New Orleans.

Jacob J. Haman (1850 to 1855), professor of music.

Lewis R. Huebner (1851 to 1858), assistant pastor of Moravian Church, Bethlehem, Pa.

Edward T. Kluge (1852 to 1856), pastor of Moravian Church, Litiz, Pa.

John Eberman* (1852 to 1854), Lutheran clergyman, deceased September 23, 1868, at Schuylkill Haven, Pa.

Parmenio Leinbach (1852 to 1858), pastor of Moravian Church, Friedburg, N. C.

Lorenzo Finn, 1852 to 1853.

Herman A. Brickenstein (1853 to 1859), editor of *Moravian*, Bethlehem, Pa.

C. Edward Kummer (1853 to 1856), teacher, Bethlehem, Pa.

Eugene Leibert (1853 to 1858), Principal Nazareth Hall.

Clement L. Reinke (1854 to 1859), pastor of Moravian Church at Chaska, Minn.

William Forsythe, 1854 to 1856.

E. Warner Carpenter, 1855.

F. Agthe (1855 to 1858), professor of music, Bridgeton, N. J.

Abraham R. Beck (1855 to 1857), Principal of School for Boys, Litiz, Pa.

Benjamin Romig (1855 to 1858), missionary, Antigua, W. I.

Henry T. Bachman (1856 to 1860), pastor of Moravian Church, Graceham, Md.

Owen Rice (1856 to 1863), druggist, Lancaster, Pa.

Albert L. Oerter (1856 to 1862), pastor of Moravian Church, Salem, N. C.

Joseph Walton (1857 to 1858), farmer, Tuscarawas co., Ohio.

Lawrence C. Brickenstein (1858), attorney-at-law, Baltimore.

Obadiah T. Huebner (1858 to 1867), physician, Litiz, Pa.

Henry A. Bigler (1858), attorney-at law, New York.

C. Ernest Berger, 1858.

Frederic Pfeiffer, 1858.

J. Paraska, 1858 to 1859.

Jeremiah J. Seiss, 1858 to 1859.

Jonathan J. Hoch (1858 to 1859), missionary, Barbadoes, W. I.

Anthony Mattes, 1859.

JAMES B. HAMAN (1859 to 1860), pastor of Moravian Church, Gnadenhutten, O.

WILLIAM H. BIGLER (1859 to 1860), professor, Moravian College, Bethlehem, Pa.

SAMUEL L. LICHTENTHALER (1859 to 1862), missionary, Barbadoes, W. I.

J. CENNICK HARVEY (1859 to 1861), conveyancer, Brooklyn, N. Y.

S. C. CHITTY (1859 to 1867), professor of music, Hope, Ind.

WILLIAM REA, 1860 to 1861.

PETER J. THWAITES (1860 to 1861), farmer, Illinois.

JOSEPH SEISS, 1860.

CHARLES A. GERING (1860 to 1862), draughtsman, Union Pacific Railroad Co.

JOSEPH ROMIG (1861 to 1862), missionary, Kansas.

WILLIAM F. SCHATZ (1861 to 1863), physician, Ohio.

C. R. KONOPAK (1861 to 1863), bookkeeper, Bethlehem, Pa.

J. THEOPHILUS ZORN (1862 to 1865), missionary, Jamaica, W. I.

EDMUND A. OERTER (1862 to 1863), pastor of Moravian Church, Lebanon, Pa.

HERMAN S. HOFFMAN (1862 to 1863), pastor of Second Moravian Church, Philadelphia.

CHARLES H. BEITEL (1863 to 1868), professor of music, Peekskill, N. Y.

JOHN C. HOLDER, 1863.

JOHN T. REINECKE, 1863.

J. WESLEY SPAUGH (1863), missionary, Kansas.

THEODORE HANCE, 1863.

LEWIS P. CLEWELL (1864 to 1865), pastor of Moravian Church, Grace Hill, Iowa.

6

FRANCIS W. KNAUSS (1864), pastor of Moravian Church, Moravia, Iowa.

EDWARD RONDTHALER (1864 to 1865), pastor of Moravian Church, Brooklyn, N. Y.

CHARLES B. SHULTZ (1864), professor in Moravian College, Bethlehem.

OSCAR ELY, 1864.

EDWIN G. KLOSE (1864 to 1867), professor in Moravian College, Bethlehem.

J. ALBERT RONDTHALER (1864 to 1865).

JOSEPH J. RICKSECKER (1864 to 1867), pastor of Moravian Church, West Salem, Ill.

CHARLES NAGLE (1865 to 1868), pastor of Moravian Church, Hopedale, Pa.

EDWARD J. REGENNAS (1865), teacher, Nazareth Hall.

HENRY A. JACOBSON (1865),   do.   do.

EDWARD J. PAINE, 1865.

OLIVER L. FEHR (1865 to 1867), Easton, Pa.

HERMAN JACOBSON (1865 to 1867), Washington, D. C.

WILLIAM H. BUCHNER, 1866 to 1867.

HENRY M. CLEWELL (1867), teacher, Nazareth Hall.

EUGENE L. SHAEFER (1867), teacher in Nazareth Hall.

THEODORE M. RIGHTS (1867), do.   do.

J. BENJAMIN LEINBACH (1868), do.   do.

JACOB D. SIEWERS (1868),   do.   do.

SAMUEL BLUM (1868),   do.   do.

CATALOGUE

OF THE

PUPILS OF NAZARETH HALL

FROM 1785—1869.

The names marked * are of pupils DECEASED while inmates of the Institution.

1785.

Beckel, George F.	Bethlehem, Pa.
Becker, John L.	Litiz, Pa.
Denke, Christian F.	Bethlehem, Pa.
Hasse, William.	do.
Hauser, Christian.	Hope, N. J.
Horsefield, Thomas.	Bethlehem, Pa.
Leinbach, John F.	Hope, N. J.
Roth, John L.	York, Pa.
Roth, John D.	Nazareth, Pa.
Roth, John B.	Bethlehem, Pa.
Weiss, Francis.	Gnadenhutten, Pa.
Wilson, Philip.	New York.

1786.

Christ, Jacob.	Nazareth, Pa.
Kummer, Jacob.	St. Thomas, W. I.
Schmidt, John Jacob.	Nazareth, Pa.
Senseman, Christian D.	do.
Ten Brook, William Watson.	New York.
Van Vleck, Henry.	do.

1787.

Bagge, Charles F......................... Salem, N. C.
Bagge, Benjamin Samuel. .... do.
Henry, Matthew........................... Lancaster, Pa.
Konkaput, John........................... Stockbridge Ind., Mass.
Kunkler, Frederick....................... Bethlehem, Pa.
Morgan, George Washington............... Philadelphia.
Schweinitz, Lewis D. von................. Bethlehem, Pa.
Shaw, Joseph............................. Philadelphia.

1788.

Crane, Joseph............................ Elizabethtown, N. J.
Dealing, John A.......................... Nazareth, Pa.
Hart, Gratianus.......................... Antigua, W. I.
Krause, C. S............................. St. Croix, do.

1789.

Beach, Abraham........................... New York.
Greene, Nathaniel Ray......... .... do.
Hunt, Abraham............................ Trenton, N. J.
Matlack, White........................... New York.
Nichols, George.......................... do.
Ogden, David............................. Trenton, N. J.
Palmer, John............................. Northampton co., Pa.
Schnepf, Christian L.* .... St. Thomas, W. I.
Schweinitz, Charles H. von............... Bethlehem, Pa.
Turner, John A........................... New York.
Turner, Archibald........................ do.
Weiss, Jacob............................. Lehighton, Pa.
Wolle, John F............................ St. Thomas, W. I.

1790.

Billington, Thomas....................... Philadelphia.
Jarvis, James............................ New York.
Logan, Albanus........................... Stenton, Phila. co., Pa.
Nichols, John............................ Philadelphia.
Nichols, William......................... do.
Senseman, John H......................... Lebanon co., Pa.
Shaw, Alexander.......................... Jamaica, W. I.

Stansbury, Joseph...................... Philadelphia, Pa.
Ten Brook, Jesse....................... New York.
Weyle, Adam C......................... St. John's, W. I.

1791.

Bowen, William........................ Providence, R. I.
Clark, John........................... do.
Clemm, William........................ Baltimore.
Conolly, James........................ Montreal, Canada.
Conolly, Thomas....................... do.
Heyliger, Martin M.................... St. Croix, W. I.
Heyliger, John........................ do.
Heyliger, Isaac....................... do.
Heyliger, William..................... do.
Linberg, Hennig....................... do.
Lyon, John............................ Baltimore.
Nightingale, William.................. Providence, R. I.
Penrose, Isaac........................ Philadelphia.
Reinke, Jr., Abraham.................. Litiz, Pa.
Rogiers, C. S......................... St. Croix, W. I.
Stansbury, Arthur..................... Philadelphia.
Wall, William Harris.................. Savannah, Ga.
Winchester, William................... do.

1792.

Beverhoudt, John Wood van............. St. Thomas, W. I.
Kuhn, Hartman......................... Philadelphia.
Kuhn, Charles......................... do.
Lawler, John.......................... do.
Smith, John R. C...................... do.
Warner, Joseph.... .... do.

1793.

Connor, John Payne.................... St. Croix, W. I.
Fromberger, George.................... Philadelphia.
Hawkins, Isaac........................ St. Croix, W. I.
Heyliger, Abraham..................... do.
O'Neill, Arthur....................... Philadelphia.
O'Neill, Tully........................ do.

1794.

Billis, James............................ St. Thomas, W. I.
Care, Peter............................. Philadelphia Co.
Cist, Jacob............................. Philadelphia.
Cist, Lewis............................. do.
Haman, John S.......................... Barbadoes, W. I.
Haman, Adam........................... do.
Heckewelder, Thomas.................... Bethlehem, Pa.
Hornig, Christian....................... do.
King, James............................ Philadelphia.
Reichel, Charles F...................... Nazareth, Pa.
Schneller, David P...................... Bethlehem, Pa.
Smith, John T.......................... Philadelphia.

1795.

Bardill, George R....................... Antigua, W. I.
Chabert, Charles....................... St. Croix, W. I.
Davoué, Frederick...................... New York.
Markoe, Abraham....................... St. Croix, W. I.
Mueller, John L........................ do.
Mueller, Ernest F...................... do.
Reeve, Aaron Burr...................... Litchfield, Conn.
Schweinitz, Christian R. von............ Bethlehem, Pa.
Wolle, Jacob........................... St. Croix, W. I.

1796.

Bartow, John B......................... Bethlehem, Pa.
Beitel, Frederic W..................... do.
Beverhoudt, Peter C. van............... St. Thomas, W. I.
Etwein, John.......................... Bethlehem, Pa.
Haga, Jr., Godfrey..................... Philadelphia.
Heitman, William...................... Bethlehem, Pa.
Heitman, George H..................... do.
Joyce, Thomas......................... New York.
Krause, John G........................ St. Croix, W. I.
Meyer, John G.* .... do.

1797.

Bininger, Abraham..................... New York.
Dam, John............................. St. John, W. I.

Etwein, John G. .... Bethlehem, Pa.
Eyerly, Jacob. .... Nazareth, Pa.
Heyliger, Peter A. .... St. Croix, W. I.
Ten Brook, Henry. .... New York.

1798.

Henry, John Joseph. .... Nazareth, Pa.
Joyce, Benjamin K. .... New York.
Kœhler, John D. .... Salem, N. C.
Kummer, John G. .... Bethlehem, Pa.
Pratt, James D. .... Philadelphia.
Rice, Joseph. .... Bethlehem, Pa.
Roebuck, Peter P. .... New York.

1799.

Beck, John. .... Lebanon co., Pa.
Behagen, Simon H. .... St. Croix, W. I.
Davidson, George. .... Bethlehem, Pa.
Depui, Nicholas. .... Northampton co., Pa.
Gill, Jacob Dickert. .... Lancaster, Pa.
Kampman, Francis C. .... Bethlehem, Pa.
King, Charles Bird. .... Newport, R. I.
Mosely, Charles. .... Hartford, Conn.
Reinke, Samuel. .... Hope, N. J.
Schneckenberger, John T. .... Bethlehem, Pa.
Stroud, Jacob M. .... Stroudsburg, Pa.
Van Vleck, William Henry. .... Bethlehem, Pa.

1800.

Douglas, Ephraim. .... Uniontown, Pa.
Huber, Jacob. .... Strasburg, Pa.
Murray, George W. .... Newtown, Pa.
Rathbone, James M. .... New York.
Perkins, Elisha B. .... Strasburg, Pa.
Reichel, G. Benjamin. .... Nazareth, Pa.
Reichel, Samuel R. .... do.
Schneller, George C. .... Bethlehem, Pa.
Stake, George R. .... Lancaster, Pa.
Wolle, Peter. .... St. Thomas, W. I.

1801.

Bethell, William..................... New York.
Burn, Joseph........................ Philadelphia.
Conkling, Thomas C. .... New York.
Davidson, John E..................... Bethlehem, Pa.
Erwin, John......................... Easton, Pa.
Haman, Christian R.................. Bethlehem, Pa.
Mitchelson, William................ New York.
Molther, William H................. York, Pa.
Peter, Joseph G.................... Bethlehem, Pa.
Sommer, John....................... Moreland, Phila. Co.

1802.

Baker, John C...................... Philadelphia.
Bickley, Daniel.................... do.
Bickley, Jacob..................... do.
Bininger, Jacob.................... New York.
Campbell, John..................... do.
Davidson, James.................... Newark, N. J.
Erwin, Scott R..................... Bucks co., Pa.
Freitag, Daniel C.................. Bethlehem, Pa.
Frick, William.................... Baltimore, Md.
Henry, Matthew S................... Nazareth, Pa.
Mueller, George B.................. Emmaus, Pa.
Scott, James...................... Philadelphia.
Sibbald, Charles.................. Augusta, Ga.
Stake, Thomas..................... Lancaster, Pa.
Van Vleck, Charles A.............. Bethlehem, Pa.
West, Charles..................... Philadelphia.

1803.

Bogardus, Archibald R............. New York.
Bohn, Charles..................... Baltimore, Md.
Brackenridge, Alexander........... Carlisle, Pa.
Hilton, George.................... Woodlands, Phila. Co.
Huebener, Samuel R................ York, Pa.
Hurel, François F................. Guadaloupe, W. I.
Molther, Augustus................. Schœneck, Pa.
Scott, Robert..................... Philadelphia.

1804.

Allen, Cornelius............................ New York.
De Hart, John............................. Philadelphia.
Herbst, Henry R........................... Salem, N. C.
Kampman, Lewis F....................... Hope, N. J.
Jessop, William........................... Baltimore.
Reiniker, Henry........................... do.
Vos, John II............................... Charleston, S. C.
Vos, Andrew............................... do.

1805.

Frick, George............................. Baltimore, Md.
Hilton, William........................... Woodlands, Phila. co.
Ireland, John............................. New York.
Knevels, D'Jurco V....................... St. John, W. I.
Knevels, John W.......................... do.
Landreth, Cuthbert....................... Philadelphia.
Lea, John................................. Wilmington, Del.
Logan, Algernon S........................ Stenton, Phila. co.
Saladé, Frederic.......................... Philadelphia.
Sholten, Frederic von..................... St. Thomas, W. I.
Sholten, William von...................... do.
Smith, George W.......................... Philadelphia
Stall, George............................. do.
Uhler, John............................... Baltimore.
Unangst, Joseph........................... Northampton co.
White, Thomas............................ Caroline co., Md.

1806.

Allen, John............................... New York.
Chanceller, William....................... —— W. I.
Conkling, Joseph H....................... Baltimore, Md.
Davis, James.............................. Smyrna, Del.
Dougherty, Felix.......................... St. Croix, W. I.
Dougherty, Charles S...................... do.
Dougherty, Martin......................... do.
Fay, Samuel B............................ New York.
Fay, Henry A............................. do.
Geib, William............................. do.
Huetter, Charles L........................ Philadelphia.

Knevels, H. Torris...................... St. John, W. I.
Lawson, Richard........................ —— W. I.
Leffingwell, L. W...................... New York.
Logan, Charles F...................... Goochland co., Va.
Man, James........................... Philadelphia.
Pluymert, Joseph F................... Meriden, Conn.
Potter, Peter M....................... Philadelphia.
Potter, Samuel C..................... do.
Price, George H. S.................... ——
Singer, Thomas*.................... Lancaster, Pa.
Singer, Richard....................... do.
Wilson, William...................... New York.
Wolle, Samuel H...................... St. John, W. I.
Worrell, George W.................... Wilmington, Del.

1807.

Benninghove, John..................... Philadelphia.
Blackiston, R. H...................... Smyrna, Del.
Cronenberg, Christian H. von.......... St. John, W. I.
Graeff, George T.*................ Lancaster, Pa.
Kluge, Charles F...................... White River, Ind.
Latimer, James........................ Newport, Del.
Lea, Edward........................... Brandywine, Del.
Mortimer, David B..................... Goshen, O.
Mummey, Samuel I..................... Baltimore.
Oppelt, Charles H..................... Fairfield, U. C.
Sevier, William....................... Tennessee.
Sevier, James......................... do.
Taylor, Peter D....................... St. Domingo.
Woolston, John........................ Wilmington, Del.
Yundt, Jacob.......................... Baltimore.

1808.

Barclay, David W...................... Philadelphia.
Beckel, George C...................... do.
Breban, John J........................ do.
Grossman, Lewis....................... do.
Jennings, Stephen..................... New York.
Latimer, William...................... Philadelphia.
Michler, Peter S...................... Northampton co., Pa.

Michael, John.............................. Lancaster, Pa.
Schropp, Christian R...................... Litiz, Pa.
Thebaud, John............................. New York.
Thebaud, Edward.......................... do.
Vickery, Thomas........................... Baltimore.

1809.

Allard, Lewis.............................. St. Domingo.
Angué, Anthony........................... Philadelphia.
Angué, Louis.............................. do.
Bellach, James J.......................... Wilmington, Del.
Bryan, William............................ Germantown, Pa.
Bryan, Samuel S........................... Philadelphia.
Chambers, George......................... do.
Drinker, Joseph D......................... do.
Dutilh, Edward G.......................... do.
Dutilh, Edmund............................ do.
France, James............................. Baltimore.
Heide, George............................. do.
Landreth, Thomas O........................ Philadelphia.
Lee, Joseph O'Sullivan..................... do.
Low, William.............................. New York.
Molther, Charles.......................... York, Pa.
Oppelt, William........................... Fairfield, U. C.
Picquet, Caius M.......................... —— France.
Reinke, Benjamin R.*.................. Hope, N. J.
Silliman, Joseph A......................... Philadelphia.
Souder, Thomas R.......................... do.
St. Ange, Francis.......................... West Indies.
Thum, George............................. Philadelphia.
Warner, Joseph............................ do.
Wortman, George.......................... Pottsgrove, Pa.

1810.

Abbott, George............................ Philadelphia.
Edmonson, James N........................ Montgomery co., Pa.
Grossman, John............................ Philadelphia.
Guillard, Joseph A......................... —— France.
Halberstadt, John.......................... Philadelphia.
Keasby, John R............................ do.

Levering, Abraham...................... Litiz, Pa.
Porter, Giles......................... Albany, N. Y.
Ross, Frederic A...................... Richmond, Va.
Smith, James.......................... Baltimore.
Walter, Jacob......................... Antigua, W. I.

1811.

Bleck, Charles A................. ..... Graceham, Md.
Chesterman, Edwin..................... New York.
Clymer, Andrew........................ Philadelphia.
France, John.......................... Baltimore.
Herwig, Ernest C...................... do.
Martin, Jacob L....................... Charleston, S. C.
Martin, John P........................ do.
Meakings, Benjamin H.................. New York.
Myers, D. W. Ross..................... Columbia, S. C.
Verneuil, Bernard P.............. ...... Jamaica, W. I.
White, James.......................... Philadelphia.

1812.

Albrecht, Daniel...................... Litiz, Pa.
Algieux, Celestin..................... Philadelphia.
Boller, Henry J....................... do.
Collins, Edmund....................... Wilmington, Del.
Collins, John......................... do.
Harple, Jacob......................... Philadelphia.
Mortimer, Charles Edward.............. New York.
Rohr, Charles H.... .... Bucks co., Pa.
Schlichter, Enos...................... do.
Sievers, Jacob F...................... St. John, W. I.
Smith, Arnold......................... Baltimore.
Sturges, Jonathan S................... New York.
Sturges, Henry A. C................... do.
Tinsfield, Frederic................... Baltimore.
Zorn, Jacob........................... St. Croix, W. I.

1813.

Adams, Gilbert........................ Pittsburg.
Baker, William Howard...... .... New York.

Baker, Henry H.............................. New York.
Butler, L. M. Harris........................ do.
Butler, William Henry...................... do.
Clench, Ralph.............................. Albany, N. Y.
Graeff, Charles............................ Lancaster, Pa.
Graeff, Henry..... .... do.
France, Lewis............................. Baltimore.
Heraud, Jean.............................. Philadelphia.
Hopkins, Charles.......................... Athens, Pa.
Leibert, John S........................... Germantown, Pa.
Levering, C. Henry........................ Litiz, Pa.
Llewellyn, S. D........................... Lancaster, Pa.
Oppelt, Conrad B.......................... Ohio.
Schropp, John............................. Bethlehem, Pa.
Sevier, Samuel............................ Tennessee.
Shurlock, P............................... Easton, Pa.
Stadiger, John F.......................... Bethlehem, Pa.
Stafford, John............................ Albany, N. Y.
Taylor, John.............................. Philadelphia.
Thorp, Issachar........................... do.

1814.

Bleck, Ernest F........................... Graceham, Md.
Brooks, Robert B.......................... Savannah, Ga.
Cagnet, Arthur............................ Philadelphia.
Desauque, Louis F......................... do.
Draper, William........................... do.
Draper, Edmund............................ do.
Eggert, Samuel R.......................... Bethlehem, Pa.
Heartly, William.......................... Philadelphia.
Lichtenthaeler, Christian................. Litiz, Pa.
Monges, John A............................ Philadelphia.
Ogden, Augustus O. B...................... New Germantown, N. J.
Richards, Anthony......................... Savannah, Ga.
Richards, James........................... do.
Smith, Henry.............................. New York.
Taylor, Archibald......................... Baltimore.
Tyson, Charles............................ do.
Willis, Charles........................... Philadelphia.

7

1815.

Andress, Abraham	Bethlehem, Pa.
Bidleman, William A.	Easton, Pa.
Butler, George	New York.
Doyle, Francis	Savannah, Ga.
Earle, Henry	Pittsburg, Pa.
Eyre, Joseph K.	Philadelphia.
Fetter, John G.	Bethlehem, Pa.
France, Richard	Baltimore.
Goundie, George H.	Bethlehem, Pa.
Hendrickson, Jos. S.	New York.
Hornor, Henry C.	Philadelphia.
Mankin, George	Baltimore.
Mayland, Samuel	Philadelphia.
Miles, Joseph M.	Baltimore.
Mix, Elihu L.	New Haven, Conn.
Molther, Lewis	Schœneck, Pa.
Norris, William	Baltimore.
Stringham, John B.	New York.
Sturges, Josiah	do.
Tschudy, Jacob B.	Litiz, Pa.

1816.

Brown, Edward P.	Philadelphia.
Butz, Daniel	Easton, Pa.
Cole, William J.	Baltimore.
Draper, John	Philadelphia.
Duval, Wm. B.	do.
Fenwick, Thomas	New York.
Gibney, Richard	Baltimore.
Gibney, John	do.
Heyliger, Christian	St. Croix, W. I.
Homiller, Joseph	Germantown, Pa.
Huebner, Abraham I.	Bethlehem, Pa.
Jacot, Richard	New York.
Leypold, John G.	Baltimore.
Miller, John P.	do.
Nelms, George P.	do.
Oakley, George	Philadelphia.
Old, Morgan P.	Berks co., Pa.

Peck, Robert	New Haven, Conn.
Sevier, Thomas R	Tennessee.
Short, George	Baltimore.
Shuman, Parmenio	Salem, N. C.
Sitgreaves, Theodore R	Easton, Pa.
Smith, Lewis Edwin	Baltimore.
Wilhelm, Abraham	do.

1817.

Badger, Bela	Bristol.
Backus, George P	Athens.
Cooper, Daniel S	Philadelphia.
Dubarry, John S	do.
Hastings, John	Chester, Pa.
Jordan, William H	Philadelphia.
Kitchell, John S	Bethlehem, Pa.
La Roche, Julius	Paris, France.
Levy, Abraham	Philadelphia.
Leypold, William F	Baltimore.
Maison, Peter	Germantown, Pa.
McCall, Samuel R	Easton, Pa.
McIlhenny, William H	Philadelphia.
McIlhenny, James	do.
Minturn, Edward	New York.
Randel, William	———
Riesch, David P	Philadelphia.
Ridgely, Richard	Baltimore.
Robinson, William	do.
Schaum, Benjamin	Lancaster, Pa.
Schnierle, John	Charleston, S. C.
Schnierle, Frederic	do.
Shultz, Henry A	Schœneck, Pa.
Smith, Washington G	Delaware.
Walker, George J. S	Augusta, Ga.
Walker, John V. F	do.

1818.

Barton, G. Washington	Lancaster, Pa.
Brown, Charles B	Philadelphia.
Brown, William Linn	do.

Busch, Henry A........................... Bethlehem, Pa.
Callanan, George D....................... Philadelphia.
Cooper, James M.......................... Baltimore.
Dancy, Daniel M.......................... Petersburg, Va.
George, Daniel........................... New Orleans.
Harris, Edward Denney.................... Norfolk, Va.
Hutter, Ferdinand Q...................... Easton, Pa.
Jarvis, James............................ New York.
Luckenbach, Charles Augustus............. Bethlehem, Pa.
Lyons, Solomon........................... Philadelphia.
Muller, Caspar O......................... do.
Oppelt, Godfrey H........................ Nazareth, Pa.
Paine, Thomas Edward..................... Athens.
Prill, Frederick......................... Baltimore.
Siewers, Joseph H........................ West Indies.
Schneider, Christian F................... Bethlehem, Pa.
Southall, Peyton A....................... Williamsburg, Va.
Stringham, Joseph........................ St. Croix, W. I.
Voute, Louis C........................... Germany.

1819.

Boller, John J........................... Philadelphia.
Crawbuck, Stephen........................ New York.
Croeger, Timothy....,.................... Graceham, Md.
Dodd, Moses.............................. New York.
Dodd, Edward D........................... do.
Frueauff, Eugene A....................... Bethlehem, Pa.
Gillies, Thomas U........................ New York.
Hains, William D......................... Berks co., Pa.
Kluge, J. Henry.......................... Graceham, Md.
Krimmel, Henry........................... Philadelphia.
Mayerhoff, Charles F..................... Columbia, N. J.
Mortimer, Daniel D....................... New York.
Richards, Jacob.......................... Chester, Pa.
Roebuck, Peter........................... St. Croix, W. I.
Roebuck, Jarvis.......................... do.
Roebuck, Jones........................... do.
Schulz, Samuel........................... York, Pa.
Wise, Joseph............................. Germantown, Pa.

1820.

Baron, John C............................	New Orleans.
Baron, Stephen K.........................	do.
Eyre, John C.............................	Philadelphia.
Kimmel, Henry...........................	Baltimore.
Lloyd, John Ambrose......................	Northumberland co., Pa.
Lucas, William A.........................	New York.
Lyons, Samuel...........................	Philadelphia.
Rudenstein, Wm. F.......................	Baltimore.
Sempf, Albert M.........................	do.
Sievers, Charles G.......................	St. Thomas, W. I.
Smith, Henry J..........................	Nazareth, Pa.

1821.

Brenan, Matthew.........................	Charleston, S. C.
Bryan, George S..........................	do.
Demuth, Emanuel........................	Lancaster, Pa.
Gurlic, Clovis...........................	New Orleans.
Henry, James............................	Philadelphia.
Kelly, Philip.............................	do.
Reardon, Richard K......................	Baltimore.
Rondthaler, Ambrose.....................	Nazareth, Pa.
Schnierle, William.......................	Charleston, S. C.
Stadiger, Herman L......................	Bethlehem, Pa.
Trout, Samuel B.........................	Philadelphia.
West, George W.........................	Baltimore.

1822.

Baker, David............................	New York.
Butz, Abraham H........................	Northampton co., Pa.
De Bow, William........................	Charleston, S. C.
Humphreys, Clement.....................	Philadelphia.
Humphreys, Andrew A...................	do.
Jordan, Edward.........................	do.
Lyons, Henry............................	do.
Oppelt, Francis..........................	Nazareth, Pa.
Pell, William James.....................	New York.
Seidel, Charles E........................	Bethlehem, Pa.
Sibley, George..........................	Charleston, S. C.

7 *

1823.

Fry, Joshua	Lehigh co., Pa.
Geer, Edward W	New York.
Hildeburn, Joseph H	Philadelphia.
Meinung, William L	Salem, N. C.
Paine, Seth W	Athens, Pa.
Patterson, Charles W	Philadelphia.
Pell, George W	New York.
Rondthaler, Jr., Emanuel	Nazareth, Pa.
Slesman, Henry	Philadelphia.
Slesman, Benjamin	do.
Yundt, Samuel	Baltimore.

1824.

Beckler, Julius T	Litiz, Pa.
Cooper, Erwin J	Philadelphia.
Cummings, Charles R	do.
Gillender, Theophilus	New York.
Hiester, Charles	——
Holm, Martin L	St. Croix, W. I.
Mitchell, Benjamin G	Philadelphia.
Smith, Eugene T	New York.
Van Beuren, Michael B	do.
Yundt, Joseph	Baltimore.

1825.

Arnoux, Alfred M	New York.
Berg, Joseph F	West Indies.
Bininger, Abraham	New York.
Boner, Joshua	Salem, N. C.
Chandler, Asbury H	Mobile, Ala.
Cunningham, Nathaniel S	New York.
Decker, Matthias	do.
Donley, Joseph	Philadelphia.
Draper, Robert	do.
Gassner, Daniel D	New York.
Gillender, Arthur	do.
Herrick, Castle H	Athens, Pa.
Horner, Charles W	Philadelphia.

Lippincott, Benjamin I...................... New York.
Maybin, David C........................... Philadelphia.
McKean, Addison.......................... Bradford co., Pa.
Mecaskey, Charles A....................... Philadelphia.
Perit, John W. C.......................... do.
Rauch, Reuben............................ Bethlehem, Pa.
Ricksecker, Moses......................... do.
Ridgway, Joseph.......................... St. Croix, W. I.
Rice, Edward.............................. Bethlehem, Pa.
Rondthaler, Edward........................ Nazareth, Pa.
Schweinitz, Emile A. de.................... Bethlehem, Pa.
Walter, Isaac. .... Antigua, W. I.
Wilton, Henry J........................... Philadelphia.

1826.

Baker, John............................... New York.
Beckler, Francis E......................... Litiz, Pa.
Clark, Jeremiah S.......................... New York.
Decker, Benjamin.......................... do.
Dungan, John.............................. Allentown, Pa.
Frazee, Augustus.......................... New York.
Friese, P. C............................... Baltimore.
Geisse, Augustus H......................... Philadelphia.
Heyliger, Frederic W....................... St. Croix, W. I.
Hildeburn, William L....................... Philadelphia.
Humphreys, Joshua......................... do.
Kissam, Daniel E........................... New York.
Kissam, Benjamin T........................ do.
Lennert, William L......................... Litiz, Pa.
Lippincott, William........................ Shrewsbury, N. J.
Mallory, Stephen R......................... Thompson's Island, Fla.
Paine, James A............................ Athens, Pa.
Philip, Frederic W......................... Brooklyn, L. I.
Philip, George A........................... do.
Post, William F............................ New York.
Prall, Ichabod............................. do.
Ralston, Robert............................ Philadelphia.
Reed, Samuel F............................ do.
Ritter, Jacob B............................ do.
Seltzer, Christian A........................ Jonestown, Pa.

Thompson, George H. . . . . Philadelphia.
Van Beuren, Daniel B. . . . . New York.
Von Hoff, Augustus H. Jonestown, Pa.

1827.

Albert, Fanning T. . . . . Brooklyn, L. I.
Aymar, Augustus J. M. . . . . New York.
Aymar, John Q. . . . .   do.
Clark, Richard M. . . . .   do.
Conger, John P. . . . .   do.
Da Costa, Jacob M. . . . . St. Thomas, W. I.
Demuth, Lawrence J. Lancaster, Pa.
Devereux, Benjamin H. . . . . Philadelphia.
De Young, Benjamin. . . . . Baltimore.
Dyer, Samuel O. . . . . New York.
Eckford, Henry. . . . .   do.
Fries, Francis I. . . . . Salem, N. C.
Hall, Richard. . . . . Allentown, Pa.
Jordan, Francis. . . . . Philadelphia.
Lippincott, Shepherd. Shrewsbury, N. J.
Man, William. . . . . Philadelphia.
McMullin, John A. . . . .   do.
Penington, Hyland B. Cecilton, Md.
Penington, Samuel. . . . . Cantwell's Bridge, Del.
Quin, George W. . . . . New Jersey.
Reppert, Jacob. . . . . Baltimore.
Richards, George N. . . . . Montgomery co., Pa.
Senseman, Christian D. . . . . Nazareth, Pa.
Sievers, John D. . . . . West Indies.
Van Beuren, Thomas P. . . . . New York.

1828.

Beisel, John P. . . . . Northampton co., Pa.
Benade, William H. . . . . Salem, N. C.
Bowie, William D. . . . . Philadelphia.
Dash, John B. . . . . New York.
Fraley, Jr., John U. . . . . Philadelphia.
Forbush, John H. . . . . Brooklyn, L. I.
Gleize, William Mc I. . . . . Charleston, S. C.
Graham, John E. . . . . New York.

Haynes, William	New York.
Hildeburn, John M	Philadelphia.
Jones, Maurice C	Old England, Wales.
Kohler, John F	Philadelphia.
Kohler, Andrew	New York.
Lidgerwood, John	Troy, N. Y.
Lidgerwood, Thomas	do.
Rogers, William J	Northampton co., Pa.
Rondthaler, Comenius	Nazareth, Pa.
Sheets, Frederic B	Holmesburg, Pa.
Shober, George	Philadelphia.
Simon, John	do.
Slesman, George J. S	do.
Sparks, Jr., Thomas	do.
Van Voorhis, William R	New York.
Wilstach, Charles M	Philadelphia.
Wolle, Sylvester	Bethlehem, Pa.

1829.

Albert, William J	Baltimore.
Berg, Charles M	Barbadoes, W. I.
Eberman, Francis	West Indies.
Hagen, Francis F	Salem, N. C.
Helm, William	St. Thomas, W. I.
Huddell, Washington A	Philadelphia.
Kampman, Lewis F	do.
Kissam, Philip	New York.
Levy, William P	Philadelphia.
Lippincott, Benjamin	Shrewsbury, N. J.
McCarty, William	Philadelphia.
Peters, John C	New York.
Porter, William H	Nashville, Tenn.
Rees, John P	Philadelphia.
Riter, George W	do.
Scott, John G	do.
Vogel, Albert	do.
Wilstach, William P	do.

1830.

Bininger, William B	New York.
Blickensderfer, Jr., Jacob	Ohio.

F

Bolmer, T. Manuel........................ New York.
Denckla, Henry........................... Philadelphia.
Ducommun, Jr., Henry..................... do.
Franklin, Philip......................... do.
Garvin, John J........................... do.
Geisse, Paul D........................... do.
Hiester, Levi............................ Reading, Pa.
Henry, Reuben A.......................... Stroudsburg, Pa.
Horton, N. Miller........................ Wilkesbarre, Pa.
Johnson, John J.......................... Germantown, Pa.
Kirkpatrick, Robert B.................... Philadelphia.
Leslie, Edmund A......................... New York.
McCarty, James........................... Philadelphia.
Newman, Joseph........................... Tennessee.
Newman, Rush............................. do.
Oakley, Cyrus H.......................... New York.
Oldfield, Granville S.................... do.
Porter, George P......................... Wilkesbarre, Pa.
Pott, John............................... Pottsville, Pa.
Pott, Frank.............................. do.
Reinke, Amadeus A........................ Graceham, Md.
Ronalds, Thomas H........................ New York.
Seidel, Henry A.......................... Bethlehem, Pa.
Seidel, Frederic......................... do.
Schweinitz, Robert de.................... do.
Scott, Thomas............................ Philadelphia.
Smith, Nehemiah D........................ New York.
Smith, Edward G.......................... Philadelphia.
Smyth, Isaac............................. Quakertown, Pa.
Strauch, Henry........................... Pottsville, Pa.
Underwood, William J..................... Philadelphia.
Value, Jesse R........................... do.

1831.

Bininger, Andrew G....................... New York.
Cassidy, Andrew.......................... do.
Clark, William J......................... do.
Dodson, Washington....................... Mauch Chunk, Pa.
Franks, Edward........................... New York.
Freed, Joseph M.......................... Philadelphia, Pa.

Hagerty, Isaiah........................... Georgetown, D. C.
Herbach, Andrew J....................... Pottstown, Pa.
Hoffman, George W....................... Philadelphia.
Kern, Julius.............................. Nazareth, Pa.
Kern, Jr., Andrew G...................... do.
Lawrance, James.......................... New York.
Lewis, Thomas D......................... Wilkesbarre, Pa.
Reppert, George.......................... Baltimore.
Richards, John F......................... Pottstown, Pa.
Ricksecker, Benjamin..................... Bethlehem, Pa.
Shoemaker, Lazarus D.................... Wilkesbarre, Pa.
Solms, Sidney J.......................... Philadelphia.
Solms, John.............................. do.
Streater, William........................ Wilkesbarre, Pa.
Trexler, William......................... Bucks co., Pa.
Vogel, William........................... Philadelphia.
Wolle, Nathaniel S....................... do.

1832.

Baker, Abner R. L........................ New York.
Benade, James A.......................... Lititz, Pa.
Bennet, Charles.......................... Wilkesbarre.
Bininger, Jr., Jacob* .... New York.
Brodrick, Thomas......................... Mauch Chunk, Pa.
Brown, Robert............................ Northampton co., Pa.
Butler, William H........................ Wilkesbarre, Pa.
Clark, George W.......................... Washington, D. C.
Day, William B........................... New York.
Garvin, Benjamin F....................... Philadelphia.
Herriman, John F......................... New York.
Kohier, George A......................... Philadelphia.
Kunckle, John............................ Nescopeck, Pa.
Kunckle, Aaron........................... do.
Lafourcade, Charles...................... Philadelphia.
Lee, Hattrick............................ New York.
Lee, James, Jr........................... do.
Meyer, William.......................... do.
Miller, Simon............................ Northampton co., Pa.
Overton, Thomas B....................... Towanda, Pa.
Paine, Charles C......................... Athens, Pa.

Quin, Emmet.............................. New Jersey.
Ripka, Jr., Joseph........................ Philadelphia.
Ripka, John............................... do.
Romig, William J.......................... Allentown, Pa.
Shants, Hiram J........................... Lehigh co., Pa.
Shankland, Alexander T.................... Philadelphia.
Shimer, Samuel C.......................... Northampton co., Pa.
Smith, William P.......................... Philadelphia.
Thompson, William H....................... Easton, Pa.
Van Vleck, Henry J........................ New York.

1833.

Bourne, John.............................. Philadelphia.
Brooks, George K.......................... New York.
Brooks, H. J.............................. do.
Burger, Samuel............................ Staten Island, N. Y.
Chamberlin, William....................... Philadelphia.
Colgate, Jr., William..................... New York.
Colgate, Samuel........................... do.
Davis, Robert C........................... Philadelphia.
Denckla, William.......................... do.
Dennison, Henry M......................... Wilkesbarre, Pa.
Horton, Thomas M.......................... do.
Kissam, William........................... New York.
Ludwigsen, John H......................... St. Croix, W. I.
Lynch, Edward P........................... Wilkesbarre, Pa.
McVickar, John J.......................... New York.
McVickar, Nathan.......................... do.
Meredith, Samuel R........................ Carbondale, Pa.
Mitchell, Henry........................... Natchez, Miss.
Overton, Giles B.......................... Towanda, Pa.
Partenheimer, H. R........................ Philadelphia.
Philip, George A.......................... Brooklyn, L. I.
Philip, John C............................ do.
Philip, Jacob............................. do.
Rea, John................................. Philadelphia.
Reichel, Edward H......................... Salem, N. C.
Reinke, Edwin E........................... Graceham, Md.
Rice, Samuel.............................. Bethlehem, Pa.
Searle, Roger............................. Montrose, Pa.

Senseman, Edwin T. . . . . Salem, N. C.
Smith, Charles E. . . . . New York.
Steinhauer, Henry F. Philadelphia.
Tennent, John. . . . . do.
Wagner, George M. . . . . do.
Wagner, Paul M. . . . . do.
Whitney, Charles F. . . . . Binghamton, N. Y.

1834.

Bassford, Joseph. . . . . New York.
Beekman, Stephen F. do.
Fullmer, John J. . . . . Philadelphia.
Gillingham, Henry. . . . . New York.
Kirk, John R. . . . . Philadelphia.
Maxwell, James. . . . . do.
Meyer, Thomas. . . . . New York.
Reichel, William C. . . . . Salem, N. C.
Renshaw, Atlantic. . . . . Long Branch, N. J.
Ritter, Isaac L. . . . . Philadelphia.
Schweinitz, Edmund de. . . . . Bethlehem, Pa.
Stein, Albert. . . . . New Orleans.
Stevens, William. . . . . Natchez, Miss.
Warren, William. . . . . Philadelphia.
Warner, William H. . . . . Bethlehem, Pa.
Whalton, Joseph C. . . . . Indian Key, Fla.
Zippel, Gustavus E. . . . . Barbadoes, W. I.

1835.

Arthurton, Samuel L. Nevis, W. I.
Baker, Joseph A. . . . . New York.
Bassford, George W. do.
Barkaloo, John. . . . . Brooklyn, N. Y.
Buttner, Albert J. . . . . Bethania, N. C.
Clark, James G. . . . . Staten Island, N. Y.
Cook, Albert G. . . . . Philadelphia.
Eberman, Jacob F. . . . . Litiz, Pa.
Gassner, John A. . . . . New York.
Hall, Edward S. . . . . Philadelphia.
Hampton, Francis. . . . . do.
Haughwout, John. . . . . Staten Island, N. Y.
8

Haughwout, Nicholas..................... Staten Island, N. Y.
Higgins, William........................ New York.
Huebner, Matthias T.................... Gnadenhutten, O.
Kummer, Joseph II..................... Bethlehem, Pa.
Lambert, Emile S....................... Schœneck, Pa.
Lilliendahl, Charles W................. New York.
Lippincott, John M..................... Shrewsbury, N. J.
Lippincott, Charles A.................. do.
Mancius, George W..................... Albany, N. Y.
Neuville, Clarence..................... Staten Island, N. Y.
Peters, John Jordan.................... Philadelphia.
Reynegom, John V...................... do.
Smith, David Z........................ Salem, N. C.
Tillou, Charles G...................... New York.
Van Beuren, William H................. do.
Van Beuren, George F.................. do.
Vanname, Henry....................... Staten Island, N. Y.
Van Vleck, Arthur L................... Lancaster, Pa.
Vredenburg, John V.................... Staten Island, N. Y.
Wattley, George....................... St. Kitts. W. I.
Wichelhausen, Peter................... New York.
Wolle, Samuel C....................... Philadelphia.
Wray, Samuel......................... Jamaica, W. I.

1836

Albert, Jacob......................... Baltimore.
Bauersachs, Lewis C................... Philadelphia.
Chamberlin, John...................... do.
Cook, Thomas W...................... New York.
Dunbar, Samuel....................... do.
Gunther, C. Godfrey................... do.
Gunther, John C....................... do.
Hooper, Jr., John*.................. Philadelphia.
Ihrie, George P........................ Easton, Pa.
Ireland, Robert W..................... New York.
Jenks, Abraham S...................... Newtown, Pa.
Jackson, Samuel....................... New York.
Keehln, Theodore F.................... Salem, N. C.
Kein, James T......................... Philadelphia.
Kimberly, John II..................... Greene co., N. Y.

Klauberg, Daniel........................ New York.
Lytle, John D........................... Philadelphia.
Maslin, Edward V....................... do.
Maslin, Alexander...................... do.
McIntosh, Leonidas..................... Georgia.
Michler, Nathaniel..................... Easton, Pa.
Moore, Michael M....................... New York.
Morrison, James........................ Philadelphia.
Riter, Michael M....................... do.
Riter, Frederick G..................... do.
Roebuck, John Jarvis................... St. Croix, W. I.
Seaman, John........................... Mobile, Ala.
Scull, William......................... Arkansas.
Scull, Benjamin........................ do.
Shoemaker, Austin D.................... Wilkesbarre, Pa.
Tennent, Charles....................... Philadelphia.
Tennent, Sidney........................ do.

1837.

Baldwin, Jr., John..................... Vera Cruz, Mexico.
Blydenburgh, William L................. New York.
Brickman, Jr., George.................. Philadelphia.
Capron, Augustus S..................... Easton, Pa.
Chamberlin, Richard.................... Philadelphia.
Crease, Orlando........................ Roxborough, Phila. co.
Cruger, Frederick H.................... Easton, Pa.
Davis, Joseph D........................ Allentown, Pa.
Day, George W.......................... New York.
Dekay, George A........................ do.
Deringer, Calhoun M.................... Philadelphia.
Farlee, John R......................... Flemington, N. J.
Finlayson, William..................... Holmesburg, Pa.
Gunther, Henry Wm...................... New York.
Henry, Eugene T........................ Stroudsburg, Pa.
Hyslop, George Paulding................ New York.
Hyslop, Frederic Knox.................. do.
Leimer, Jr., Alexander................. Philadelphia.
Lewis, Richard B....................... Pottsville, Pa.
McIntosh, James McQueen................ Georgia.
McIntosh, John Baillie................. do.

McNair, James	Oswego, N. Y.
Philip, Joseph Dean	Brooklyn, N. Y.
Ponte, Jean Durant da	New York.
Schweinitz, Bernard de	Bethlehem, Pa.
Scherr, Philip R	Philadelphia.
Smith, Horace W	do.
Snyder, Mifflin H	Northampton co., Pa.
Waterbury, Julius H	Philadelphia.
Winpenny, Joseph	Manayunk, Pa.
Woods, William H	St. Croix, W. I.

1838.

Bates, Jr., John M	Greensboro', Ala.
Briggs, Gilbert C	New York.
Brodrick, Jr., James	Mauch Chunk, Pa.
Brower, Isaac L	New York.
Chapman, Lebbeus, Jr.	Schuylkill Haven, Pa.
Eckstein, William A	Philadelphia.
Eckstein, Charles H	do.
Eckstein, Horatio G	do.
Lambert, Emile	Nazareth, Pa.
Marsh, Charles	Philadelphia.
Marsh, Thomas T	do.
Michler, Francis	Easton, Pa.
McAlpin, Thaddeus*	Mobile, Ala.
Molony, George H	Philadelphia.
Moore, William H	do.
Perry, William F	New York.
Stem, James M	Bath, Pa.
Wilmer, Jr., John	Philadelphia.
Winder, Moses	Attleboro', Pa.
Wolle, James H	Litiz, Pa.

1839.

Blake, Harvey B	New York.
Bourne, James H	do.
Briggs, George H	do.
Carsten, Philip	Charleston, S. C.
Dickson, Charles W	Easton, Pa.
Dickson, William J	do.

Edwards, William...................... New York.
Hall, Robert S........................ Philadelphia.
Hitz, John............................ Wurtsboro', N. C.
Huebner, Lewis R...................... Graceham, Md.
Innes, Edward......................... Easton, Pa.
Jones, Elias H........................ Philadelphia.
Keen, Alfred.......................... do.
Keen, Clement......................... do.
Kluge, Charles E...................... Nazareth, Pa.
Lawrence, Jr., Alexander.............. New York.
McIntosh, William A................... Georgia.
McKinley, George...................... Chester co., Pa.
Parke, Horatio S...................... Philadelphia.
Parke, Cornelius...................... do.
Philip, William....................... Brooklyn, N. Y.
Pitcher, Charles H.................... New York.
Richardson, George J. B............... Wayne co., Pa.
Rights, Constantine L................. Salem, N. C.
Tappen, Charles L..................... Staten Island, N. Y.
Ten Eyck, Richard..................... New York.
Townsend, Benjamin B.................. do.
Wallace, Samuel....................... Philadelphia.

1840.

Armstrong, William H.................. Newburg, N. Y.
Barnet, William....................... Easton, Pa.
Beear, Benjamin B..................... Bethlehem, Pa.
Cooper, Thomas L...................... Columbus, Ga.
De Forest, Othniel.................... Pottsville, Pa.
De Forest, David...................... do.
Fisher, Joseph C...................... New York.
Fitler, Washington.................... Philadelphia.
Hunter, David H....................... Allentown, Pa.
Lambert, Theodore A................... Hopedale, Pa.
McCawley, Charles G................... Philadelphia.
McKeen, Jr., Thomas L................. Easton, Pa.
Pomp, Charles......................... do.
Prior, Volney......................... New York.
Scott, George......................... Wilkesbarre, Pa.
Shouse, Samuel Opp.................... Easton, Pa.
8 *

Spackman, John	Philadelphia.
Tennent, Sidney	do.
Tennent, Albert	do.
Thomas, Samuel	Catasauqua, Pa.
Van Buren, David H	Clarksville, Ga.
Van Beuren, George F	New York.
Van Beuren, Charles E	do.

1841.

Acord, John H	Huntsville, Ala.
Beck, James N	Litiz, Pa.
Bodine, Jacob	Staten Island, N. Y.
Brown, John M	New York.
Disdier, Frederic	Havana, Cuba.
Eberman, John H	Hope, Ind.
Eisenbrey, Edwin T	Philadelphia.
Geisse, George F	do.
Geisse, Louis	do.
Goepp, R. Max	Bethlehem, Pa.
Harrison, Charles T	New York.
Hunter, John N. N	Allentown, Pa.
Jacobson, William A	Salem, N. C.
Klosè, Charles	Barbadoes, W. I.
Klosè, Martin*	do.
Parker, Edmund	Philadelphia.
Parker, William	do.
Parker, Charles	do.
Prince, Abraham	Jamaica, W. I.
Ritter, Bradford	Philadelphia.
Scull, Joseph	Pine Bluff, Ark.
Stockton, James	New Orleans.
Stockton, George	do.
Stout, Charles M	Bethlehem, Pa.
Thomas, John	Catasauqua. Pa.
Womrath, George K	Philadelphia.
Zane, Charles	Easton, Pa.

1842.

Bachman, Edwin J	Fairfield. U. C.
Bigler, John F	New York.
Birdsall, John F	Brooklyn, N. Y.

Boyd, James G. S...................... Lynchburg, Va.
Brickenstein, Lawrence C.................... Bethlehem, Pa.
Davis, Benjamin J. B...................... Philadelphia.
Kluge, John P...................... Bethlehem, Pa.
Koons, Edward A...................... Philadelphia.
Lapsley, Edward...................... do.
Larcade, Gustave...................... Port-au-Prince, Hayti.
Phelps, Joseph F...................... New York.
Ripka, Robert A...................... Manayunk, Pa.
Ripka, Andrew A...................... do.
Ryan, James...................... Philadelphia.
Shober, Charles E...................... Salem, N. C.
Troeger, Henry A...................... Nazareth, Pa.
Trucks, William...................... Philadelphia.
Winpenny, John M...................... Manayunk, Pa.
Wolle, Theodore F...................... Philadelphia.

1843.

Clauder, Amos C...................... Staten Island, N. Y.
Clauder, Charles J...................... do.
Clewell, Eugene F...................... Salem, N. C.
Davis, Samuel T...................... Philadelphia.
Doyle, Staughton F...................... do.
Innes, Joseph M...................... Easton, Pa.
Jacobson, Edward H...................... Salem, N. C.
Michler, Clarence...................... Easton, Pa.
Overington, Thomas...................... Frankford, Pa.
Thomas, William...................... Beaver Meadow, Pa.

1844.

Bachman, Henry T...................... Westfield, Mo.
Biddle, Henry D...................... New York.
Brickenstein, Herman A...................... Bethlehem, Pa.
Davis, Jr., Collin K...................... Philadelphia.
Davis, Alfred B...................... do.
Dearie, Jr., John...................... do.
Denniston, James...................... Lockport, N. Y.
Eberman, Edward M...................... Bethlehem, Pa.
Egbert, Augustus...................... Manayunk, Pa.
Hess, John J...................... Philadelphia.

Hood, Edmund B.	New York.
Lilliendahl, William A.	do.
Lockwood, Philip E.	do.
Marston, Edward E.	Philadelphia.
McKinley, John H.	New York.
Prince, Isaac.	Jamaica, W. I.
Reinke, Clement L.	Bethlehem, Pa.
Spackman, Samuel G.	Philadelphia.
Sutton, Stephen.	Luzerne co., Pa.
Townsend, Samuel T.	New York.
Troeger, Jeremiah.	Nazareth, Pa.

1845.

Balliet, Louis B.	Lehigh co., Pa.
Bewley, John B.	Philadelphia.
Denniston, Edward.	North Providence, R. I.
Drinker, Joseph D.	Montrose, Pa.
Eldridge, G. Morgan.	Cecilton, Md.
Ingersoll, George K.	New York.
Kluge, William C*	Bethlehem, Pa.
Kummer, C. Edward.	Litiz, Pa.
Lee, Jr., Franklin.	Philadelphia.
Maison, William A.	do.
Mitchell, Robert W.	do.
Perkin, John J.	do.
Peters, Charles F.	do.
Pinkney, Charles.	New York.
Rex, Jacob L.	Montgomery co., Pa.
Shober, Francis E.	Salem, N. C.
Steinberger, Charles M.	Philadelphia.
Widmayer, George A.	New York.
Wilson, Henry C.	Bethania, N. C.
Womrath, Andrew K.	Philadelphia.
Yaeger, George A.	Berks co., Pa.
Zippel, Edwin T.	Barbadoes, W. I.

1846.

Beard, Oliver T.	Brooklyn, N. Y.
Brown, Jacob O.	Monroe co., Pa.
Chidsey, George W.	Easton, Pa.

Freitag, Theodore E...................... Allentown, Pa.
Heilig, Daniel B......................... Monroe co., Pa.
Henry, Granville......................... Boulton, Pa.
Housel, Edwin........................... Easton, Pa.
Hutchinson, Charles H................... Philadelphia.
Kluge, Edward T........................ Salem, N. C.
Reinke, Samuel F*................... Bethlehem, Pa.
Stevenson, Richard J.................... New York.
Talmadge, T. Van Pelt.................. Brooklyn, N. Y.
Thomae, George F....................... New York.
Thomae, Henry K........................ do.
Vogler, Lawrence....................... New Fairfield, Canada.
Wilson, George.......................... New York.
Wolle, Henry H......................... Litiz, Pa.

1847.

Babcock, Charles W..................... New York.
Bartram, John.......................... Philadelphia.
Bigler, Henry A........................ New York.
Brittain, Henry........................ Bucks co., Pa.
Chapman, Robert........................ New York.
Clarke, Henry T........................ Easton, Pa.
Crawford, William H................... do.
Crawford, John......................... do.
Crease, Henry.......................... Roxborough, Pa.
Eldridge, Edwin J...................... Cecil co., Md.
Gerber, John........................... Pottsville, Pa.
Gilbert, John.......................... Jersey City.
Hart, Walter H......................... New York.
Hart, John M........................... Philadelphia.
Huffnagle, Allen....................... Bethlehem, Pa.
Keiffer, John.......................... Charleston, S. C.
Knox, J. Charles....................... Philadelphia.
Lambert, Lewis D....................... Nazareth, Pa.
Levan, Albert.......................... Lehigh co., Pa.
Lewis, Charles M....................... Philadelphia.
Mecke, George A........................ Minersville, Pa.
Mixsell, Jacob C....................... Easton, Pa.
Napier, Thomas L....................... Macon, Ga.
Napier, Nathan M....................... do.

Oerter, Albert L.......................... Litiz, Pa.
Paine, Clement T........................ Bradford co., Pa.
Plumb, James............................. New York.
Pretz, Philip S........................... Allentown, Pa.
Schols, Clayton........................... Brooklyn, N. Y.
Smeidle, Charles L........................ Philadelphia.
Spearing, Edward J....................... New Orleans.
Steinle, Frederick E...................... New York.
Stevenson, James.......................... do.
Taggart, Joseph.......................... Tamaqua, Pa.
Trucks, Jr., John........................ Philadelphia.
Tschudy, Richard R....................... Litiz, Pa.
Turner, Jr., John......................... Luzerne co., Pa.
Vancourt, Robert A....................... Philadelphia.
Wohlgemuth, Otto......................... Allentown, Pa.
Womrath, Frederic K...................... Philadelphia
Yaeger, Robert J......................... Allentown, Pa.

1848.

Anderson, Charles J...................... New York.
Barnum, Freeman......................... St. Louis, Mo.
Beck, Abraham R......................... Litiz, Pa.
Burke, Joseph............................ Easton, Pa.
Clauder, Frederic A...................... Staten Island, N. Y.
Drinker, Charles J....................... Montrose, Pa.
Elliott, Edward T................. ...... Towanda, Pa.
Foster, William R........................ Philadelphia.
Gaylord, Asher........................... Luzerne co., Pa.
Hawley, Christopher E.................... Binghamton, N. Y.
Huebner, Obadiah T....................... Salem, N. C.
Irion, William M......................... New Castle, Tenn.
Keyser, Eyre............................. Philadelphia.
Keyser, Peter D.......................... do.
Leibert, Eugene M........................ Bethlehem, Pa.
Montayne, George D....................... Towanda, Pa.
Oerter, J. Eugene........................ Bethlehem, Pa.
Philips, Louis........................... New Orleans.
Philips, James........................... do.
Thomas, Jr., David....................... Catasauqua, Pa.
Yaeger, Samuel T......................... Berks co., Pa.

1849.

Audenried, Thomas	Northampton co., Pa.
Audenried, James E.	do.
Bachman, Joseph P.	Westfield, Mo.
Byrnes, Thomas H.	New York.
Davenport, Abraham M.	do.
Finn, Lorenzo	Laguayra, S. A.
Förste, Charles	do.
Gillender, William C.	New York.
Haman, James B.	Salem, N. C.
Hollenback, John M.	Wilkesbarre, Pa.
Huebner, Samuel A.	Salem, N. C.
Huntzinger, Henry H.	Orwigsburg, Pa.
Kenton, Henry C.	Philadelphia.
Mayo, Archibald	do.
McClatchey, Robert J.	do.
Pfohl, Augustus F.	Salem, N. C.
Philip, Benjamin D.	New York.
Rahn, Oscar	Philadelphia.
Rice, Jr., Owen	Bethlehem, Pa.
Siewers, Clarence E.	Mauch Chunk, Pa.
Stauffer, Isaac	Monroe co., Pa.
Taylor, William Ralph	New York.
Taylor, Horace E.	do.
Wainwright, Charles B.	Philadelphia.
Walls, Abbot	Lewisburg, Pa.

1850.

Cameron, William	Lewisburg, Pa.
Dubosq, Robert	Philadelphia.
Fenner, William Henry	Monroe co., Pa.
Kent, Francis S.	Philadelphia.
Spearing, Robert	New Orleans.
Titze, Henry A.	Bethlehem, Pa.

1851.

Browning, Newton	Philadelphia.
Bute, Jr., Charles L.	do.
Cathrall, Eugene	do.
Chamberlin, Henry	Nazareth, Pa.

Chapman, Richard H...................... Philadelphia.
Cortelyou, Eugene A...................... Staten Island, N. Y.
Cummins, William*...................... New York.
Cummins, T. Eugene...................... do.
Dorney, Theodore P...................... Philadelphia.
Fiechtner, Frederic J. R................... do.
Frueauff, J. Frederic...................... Litiz, Pa.
Gratz, Robert........................... Philadelphia.
Heilig, Augustus......................... Monroe co., Pa.
Hering, Maximilian...................... Philadelphia.
Lichtenthaler, Samuel.................... Chicago, Ill.
Loyd, William Henry..................... Philadelphia.
Loyd, Wilson............................ do.
Megarey, Alexander...................... Brooklyn, L. I.
Post, Charles William.................... do.
Schroeder, A. Drummond................. Red Bank, N. J.
Wenzel, John Philip..................... Bavaria.

1852.

Basham, John........................... New York.
Basham, Edmund........................ do.
Carey, George A........................ Easton, Pa.
Clauder, Henry T....................... Hope, Ind.
Davis, Hamilton........................ New York.
Georger, Lewis F....................... do.
Gosevisch, Frederic..................... Wilmington, Del.
Harris, William F....................... Philadelphia.
Harvey, John Cennick................... Brooklyn, L. I.
Heilig, Theophilus...................... Monroe co., Pa.
Henry, Dorwin D....................... Albany, N. Y.
Henry, Charles V....................... do.
Jones, Samuel M........................ Philadelphia.
Jordan, John W......................... do.
Kessler, Thomas V...................... do.
Laughlin, Robert....................... do.
Lilliendahl, Francis T.................. New York.
Michler, William Henry H.............. Easton, Pa.
Mills, John B.......................... Pottsville, Pa.
Noble, James.......................... Philadelphia.
Persse, Stratford...................... New York.

Persse, William	New York.
Shultz, Charles B.	Litiz, Pa.
Van Duzer, Daniel T.	Staten Island, N. Y.
Waldman, Thomas.	Philadelphia.
Walker, Joseph.	New York.
Walker, John	do.
White, Andrew G.	Albany, N. Y.
Widmayer, William	Staten Island, N. Y.
Widmayer, Henry	do.
Williams, George.	New York.
Woodward, William Henry	Northampton, Mass.
Zorn, J. Theophilus	Bethlehem, Pa.

1853.

Bennett, Horace C.	Minersville, Pa.
Bigler, William H.	New York.
Cook, James Renwick.	Albany, N. Y.
Culp, Jacob.	Philadelphia.
Decoursey, Marcelin L.	do.
Eplee, George H.	do.
Fiechtner, William D.	do.
Graff, Francis.	do.
Grant, Francis H.	Derby, Conn.
Harper, Andrew D.	Brooklyn, N. Y.
Henry, Horace H.	Albany, N. Y.
Hilton, Samuel M.	Brooklyn, N. Y.
Hoeber, Edward E.	Nazareth, Pa.
Homer, Horace.	Philadelphia.
Jackson, Thomas M.	do.
Jordan, William H.	do.
Jordan, Jr., Francis	do.
Kern, James D.	Nazareth, Pa.
Latimer, David Teford.	Plainfield, N. J.
Lewis, Lionel B.	Morristown, N. J.
Lichtenthaler, Edwin.	Chicago, Ill.
Longmire, Edwin	Philadelphia.
Longmire, Nathaniel C.	do.
Lyons, George W.	Louisiana.
Marsden, William	Philadelphia.
Nathans, Camillus	do.

9   G

Nixon, William Henry..................... Manayunk, Pa.
Nixon, Theodore A......... .... do.
Oerter, Edmund A....................... Bethabara, N. C.
Powell, Edmund F....................... Allentown, Pa.
Ricksecker, Joseph J...................... Tobago, W. I
Rondthaler, Jr., Edward.................. Nazareth, Pa.
Rosenbaum, Charles A.................... New York.
Shields, George W....................... Manayunk, Pa.
Shouse, Edmund A...................... Easton, Pa.
Street, William Augustus................. New York.
Tilge, Frederic Augustus................. Philadelphia.
Uhl, Herman............................. New York.
Walter, Eugene.......................... Nazareth, Pa.
Watson, George.......................... New York.
Watson, William......................... do.
Willower, Charles F...................... Philadelphia.
Witmer, John A.......................... Cincinnati.
Witmer, Elam W......................... do.

1854.

Barrett, Walter........................... Clearfield, Pa.
Bergen, Garret P......................... Brooklyn, L. I.
Bergen, Van Brunt M..................... do.
Brogden, F. L............................ New Orleans.
Buck, William F......................... Philadelphia.
Bute, William Edward.................... do.
Butler, F. A............................. Shrewsbury, N. J.
Crane, F. L.............................. Easton, Pa.
Cochran, Walter C....................... New York.
Cutler, Augustus W...................... Morristown, N. J.
Cutter, Le Clerc......................... New York.
Daily, Henry A.......................... Easton, Pa.
Drinkhouse, Joseph W.................... Philadelphia.
Drinkhouse, Samuel...................... do.
Finnall, Marion S........................ Washington, D. C.
Gilsey, Charles.......................... New York.
Gilsey, Peter............................ do.
Grafton, James Ingersoll................. Boston, Mass.
Haman, W. H. T......................... Salem, N. C.
Harlan, Richard P....................... Wilmington, Del.

Harris, James M. R.	Massillon, O.
Hendrickson, Charles	Brooklyn, L. I.
Henry, Benneville M.	Reading, Pa.
Hilton, John W.	Brooklyn, L. I.
Horton, Nathan Waller	Wilkesbarre, Pa.
Kenney, Joseph R.	Philadelphia.
Klose, Edwin G.	St. Kitts, W. I.
McIlroy, Matthew	Philadelphia.
Moore, William A.	Richmond, Mo.
Moore, Alexander P.	do.
Place, Charles A.	New York.
Purdy, Lovell	Staten Island, N. Y.
Purdy, Charles	do.
Reed, Thomas H.	Pottsville, Pa.
Remick, Albert	Philadelphia.
Richards, Jr., Daniel	New York.
Ridgway, Jr., Joseph	do.
Rogers, Molton C.	New Castle, Del.
Saltmarsh, Orlando T.	San Antonio, Texas.
Seidel, Charles W.	Bethlehem, Pa.
Shoemaker, Frederic M.	Wilkesbarre, Pa.
Tonnelle, Peter	New York.
Vail, Jr., Stephen	Morristown, N. J.
Vail, James Cummins	do.
Van Beuren, Thomas P.	Newburg, N. Y.
Van Beuren, Edward	Paterson, N. J.
Weimer, Lucian E.	Reading, Pa.
Wilson, Charles J.	Somerville, N. J.
Wood, John F.	Philadelphia.
Woodall, F. B.	New Orleans.
Yates, G. Clement	San Josè, Cal.

1855

Anderson, Carman E.	Brooklyn, N. Y.
Backer, James N.	Baltimore.
Bigler, D. Eugene	New York.
Bridge, Benjamin	New Orleans.
Brodrick, Henry T.	Rockport, Pa.
Coles, Edwin	New York.
Cox, Fullerton	Brooklyn, N. Y.

Ellis, Frank H.......................... Philadelphia.
Erben, Charles......................... New York.
Fasig, Daniel H......................... Reading, Pa.
Fisher, Richard......................... Philadelphia.
Fisher, Jacob B......................... New York.
Forman, Lawrence H.................... Easton, Pa.
Fry, Marcus............................ Coopersburg, Pa.
Gebhard, Julius........................ Buffalo, N. Y.
Gilchrist, Thomas McCartney............ Wilkesbarre, Pa.
Gilchrist, Harry S...................... do.
Grosclaude, L. Augustus.. .... Hoboken, N. J.
Harper, James P........................ Brooklyn, N. Y.
Held, Charles E........................ New York.
Jones, John R.......................... Montgomery co., Pa.
Kampman, Albert....................... Bethlehem, Pa.
Knecht, John N......................... Shimersville, Pa.
Kutzmeyer, Philip H.................... Jersey City, N. J.
Lorillard, Blase........................ Saugerties, N. Y.
McCartney, Washington................. Kittaning, Pa.
Michael, James H....................... Perrymansville, Md.
McKenzie, Richard...................... Charleston, S. C.
Moore, John............................ St. John, W. I.
Moore, Harrison........................ do.
Moore, Robert.......................... do.
Morrell, William A..................... New York.
Morrison, John F....................... South Orange, N. J.
Mozer, Herman H....................... Buffalo, N. Y.
Oehler, Reuben......................... Hopedale, Pa.
Paine, Charles......................... Troy, Pa.
Parker, Edward......................... Philadelphia.
Place, Newberry........................ New York.
Regennas, Edward J..................... Emmaus, Pa.
Remsen, William R...................... New York.
Rogers, Thomas W...................... New Castle, Del.
Rondthaler, J. Albert................... York, Pa.
Ryerson, Charles....................... New York.
Seitzinger, Franklin.................... Reading, Pa.
Silliman, Thomas H..................... Pottsville, Pa.
Silver, Marcus......................... Philadelphia.
Simonson, Cornelius A.................. New York.
Simonson, Jeremiah V.................. do.

Staats, Bernardus E., Jr..................... Norwalk, Conn.
Stearns, William W....................... Elizabeth, N. J.
Uhl, Edward............................. New York.
Van Beuren, Thomas P.................... Newburg, N. Y.
Whitehurst, Clarence..................... Key West, Fla.
Youngs, George.......................... New York.
Youngs, Washington...................... do.

1856.

Anderson, Jansen H...................... Saugerties, N. Y.
Benners, Samuel C....................... Philadelphia.
Berks, Theodore W....................... Germantown, Pa.
Berks, Samuel H......................... Philadelphia.
Caldwell, Samuel W...................... Camden, N. J.
Corell, Daniel........................... Easton, Pa.
Close, William Henry.................... New York.
Close, Charles Augustus.................... do.
Fream, George Lorillard.................... do.
Frueauff, W. Herman T................... Bethlehem, Pa.
Georger, C. Emile....................... New York.
Gunther, Charles B...................... do.
Henry, Edward T........................ Bolton, Pa..
Jacobson, Henry A...................... Bethlehem, Pa.
Jarvis, Jay............................. New York.
Kampman, Clarence..................... Lancaster, Pa.
Knox, Edward M........................ New York.
Landell, Benjamin F....... .... Philadelphia.
Manly, Louis............................ Woodbury, N. J.
Moss, Edgar W.......................... Philadelphia.
Moss, Frank V.......................... do.
Morrell, William A...................... New York.
Ostrom, Charles......................... Brooklyn, N. Y.
Purdy, Charles.......................... New York.
Raborg, Frank.......................... St. Louis, Mo.
Renshaw, William H..................... Philadelphia.
Robbins, John T........................ do.
Rohn, Jacob P.......................... Nazareth, Pa.
Schoelkopf, Henry....................... Buffalo, N. Y.
Sellers, George......................... Philadelphia.
Sigel, Charles, Jr....................... White's Corner, N. Y.

9 *

Sigel, Frederic	White's Corner, N. Y.
Shoemaker, Richard M., Jr	Philadelphia.
Silver, Marcus	do.
Sneckner, William H	New York.
Stadiger, John F	Friedensville, Pa.
Thomas, Abraham W	Germantown, Pa.
Trautwine, William	Philadelphia.
Tschudy, Haydn H	Litiz, Pa.
Tyng, Dudley	Morristown, N. J.
Valliant, George A	Philadelphia.
Van Harlinger, John	Millstone, N. J.
Walker, Augustus E	Ottawa, Ill.
Weaver, Thomas M	Philadelphia.
Wetherill, Samuel Price	Bethlehem, Pa.
Wetherill, John Price	do.
Wood, Irving D	Philadelphia.
Williams, Harding	do.
Wright, Charles	New York.
Yohe, William W	Bethlehem, Pa.
Yohe, George A	do.
Youngs, William	New York.

1857.

Bain, Henry	Philadelphia.
Barret, Frederic	Mauch Chunk, Pa.
Beckler, Henry B	Litiz, Pa.
Benade, James Arthur	Reading, Pa.
Benade, Patrick Henry	do.
Berrien, Theodore	New York.
Berrien, George	do.
Bininger, Abraham M	do.
Burnham, James M	do.
Burnham, Thomas	do.
Caldwell, James R	Camden, N. J.
Colladay, Samuel R	Philadelphia.
Davis, Chambers C	Nesquehoning, Pa.
Disbrow, William H	New York.
Drinkhouse, Albert	Easton, Pa.
Flammer, Edwin F	Nazareth, Pa.
Gunther, Frederic W	New York.

Gunther, Christian G...................... New York.
Havemeyer, William A..................... do.
Hicks, Elias.............................. do.
Hindes, Joseph H......................... Brooklyn, L. I.
Knauss, Charles E........................ Nazareth, Pa.
Ladd, William W.......................... Woodbury, N. J.
Le Conte, William........................ Washington, D. C.
Lichtenthaler, Adolphus................... Jamaica, W. I.
McCalla, Bowman H....................... Camden, N. J.
Moss, Walter L........................... Philadelphia.
Moss, Jacob A............................ do.
Palmer, Henry A.......................... New Market, N. J.
Pfefferle, John F......................... Hoboken, N. J.
Pitt, William A........................... Stamford, Conn.
Pitt, Charles B........................... do.
Purdy, John F............................ San Francisco, Cal.
Purdy, Charles T......................... do.
Remsen, Phœnix.......................... New York.
Richards, Daniel E....................... Easton, Pa.
Ridgway, Joseph, Jr....................... New York.
Ritter, James Morrison.................... Philadelphia.
Rohn, Jacob P............................ Nazareth, Pa.
Rowland, James Day....................... Philadelphia.
Rowland, Frank Sheets.................... do.
Scheu, Jacob.............................. Buffalo, N. Y.
Schneider, Peter.......................... Hoboken, N. J.
Sheets, Henry............................ Washington, D. C.
Simonson, George L....................... Staten Island, N. Y.
Stickle, D. Edgar......................... Rockaway, N. Y.
Streater, Charles......................... Wilkesbarre, Pa.
Thompson, William........................ Philadelphia.
Tilge, George Edward..................... do.
Warmkessel, Theobald..................... New York.
Yates, Rudolph B......................... Schenectady, N. Y.

1858.

Allaire, Frederic......................... New York.
Bahnson, Henry T......................... Salem, N. C.
Bishop, Charles D........................ Springplace, Ind. Ter.
Blickensderfer, Ulric..................... Hospitality, Erie co., Pa.

Bryan, Augustus W	New York.
Clark, Thomas L	do.
Clark, Henry F	do.
Conrad, William Augustus	Huntsville, N. C.
Dreher, Henry E	New York.
Duer, William A	Morristown, N. J.
Grote, August H	Fordham, N. Y.
Gunther, Frederic W	New York.
Hagen, John C	York, Pa.
Heiser, Godfrey C	Buffalo, N. Y.
Held, Robert L	New York.
Hibbler, George H	Newark, N. J.
Illig, M. Charles	Williamsburg, L. I.
Jones, Abraham G	Bethania, N. C.
Jones, James J. B	do.
Jordan, Ewing	Philadelphia.
Kuntz, Joseph	New York.
Lafourcade, P. M	Philadelphia.
Lash, Flavius H	Bethania, N. C.
Lee, George F	Philadelphia.
Lennert, Edward F	Nazareth, Pa.
Lewis, George C	Wilkesbarre, Pa.
Loutey, Joseph A	Philadelphia.
Mack, Ephraim H	Canaan, Indian Ter.
Mayer, Norman J	New York.
Mayer, Ferdinand C	do.
Meurer, William A	Philadelphia.
Mimmes, Frank W	Cincinnati.
Munro, Nathan C	Macon, Ga.
Newton, Alfred W	Philadelphia.
Sargent, Thomas B	Baltimore.
Scheu, William D	Buffalo, N. Y.
Senseman, John H	New York.
Siewers, Nathanial S	Salem, N. C.
Shuttmeister, Victor R	San Francisco, Cal.
Smylie, Matthew C	Easton, Pa.
Snyder, Peter	do.
Stone, Louis V. P	New York.
Stanton, Edward T	do.
Steiner, John L	Philadelphia.
Stiles, William, Jr	do.

Tilge, Louis T.............................. Philadelphia.
Van Reed, Joshua........................ Sinking Spring, Pa.
Vastine, Benjamin P..................... Pottsville, Pa.
Vetterlein, Herman G.................... Philadelphia.

1859.

Albert, Joseph Taylor..................... Baltimore.
Albert, Jacob.............................. do.
Barnes, Edward........................... New York.
Barnes, Albert............................ do.
Bast, George.............................. Schuylkill Haven, Pa.
Birkle, George............................ Stapleton, Staten Island.
Blickensderfer, James C.................. Erie co., Pa.
Clarke, George L......................... New York.
Cooke, Robert Fulton..................... Brooklyn, N. Y.
Deal, Elias................................ Philadelphia.
Deal, Benjamin C......................... do.
Dusenberry, Edwin....................... New York.
Engel, Theodor C......................... Philadelphia.
Guiterman, Marcus H..................... Port Carbon, Pa.
Hagen, F. Benjamin....................... York, Pa.
Hess, Robert J............................ Easton, Pa.
Hilman, William H........................ New York.
Hooley, John.............................. Philadelphia.
Hornblower, Arthur E..................... Newark, N. J.
Howell, Edward D........................ New York.
Hyatt, George E. L....................... do.
Johnson, Lewis Cass...................... Philadelphia.
Johnston, Thomas A....................... Madison, N. J.
Kampman, Joseph......................... Bethlehem, Pa.
Kase, Charles M.......................... Newark, N. J.
Landenberger, Jr., Martin................ Philadelphia.
Landenberger, Charles H................. do.
Lemon, James H.......................... do.
Longmire, Joseph W...................... do.
Mayer, Bruno F........................... New York.
McIlvain, R. Emmet....................... Philadelphia.
Nathans, Cornelius C..................... do.
Nottingham, Leonard B................... Macon, Geo.
Paine, Edward J.......................... Troy, Pa.

Parkinson, T. McKean	Philadelphia.
Pollitz, Herman W	New York.
Rank, David F	Jonestown, Pa.
Reichel, Edward B	Nazareth, Pa.
Ricksecker, Henry C	Washington co., N. Y.
Rights, Theodore M	Friedberg, N. C.
Schnitzel, Anthon	Philadelphia.
Siewers, Jacob D	Bethania, N. C.
Smith, Benjamin P	Memphis, Tenn.
Vetterlein, Julius	Philadelphia.
Vetterlein, Ferdinand T	do.
Vetterlein, Willie B	do.
Vogler, William H	Salem, N. C.
Waters, George F	Baltimore.
Whyte, Elias W. E	Wilkesbarre, Pa.
Whitney, Benjamin P	Port Carbon, Pa.
Winslow, Stephen N	Philadelphia.
Wilkes, William H. H. C	Wheeling, Miss.
Wolle, Herbert W	Nazareth, Pa.
Zollner, Charles	New York.
Zollner, Eugene	do.

1860.

Bayley, John Thomas	Norristown, Pa.
Beitel, John F	Nazareth, Pa.
Bininger, Abraham M	New York.
Boyd, Theron	do.
Brintzinghoffer, Theodore C	Newark, N. J.
Capers, William W	New York.
Cozzens, William B	West Point, N. Y.
Coulter, William A	New York.
Deal, John F	Philadelphia.
Ebbinghousen, George H	New York.
Garner, George	Brooklyn, N. Y.
Goundie, William Tell	Bethlehem, Pa.
Groetzinger, Charles	Easton, Pa.
Haight, Edward G	New York.
Haight, Ogden	do.
Harper, Fletcher U	do.
Harper, Joseph H	do.

Hepburn, Charles W...................... Philadelphia.
Hepburn, Martin....................... do.
Jewett, Jr., Pliny A...................... New Haven, Conn.
Jordan, Gilbert........................ Philadelphia.
Landenberger, John.................... do.
Lerch, Daniel D....................... Pottsville, Pa.
Miner, Charles......................... Reading.
Neal, Harry........................... Philadelphia.
Nenzel, Frederic W..................... do.
O'Hara, Samuel J...................... New York.
Pfohl, Charles B....................... Salem, N. C.
Rhine, Benjamin....................... Philadelphia.
Richards, James D..................... Augusta, Ga.
Richardson, George W.................. Philadelphia.
Rowland, Thaddeus.................... do.
Setley, Harry.......................... Camden, N. J.
Stone, Adolphus P..................... Nevada, Cal.
Stone, William........................ do.
Stow, James S........................ Eufaula, Ala.
Tucker, Henry W...................... Philadelphia.
Walter, Alfred........................ New York.
White, David P....................... Norristown, Pa.

1861.

Brautigam, T. Augustus.................. Jersey City, N. J.
Clyde, John J......................... Harrisburg, Pa.
Coggeshall, Elwood.................... New York.
Elliott, William S...................... Milton Hill, Mass.
Evans, Frank B........................ Philadelphia.
Fiechtner, Lewis C.................... do.
Grote, Frederic J..................... New York.
Gunther, William H.................... do.
Gunther, John Jacob................... do.
Hagen, Samuel E...................... Bethlehem, Pa.
Hamilton, Howard..................... Harrisburg, Pa.
Hamilton, Hugh....................... do.
Holzerman, John H.................... Baltimore.
Holzerman, Charles F.................. do.
Kennedy, Theodore Frelinghuysen.......... Bloomsbury, N. J.
Kenner, Frederic B.................... New Orleans.

Lawall, Harry C........................... Easton, Pa.
Love, Samuel H........................... Hagerstown, Md.
Meredith, Samuel R....................... Brooklyn, N. Y.
Miller, George M.......................... Reading, Pa.
Mushler, Jacob S.......................... Jonestown, Pa.
Pollitz, J. Rudolph....................... Brooklyn, N. Y.
Prince, James G........................... do.
Rowland, William Day..................... Philadelphia.
Rowland, Joseph S........................ do.
Sallade, Israel B......................... Reading, Pa.
Sallade, Christian A...................... do.
Skirving, Edwin H........................ Washington, D. C.
Sullivan, Charles A....................... Butler, Pa.
Sullivan, Moses........................... do.
Thorbecke, Edward........................ Philadelphia.
Thorbecke, Herman........................ do.
Vogler, Anson S........................... New Fairfield, C. W.
Watson, Nicholas W....................... Harlem, N. Y.
Welsh, Henry J........................... New York.

1862.

Allaire, Joseph B......................... Green Point, L. I.
Arnold, Alfred............................ New York.
Balliet, Edward H......................... Allentown, Pa.
Bishop, Edwin P.......................... Bethlehem, Pa.
Bleck, Charles H.......................... Canal Dover, Ohio.
Breder, Hugo.............................. New York.
Coyne, George T.......................... Richmond, Staten Isl.
Coutin, Henri............................. Baracoa, Cuba.
Dearie, William A......................... Philadelphia.
Deringer, Henry........................... do.
Fassitt, Edward F......................... do.
Fontanè, Joseph A. C...................... Key West, Fla.
Grote, William H.......................... New York.
Hartman, Thomas T........................ Philadelphia.
Howell, Charles T......................... do.
Hull, Thomas H. B........................ San Francisco, Cal.
Justice, Howard R......................... Philadelphia.
Knight, George R......................... Buffalo, N. Y.
Landenberger, George W................... Philadelphia.

Lockwood, J. Delos...................... Plymouth, Ind.
Mack, John A........................... Indian Territory.
Marsh, Charles C....................... Jersey City, N. J.
Meyers, Lawrence P..................... Easton, Pa.
Oehler, Clement T...................... Bethlehem, Pa.
Oehler, Albert E....................... do.
Ogden, Harvey S........................ New York.
Ridgway, Edward........................ South Amboy, N. J.
Ridgway, Charles....................... do.
Russell, Charles S..................... Philadelphia.
Senseman, Wilson....................... do.
Staats, William C. M................... Norwalk, Conn.
Stuart, William C...................... Roslyn, L. I.
Stuart, Robert......................... Brooklyn, L. I.
Trumbower, John........................ Hokendauqua, Pa.

1863.

Allaire, Henry Clay.................... Green Point, L. I.
Anathan, Nathan........................ Philadelphia.
Bardsley, George H..................... do.
Berg, Alfred M......................... do.
Bley, Alphonso A. W.................... do.
Bucher, Silas W........................ Massillon, O.
Collins, Richard....................... New York.
Conkle, Harry C........................ Philadelphia.
Conrades, Henry........................ New York.
Coston, William F...................... do.
Dade, Morris........................... Mobile, Ala.
Denmead, William C..................... Baltimore.
Eliason, John F........................ Middletown, Del.
Ellwanger, Emanuel..................... Philadelphia.
Georger, Eugene A...................... Buffalo, N. Y.
Georger, Charles F..................... do.
Hamilton, William J.................... Philadelphia.
Hardy, Harold J. W..................... Norfolk, Va.
Hark, J. Maximilian.................... Nazareth, Pa.
Hartman, George V...................... New York.
Hess, Harlan P......................... Easton, Pa.
Hoguet, Albert......................... Bristol, Pa.
Hoguet, William....................... do.

10

Hope, James W.	Clinton, N. J.
Hurxthal, Charles B.	Massillon, Ohio.
Johnson, Lewis C.	Grand Rapids, Mich.
Kern, Joseph C.	Philadelphia.
Kern, William P.	do.
Kipling, Francis J.	New York.
Kountz, Albert J.	Pittsburg.
Kunkle, John J.	Frederic, Md.
Kurtzman, Charles F.	Buffalo, N. Y.
Lawrence, Edward H.	Philadelphia.
Lawrence, William T.	Brooklyn, N. Y.
Lee, Henry A.	Philadelphia.
Lefevre, Charles H.	do.
Lehmaier, Marcus B.	New York.
Lerch, William J.	Reading, Pa.
Linn, James.	Bellefonte, Pa.
Luckenbach, Jacob W.	Bethlehem, Pa.
Mackey, Philip B.	Milford, N. J.
Mars, Walter W.	Pottsville, Pa.
McKenzie, Alexander.	Stamford, Conn.
Miksch, Lewis.	Nazareth, Pa.
Miksch, J. Jacob.	Bethlehem, Pa.
Motz, Henry A.	Brooklyn, L. I.
Nixon, William R.	Springfield, Ohio.
Phillips, Frank C.	Philadelphia.
Phillips, Charles D.	do.
Poole, George.	Baltimore.
Price, Richard L.	Middletown, Del.
Rader, Robert P.	Easton, Pa.
Ridgway, James W.	Brooklyn, N. Y.
Ridgway, James V.	South Amboy, N. J.
Riegel, Thomas M.	Easton, Pa.
Ritter, Oliver H.	Bethlehem, Pa.
Ross, John.	Indian Territory.
Ross, William D.	Leavenworth City, Kan.
Russell, Charles W.	Massillon, Ohio.
Schimpf, Charles H.	Allentown, Pa.
Scobie, Douglas D.	New York.
Skirving, John J.	Washington, D. C.
Skirving, Samuel M.	do.
Stapler, H. Bascom.	Indian Territory.

Steever, Ambrose W. T.................... Washington, D. C.
Thomas, William M...................... Belvidere, N. J.
Turner, Robert McC..................... Bethlehem, Pa.
Underhill, J. Albert...................... Boston.
Vogler, Charles F.* .... New Fairfield, C. W.
Vorhees, Thomas......................... Trenton, N. J.
Walden, Duncan.... .... Philadelphia.
Walker, John C........................ La Porte, Ind.
Warman, Thomas E...................... Westfield, N. J.
Warthman, Edgar B..................... Philadelphia.
Weiler, Peter R........................ Belville, N. J.
Wetjen, G. Henry...................... New York.
Wetjen, John........................... do.
White, John............................ Belvidere, N. J.
Wilson, James W....................... Easton, Pa.
Wolle, Robert H....................... Bethlehem, Pa.
Wolle, Francis L........................ do.
Wolle, Clarence A...................... do.
Wolle, Charles E....................... Litiz, Pa.
Wolle, Robert N........................ do.
Yohe, Samuel S........................ Bethlehem, Pa.

1864.

Ackerman, Walter H..................... New York.
Bachman, Charles C..................... Hope, Ind.
Bell, Edmund C........................ Alexandria, Va.
Berens, Joseph......................... Philadelphia.
Bishop, James N....................... Bethlehem, Pa.
Brown, George S. A..................... Philadelphia.
Brown, Joseph U....................... Easton, Pa.
Brown, William Frank.................. Massillon, O.
Brown, Huntington..................... do.
Brown, John H......................... Philadelphia.
Burr, Henry Clay....................... do.
Bussey, Robert H...................... York co., Pa.
Cameron, William T.................... New York.
Chapman, William...................... Chapmansville, Pa.
Carlisle, William D..................... Clarkesburg, West Va.
Connor, Andrew G...................... Philadelphia.
Cornell, John J........................ Fordham, N. Y.

Davis, George H........................ Nesquehoning, Pa.
Denman, Isaac R....................... Newark, N. J.
Denman, George H..................... do.
Dimond, Cornelius R................... Washington, D. C.
Duncan, David B....................... Philadelphia.
Earl, John Ogden...................... New York.
Early, Silas L......................... Palmyra, Pa.
Edwards, Joseph W.................... Philadelphia.
Eisendrath, Bernhard W............... Chicago.
Eisendrath, William................... do.
Emanuel, Solomon..................... Easton, Md.
Erben, Louis D........................ Philadelphia.
Erben, Walter......................... do.
Ervin, Spencer........................ do.
Evans, John F. R...................... Fort Wayne, Ind.
Fassitt, Thomas....................... Philadelphia.
Ford, Edward E........................ Brooklyn, L. I.
Freck, Harry Clay..................... Ashland, Pa.
Freck, Charles G...................... do.
Fulford, Charles J.................... Jamaica, W. I.
Fulford, George D..................... do.
Greig, Evelyn N....................... New York.
Grobe, William C...................... Philadelphia.
Groot, William C...................... Washington, D. C.
Harrison, James C..................... Philadelphia.
Hartman, George V.................... New York.
Henninger, Frederic J................. Reading, Pa.
Hincken, John L....................... Philadelphia.
Hincken, William W................... do.
Hook, Richard W...................... New York.
Hopping, A. Howard................... do.
Hurxthal, Frederic L.................. Massillon, O.
Jaeger, William R..................... Baltimore.
Kelley, A. Frank...................... Massillon, O.
Kiel, Arthur.......................... Hoboken, N. J.
Kinike, Albert........................ Philadelphia.
Klinefelter, William L................ York co., Pa.
Knapp, George A...................... New York.
Lytle, William F...................... New Orleans.
Lytle, Randell H...................... do.
Mitchell, John J...................... Alton, Ill.

Naudain, Richard L.	Alexandria, Va.	
Peale, Louis Titian	Washington, D. C.	
Read, Oscar	Newark, N. J.	
Regennas, Eugene J.	Schœneck, Pa.	
Rhodes, John D.	Brooklyn, N. Y.	
Ross, Lewis A.	Fort Gibson, Ind. Ter.	
Ross, Henry C.	do.	do.
Ross, Edgar P.	do.	do.
Ross, Gilbert R.	do.	do.
Saul, Mowbray	New York.	
Seitz, Frederic	Easton, Pa.	
Schneider, Edward G.	Hoboken, N. J.	
Schneider, Otto N.	do.	
Siebenman, Henry A.	do.	
Smith, Elwood	Philadelphia.	
Smith, Stephen	do.	
Snyder, Harry	do.	
Spivey, J. Hugh	Savannah, Ga.	
Steiner, Gabriel C.	Philadelphia.	
Stuyvesant, J. Reade	Schenectady, N. Y.	
Thompson, Albert F.	Philadelphia.	
Ward, Darius E.	Indian Territory.	
Waterman, James F.	New Market, N. J.	
Whitaker, Robert	Philadelphia.	
Wood, Harry	New York.	

1865.

Atlee, John Y.	Washington, D. C.
Ayres, Donald	Brooklyn, N. Y.
Barron, William H.	New York.
Berrian, Henry M.	Fordham, N. Y.
Birchall, John N. B.	Philadelphia.
Bley, John M.	do.
Browne, A. William	do.
Butz, Daniel W.	Easton, Pa.
Carter, Walter H.	Philadelphia.
Casper, E. Davis	Salem, N. J.
Clarke, William	Newark, N. J.
Conley, William C.	Philadelphia.
Cremer, Frank R.	do.

Day, Edwin C.	Peru, Ill.
Dearie, Harry C.	Philadelphia.
Forman, John E.	Milford, N. J.
Foster, Joseph L.	Bethlehem, Pa.
Gower, Charles H.	Iowa City, Ia.
Hincken, George A.	Philadelphia.
Hoffeditz, John C.	Reading, Pa.
Jaeger, George A.	Berks co., Pa.
Kegler, Frederic T.	Charleston, S. C.
Kegler, Louis P.	do.
Knipe, William B.	Harrisburg, Pa.
Leisenring, Harry S.	Philadelphia.
Leisenring, Charles R.	do.
Mack, Edwin J.	Greene co., Mo.
Manus, Carroll J.	Baltimore.
Martin, Luther	Philadelphia.
McLean, James L.	Carbon co., Pa.
Miller, Edwin W.	Easton, Pa.
Miller, Charles	Hutchinson, Mo.
Munger, Harry B.	Augusta, Ga.
Myers, Frank E.	Canton, O.
Oehler, Calvin	Coveville, Pa.
Packer, Asa A.	Nesquehoning, Pa.
Powers, Frank M.	New York.
Penoyer, Alonzo B.	Massillon, Ohio.
Phillips, Charles B.	Alleghany City, Pa.
Polhamus, Charles E. V.	Santa Cruz del Sur, Cuba
Putney, Daniel R.	Washington, D. C.
Rose, John	Jersey City, N. J.
Saclon, George D.	Canton, O.
Schantz, Tilghman D.	Lehigh co., Pa.
Schlabeck, Adam	Philadelphia.
Schneider, Alexander	Hoboken, N. J.
Schweinitz, Lewis de	Salem, N. C.
Sholder, Louis H.	Navarre, O.
Skirving, William	Philadelphia.
Smith, William C.	do.
Smith, Henry F.	do.
Smith, Charles S.	do.
Stiver, Ellwood	do.
Strowbridge, Timothy R.	New York.

Suppes, Charles H. . . . . Johnstown, Pa.
Terry, Frederic W. . . . . Bradford co., Pa.
Thomas, Oscar . . . . Belvidere, N. J.
Van Brunt, Willett C. . . . . New York.
Wessels, Henry E. . . . . do.
Wiegner, Adam . . . . Nazareth, Pa.
Ziegler, E. Howard . . . . Philadelphia.
Ziegler, Harry N . . . . do.

1866.

Altemus, Joseph T. . . . . Philadelphia.
Baxter, Henry S. . . . . do.
Benjamin, Walter R. . . . . Castleton, N. J.
Benjamin, Charles M. . . . . do.
Bishop, Julius. . . . . Bethlehem, Pa.
Boorum, Cornelius. . . . . Milford, N. J.
Boorum, Pierre Irving. . . . . do.
Clark, Charles F. . . . . Newburg, N. Y.
Coles, Willett H. . . . . Yonkers, N. Y.
Cooper, Eugene T. . . . . Philadelphia.
Coulter, William A . . . . New York.
Davis, Frank. . . . . Philadelphia.
Dech, Milton A . . . . Hecktown, Pa.
Ducker, William M . . . . Brooklyn, N. Y.
Ely, Anthony M . . . . Lebanon, Pa.
Epping, Henry. . . . . Columbus, Ga.
Forman, Lewis. . . . . Milford, N. J.
Fulford, John N . . . . Jamaica, W. I.
Glover, David. . . . . Pottsville, Pa.
Glover, Richard. . . . . do.
Harland, Charles D . . . . Philadelphia.
Heath, John S . . . . Easton, Pa.
Heintzelman, Paul B. . . . . Philadelphia.
Hemming, Robert. . . . . Jersey City, N. J.
Hemmingway, Frank. . . . . Easton, Pa.
Huart, James Edgar. . . . . Washington, D. C.
Hillman, Shimer D . . . . Bethlehem, Pa.
Hill, Robert Henry A . . . . Philadelphia.
Himes, William A. . . . . New Oxford, Pa.
Hough, Edward B. . . . . Philadelphia.

Jordan, Pierre............................	New York.
Jordan, Frank S........................	do.
Klein, Charles...........................	do.
Kolb, William W.......................	Easton, Pa.
Lord, John..............................	Philadelphia.
Martin, Otto F.........................	Nazareth, Pa.
Mattison, James C......................	Washington, N. J.
McNair, Albert.........................	Oswego, N. Y.
Milledoler, William S..................	New York.
Nelson, Edward........................	Plainfield, N. J.
Pinkney, E.............................	Weston, West Va.
Pinkney, Arthur........................	do.
Reed, John F...........................	Lancaster, Pa.
Regennas, Walter S.....................	Schœneck, Pa.
Richmond, Harry.......................	New York.
Roepper, Francis A.....................	Bethlehem, Pa.
Schmeck, W. W.........................	———
Seaman, William B.....................	Elizabeth, N. J.
Sherer, William Wirt..................	Easton, Pa.
Shotwell, S. Frank.....................	New York.
Shouse, Charles J......................	Philadelphia.
Sloat, Henry C.........................	Milford, N. J.
Slocum, Edward C......................	Wilkesbarre, Pa.
Smith, Charles H.......................	Plainfield, N. J.
Smith, Milton..........................	New York.
Snyder, Frederic Antes.................	Williamsport, Pa.
Spangler, Charles S....................	Philadelphia.
Stotz, John T..........................	Wind Gap, Pa.
Strader, Robert S......................	Washington, N. J.
Temple, J. Clayton.....................	Philadelphia.
Thompson, Major.......................	New York.
Tracy, Charles B.......................	Crumpton, Md.
Wiley, Alexander.......................	New York.
Youngs, Charles........................	do.
Youngs, Edmund.......................	do.
Zippel, Gustavus E.....................	do.

1867.

Aischman, Joseph.......................	Philadelphia.
Armstrong, Frederic W.................	Plainfield, N. J.
Arrison, Matthew.......................	Philadelphia.

Bachschmidt, Ernest C	Nazareth, Pa.
Brock, Paul	Philadelphia.
Browne, J. Andrew	Canada West.
Bruner, Daniel D	Columbia, Pa.
Campbell, George B	Philadelphia.
Carmichael, John J	do.
Chapman, Nelson	Chapmansville, Pa.
Coulter, William T	Philadelphia.
Cremer, James	do.
Cumiskey, Daniel M	New York.
Dalrymple, William R	do.
Day, D. Mortimer	do.
Demarest, Abraham	do.
Doll, Edwin P	Plainfield, N. J.
Egbert, William H	do.
Eilshemins, Gustavus	Belleville, N. J.
Eilshemins, Emil	do.
Engel, Frederic	Brooklyn, N. Y.
Gibbs, Willie St. Clair	Hyde Park, Pa.
Graham, James F	Newburg, N. Y.
Greider, Allen L	Graceham, Md.
Greider, Edwin	do.
Groff, William H	Upper Sandusky, O.
Grosholz, William H	Philadelphia.
Harper, Frederic P. P	New York.
Hess, B. Lintner	Lancaster, Pa.
Hillman, Andrew	Wilkesbarre, Pa.
Holland, Daniel	Hope, Ind.
Illig, Christian	Brooklyn, N. Y.
Kern, Walter R	Philadelphia.
Lawson, David T	New York.
Leman, Henry E	Lancaster, Pa.
Lichtenthaler, Octavius A	Jamaica, W. I.
Mayher, Jr., John	New York.
Miller, J. Edgar	Elizabeth, N. J.
Munro, David	Girardville, Pa.
Nathans, Harry J	Philadelphia.
Nickles, T. Henry	do.
Ogden, Middleton	do.
Outerbridge, Franklin	Bermuda, W. I.
Palmer, Stephen S	Newmarket, N. J.

Palmer, Edward T.	Newmarket, N. J.
Peck, Frank S.	New York.
Perot, Jr., Francis	Philadelphia.
Pharo, Charles J.	Bethlehem, Pa.
Platt, William E.	Augusta, Ga.
Potter, Samuel B.	New York.
Reichel, Charles F.	Nazareth, Pa.
Remy, Curtis H.	Hope, Ind.
Reynolds, George B.	Plymouth, Pa.
Reynolds, Harry D.	Wilkesbarre, Pa.
Ricksecker, Charles Alfred	Camden Valley, N. Y
Robinson, Franklin P.	Wilkesbarre, Pa.
Rockwell, James W.	New York.
Schneider, Lawrence	Schœneck, Pa.
Smith, Harry D.	Plainfield, N. J.
Stark, James W.	Plainsville, Pa.
Todd, Richard	Philadelphia.
Turner, William G.	Nazareth, Pa.
Warner, Edward E.	Philadelphia.
Wiegner, Josephus	Nazareth, Pa.
Weinland, George D.	Hope, Ind.
Wills, Joseph	Irvington, N. J.
Woodman, Edward	Jacksonville, Pa.

1868.

Ayer, James J.	New York.
Baeder, William A.	Jenkintown, Pa.
Baeder, Harry	do.
Benson, William H.	Colebrook, Pa.
Bishop, Rufus N.	Bethlehem, Pa.
Bohde, Charles H.	New York.
Braman, Walter F.	Philadelphia.
Buess, Rudolph	New York.
Buess, William	do.
Carey, William R.	Bethlehem, Pa.
Conway, Henry	Philadelphia.
Crohen, Theodore	Brooklyn, L. I.
Egbert, Clay	Plainfield, N. J.
Elliott, Joseph W.	Dover, N. J.
Frey, Aaron L.	Lancaster, Pa.
Frick, Gerhard	Bethlehem, Pa.

Friedel, T. Augustus	New York.
Garrettson, Frederic P.	do.
Gould, William E.	Chatham, N. J.
Grice, Francis	Philadelphia.
Grice, Charles P.	do.
Griffin, Samuel T.	Haddonfield, N. J.
Grundy, George C.	Elizabeth, N. J.
Hahn, Alfred H.	Clearfield, Pa.
Hark, Otto B.	Nazareth, Pa.
Harriott, Randolph	Plainfield, N. J.
Himes, Harry O.	New Oxford, Pa.
Huszagh, Rudolf.	Brooklyn, N. Y.
Iverson, John H.	Fort Howard, Wis.
Jones, David D.	Plainfield, N. J.
Jones, Victor S.	Bethlehem, Pa.
Kershaw, William A.	Norristown, Pa.
Kretschmar, Horatio C.	Flushing, L. I.
Loeffler, Herman W.	Massillon, Ohio.
Loovis, Joseph M.	New York.
McCay, Leroy W.	Eufaula, Ala.
McClellan, Alfred C.	Philadelphia.
McCormack, George.	New York.
Miller, Charles F.	Cleveland, Ohio.
Moore, Andrew R.	Philadelphia.
Napheggi, Rodolfo A.	New Brighton, L. I.
Napheggi, Alberto.	do.
Naylor, F. Harry	Philadelphia.
Naylor, Frank.	Tiffin, Ohio.
Niemann, Francis S.	Philadelphia.
Parkhurst, Joseph.	York, Pa.
Pounden, Francis J.	New York.
Rader, Max. W.	do.
Romig, Alvin F.	St. Johns, W. I.
Rosenheim, Otto.	St. Louis, Mo.
Take, Christian.	Easton, Pa.
Throop, George S.	Scranton, Pa.
Todd, Deringer.	Philadelphia.
Tucker, Charles A.	New York.
White, Alfred A.	do.
Willis, Allieton C.	Brooklyn, N. Y.
Wilson, Daniel T.	do.

THELOGICAL SEMINARY.

HISTORICAL SKETCH

OF THE

MORAVIAN THEOLOGICAL SEMINARY

OF THE

AMERICAN PROVINCE,

Founded October 3, 1807, at Nazareth, Pennsylvania.

WHILE the Moravian Church has never despised the services of illiterate men of God, having found among these most efficient instruments in her aggressive movements against the strongholds of Satan in heathendom, she has always recognized the importance of an educated ministry.

Its ranks were supplied at an early day by accessions of men from other evangelical denominations, who had been prepared for the Church in the seats of theological learning of Protestant Germany. First among these were the Universities of Tubingen and Jena. From both, and especially from the latter, came forth able champions and architects of the Renewed Church of the Brethren, both in this country and abroad. Spangenberg and Boehler were of this number; and we mention them because their names are identified with the first attempt of the Moravians to colonize in North America, and with their establishment as an ecclesiastical body in the British provinces of the New World.

3

The first divinity school opened by the Moravians on the Continent was in a district of Western Germany, called the Wetterau, which, between 1737 and 1749 (during Count Zinzendorf's banishment from Saxony), was the seat of the little Church of which he was the guardian and directing spirit. Here it was located successively at Herrnhaag, Lindheim and Marienborn. Bishop John Frederic Cammerhoff, Spangenberg's assistant at Bethlehem between 1747 and 1751 (until his death in April of the last-mentioned year), completed his theological studies at the school while at Herrnhaag.

In May of 1754 the Theological Seminary of the Brethren's Church, which (together with its sister Institute founded at Nazareth in 1807) now for upward of a century has supplied her pulpits with an educated ministry, was opened in the village of Barby, in Saxony. Bishop Charles G. Reichel, the first Principal of Nazareth Hall, the late Bishop Andrew Benade (tutor between 1795 and 1800) and Bishop Jacob Van Vleck, its second Principal, were graduated here. In 1789 the Institution was transferred to Nisky, in Lower Silesia. The late Rev. Charles F. Seidel, Bishops John C. Beckler and John G. Herman—and the aged Bishop John C. Jacobson—(successively Principals of Nazareth Hall), studied Theology at Nisky.

Since 1818, Gnadenfeld, in Upper Silesia, has been the seat of the Seminary. Rev. Levin T. Reichel, tenth Principal of the Hall, was graduated here.

Although the opportunities afforded at Nazareth Hall after its reopening in 1785 were of a higher order than before, there was no provision for educating young men with a view to the ministry; and accordingly those desirous of entering this career were necessitated either to repair to Germany or to avail themselves of instruction

at the hands of private tutors. A few young Americans
had gone abroad earlier; when, between 1798 and 1803,
Lewis D. De Schweinitz, Charles F. Reichel, J. D. Koehler and Samuel R. Reichel, all sons of clergymen, followed, and were entered at Nisky. Koehler and Samuel
Reichel remained in Europe; the latter, after many years
of service in England, died at Herrnhut during the sessions of the General Synod in June of 1857. Charles
Reichel was in America, between 1829 and 1834, stationed
at Lancaster (deceased in 1846); and De Schweinitz,
eminent in the field of botanical science, held positions in
both provinces of the American Church, until his death
at Bethlehem in February of 1834. Few, however, were
able to avail themselves of such a privilege, the expense
it involved being not inconsiderable; and a passage across
the Atlantic, in those days of uncertain travel, even in
times of peace, considered no ordinary undertaking.

The want of a theological seminary in the American
Province was thus forced upon the consideration of its
authorities, and by them referred to the Unity's Executive
Board at Berthelsdorf.

This body accordingly empowered Revs. John R.
Verbeck and Charles de Forestier, before setting out on a
visitation to the American churches in 1806, to act in the
matter as would best subserve the interests of all con-
cerned; and Rev. Jacob Van Vleck, then Principal of
Nazareth Hall, was by them authorized to undertake a
Divinity School in connection with the Institution over
which he presided.

On the 3d day of October, 1807, William H. Van
Vleck, Samuel Reinke and Peter Wolle entered upon a
course of theological studies in an apartment on the
second floor in the Hall. Mr. Ernest L. Hazelius, a
graduate of Nisky, and subsequently Professor of The-

11 *

ology in the Lutheran Theological Seminary at Hartwick, N. Y., next at Gettysburg, and latterly at Lexington, S. C. (where he deceased in February of 1853), was appointed professor, and Mr. John C. Beckler, instructor. Two members of this first class are at this writing living in retirement at Bethlehem (both venerable bishops of the Church). The third, Bishop William H. Van Vleck, ended his Christian warfare on the 19th of January, 1853, while pastor of the Moravian Church at that place.

In 1810 a second class of students of Theology was formed. There being no candidates for the ministry in the following years, the Institution was temporarily closed —until reopened with three students in 1820.

In 1825 it received an endowment, $20,000 having been bequeathed to the authorities of the Church, in trust for its benefit, by Mr. Godfrey Haga, merchant, of Philadelphia.

During Rev. William H. Van Vleck's administration at Nazareth Hall, in 1828, the oldest of three classes of students preparing for the ministry were temporarily provided with apartments in the Principal's house; a change which was rendered necessary by an increase in the number of pupils at the Hall. The purchase of a dwelling, near by ("The Cottage"), in 1830, obviated the inconvenience; and here it was designed to permanently locate the Institution, with Rev. Charles C. Dober, a graduate of Gnadenfeld, as Professor of Theology. Mr. Dober entered upon his duties in 1837, and was connected with the Institution, after its removal to Bethlehem in the following year, until his death in January of 1840.

In 1851 the Seminary was transferred to Nazareth. During its continuance there, the students resided successively in the Hall, in the Sisters' House and in the " Whitefield House" at Ephrata. Four members of the class of 1852 completed their theological studies at Philadelphia in 1855.

In 1858 the Institution was once more returned to Bethlehem, and arrangements made to afford special opportunities to young men desirous of entering the Church, whose previous advantages had been but limited.

The Divinity School, with its preparatory class, has since that time been conducted in connection with the Moravian College, which was then opened under the presidency of Rev. Lewis F. Kampman.

The course of study pursued in the two departments of this Church institution, whose history we have just reviewed, is calculated to well ground the student in those acquirements on which he is to draw in his professional career. In addition to an acquaintance with the great consuls of the republic of ancient letters, and with the wide field of universal history, offered him in the preparatory class, he is likewise subjected to the severer discipline of the mathematics. The knowledge of the languages here obtained is applied in the Divinity School to the critical interpretation of the Scriptures in the original. Besides lectures on Church history, on the history and science of doctrines, and on pastoral Theology in its various departments, the history of the Moravian Church, as a specialty, enters into the two years' course allotted to theological students.

The first professors and tutors in this Institution were from Germany, many of them men of solid learning ; and the *German mode of instruction, which is unostentatious, patient, laborious, and therefore likely to be thorough,* has by them been engrafted on the school of the prophets they helped to mould ; the merits of which have been recognized also by the alumni of the venerable Institution .

founded in 1785, whose tutors are usually graduates of the Moravian Seminary.

One hundred and thirty-seven students are registered since 1807 as having attended one or the other of the departments of the American Theological Seminary. Some of these were young men other than Moravians, admitted into the classical school, and there prepared in part for professional life.

Twenty-six of the above number, as far as we know, are deceased.

Sixty-one entered the Moravian Church, and served, or are serving, either as pastors or in the educational institutions of the American Province, North and South ; or as missionaries in the West Indies, or among the Christian Cherokees and Delawares of Canada and the Indian country, the feeble remnant of a once flourishing mission among the aborigines of the New World.

The following deceased while in the service of the Church :

REV. JACOB ZORN, May 27, 1843, at Fairfield Station, Jamaica, W. I.

REV. HENRY A. SEIDEL, June 10, 1844, at Hopedale, Wayne co., Pa.

REV. WILLIAM H. WARNER, June 20, 1845, at Friedensthal Station, Santa Cruz, W. I.

REV. CHARLES A. VAN VLECK, December 21, 1845, at Greenville, Tenn.

REV. EMANUEL RONDTHALER, November 30, 1848, at Philadelphia.

DR. EDWARD RICE, July 2, 1849, at Bethlehem.

REV. CHARLES A. BLECK, January 17, 1850. at Gnadenhutten, Ohio.

RT. REV. WILLIAM H. VAN VLECK, January 19, 1853, at Bethlehem.

Rev. Bernard de Schweinitz, July 20, 1854, at Salem, N. C.

Rev. Edward Rondthaler, March 5, 1855, at Nazareth.

Rev. Edwin T. Senseman, February 8, 1866, at Hope, Ind.

CATALOGUE OF STUDENTS

OF THE

MORAVIAN THEOLOGICAL SEMINARY,

Founded at Nazareth, Pa., October, 1807.

The names marked thus * are of persons DECEASED.

I.—CLASS 1807 TO 1810.

PROFS. ERNEST L. HAZELIUS AND JOHN C. BECKLER.

William H. Van Vleck* (1809), teacher, deceased January 19, 1853, while pastor of Moravian Church at Bethlehem (Bishop).

Samuel Reinke (1810), teacher, resides in retirement at Bethlehem, Pa. (Bishop).

Peter Wolle (1810), teacher, resides in retirement at Bethlehem, Pa. (Bishop).

II.—CLASS 1810 TO 1813.

PROF. JOHN C. BECKLER.

Charles A. Van Vleck* (1813), teacher, deceased December 21, 1845, while President of Greenville College, Tenn.

G. Benjamin Mueller (united with Lutheran Church), professor of Theology in Lutheran Seminary, Hartwick, N. Y.

10

III.—CLASS 1820 TO 1823.

PROFS. CHARLES A. VAN VLECK AND JOHN C. JACOBSON.

S. Thomas Pfohl (1821), teacher at Salem, N. C., warden of Moravian congregation at Salem, N. C.

Jacob Zorn* (1823), teacher, deceased May 27, 1843, while superintendent of Jamaica mission, at Fairfield Station.

Charles A. Bleck* (1823), teacher, Principal Salem Female Academy 1844 to 1848; deceased January 17, 1850, at Gnadenhutten, Ohio, while pastor.

IV.—CLASS 1823 TO 1826.

PROFS. JOHN C. JACOBSON, WM. L. BENZEIN, WM. H. VAN VLECK
AND JOHN C. BRICKENSTEIN.

J. Henry Kluge, teacher at Salem, N. C., 1826, teacher at Hope, Ind.

Henry A. Shultz, teacher at Salem, N. C., 1826, pastor of Moravian Church at Nazareth, Pa. (Bishop).

Abraham L. Huebner (1826), teacher, physician and professor in Young Ladies' Seminary at Bethlehem, Pa.

Ernest F. Bleck (1826), teacher, treasurer of Moravian congregation at Bethlehem, Pa.

Eugene A. Frueauff (1825), left for Europe, Principal of Linden Hall, Litiz, Pa.

Henry I. Schmidt (1826), teacher, Professor of German Literature in Columbia College, N. Y.

V.—CLASS 1825 TO 1829.

PROFS. JOHN C. BRICKENSTEIN AND REV. WM. H. VAN VLECK.

William L. Meinung* (1829), teacher, deceased Oct. 14, 1863, at Salem, N. C.

James Henry (1829), teacher, gun manufacturer, Bolton, above Nazareth, Pa.

Joshua Boner, left for Salem 1827, bookkeeper, Salem, N. C.

VI.—Class 1827 to 1830.
Prof. John C. Brickenstein.

Joseph H. Siewers (1830), teacher, attorney-at-law, Mauch Chunk, Pa.

Charles E. Seidel, left 1826, Pittsburg, Pa.

Joseph F. Berg (1830), teacher, Professor of Theology in Dutch Reformed Seminary, Rutgers College, New Brunswick.

Edward Rice, * left 1829, deceased July 2, 1849, while Professor in Theological Seminary at Bethlehem.

Maurice C. Jones, gentleman, Bethlehem, Pa.

VII.—Class 1828 to 1832.
Profs. Charles A. Bleck and Charles C. Dober.

William L. Lennert (1832), teacher, pastor of Moravian Church at Hope, Ind.

Francis Fries * (1832), teacher at Salem, deceased August 1, 1863, at Salem, N. C.

Ambrose Rondthaler (1832), teacher, Principal of Moravian Day-school, at Bethlehem, Pa.

Emanuel Rondthaler * (1832), teacher, deceased November 30, 1848, while pastor of Moravian Race Street Church, Philadelphia.

Julius T. Beckler (1832), teacher, Principal Linden Hall (1856 to 1862), resides at Litiz, Pa.

VIII.—Class 1830 to 1835.
Profs. George F. Bahnson and Herman J. Titze.

Sylvester Wolle (1835), teacher, Principal Young Ladies' Seminary at Bethlehem (1849 to 1851), member of Executive Board of Moravian Province North, Bethlehem, Pa.

William H. Benade (1835), teacher, pastor of Swedenborg Church, Pittsburg.

Edward Rondthaler* (1835), teacher, deceased March 5, 1855, while Professor in Theological Seminary at Nazareth.

Christian David Senseman* (1836), teacher, professor of music, deceased August 10, 1861, near Philadelphia.

Lawrence Demuth, left for Europe 1834; manufacturer, Philadelphia.

Emile de Schweinitz, left for Europe 1834; Principal Salem Female Academy (1848 to 1853), member of Executive Board of Moravian Province South, Salem, N. C.

Francis F. Hagen (1835), teacher, pastor of Moravian Church on Staten Island.

Lewis F. Kampman (1835), teacher, member of Executive Board of Moravian Province North, Bethlehem, Pa.

Edwin T. Senseman* (1839), teacher at Salem, deceased February 8, 1866, while pastor of Moravian Church at Hope, Ind.

IX.—CLASS 1834 TO 1839.

PROFS. JOSEPH F. BERG, HERMAN J. TITZE, LEVIN T. REICHEL, CHAS. C. DOBER AND GEORGE F. BAHNSON.

William B. Bininger,* deceased at Rome.

Robert de Schweinitz (1839), teacher, Principal Salem Female Academy 1853 to 1867, president of Executive Board of Moravian Province North, Bethlehem, Pa.

Henry A. Seidel* (1839), teacher, deceased June 10, 1844, while pastor of Moravian Church at Hopedale, Pa.

X.—CLASS 1836 TO 1841.

PROFS. JULIUS T. BECKLER, EMAN'L RONDTHALER, SYLVESTER WOLLE (AT NAZARETH), REV. C. C. DOBER, REV. GEORGE F. BAHNSON, DR. EDWARD RICE, REV. CHARLES A. VAN VLECK (AT BETHLEHEM).

David Z. Smith (1841), teacher at Salem, pastor of Moravian Church at Sharon, Ohio.

12

Edward H. Reichel (1841), teacher, Principal Nazareth Hall 1854 to 1867, resides at Nazareth, Pa.

Amadeus A. Reinke (1841), teacher at Bethlehem, pastor of Moravian Church in New York.

Jacob Bininger, Jr.,* deceased April 11, 1837, at Nazareth, Pa.

Albert J. Buttner (1841), teacher at Salem, N. C., manufacturer, Whitesville, N. C.

Emanuel Bolmer, left in 1837.

Nathaniel S. Wolle, left 1838, merchant, Litiz, Pa.

Andrew G. Kern, Jr.* (1842), teacher, professor of music, deceased January 6, 1861, at Lake City, Florida.

Theodore F. Keehln, left in 1839, physician, Salem, N. C.

William H. Warner,* missionary, deceased June 20, 1845, at Friedensthal Station, Santa Cruz, Danish W. I.

Henry J. Van Vleck (1841), teacher, pastor of German Moravian Mission Church, South Bethlehem.

George W. Perkin (1840), teacher, bookseller, Bethlehem, Pa.

XI.—CLASS 1839 to 1844.

PROFS. WM. H. BENADE AND EMILE DE SCHWEINITZ (AT NAZARETH), DR. EDWARD RICE AND REV. CHAS. A. VAN VLECK (AT BETHLEHEM).

William C. Reichel (1844), teacher, Principal Linden Hall 1862 to 1867, now at Bethlehem, Pa.

Edwin E. Reinke (1844), teacher, pastor of Moravian Indian congregation at Fairfield, C. W.

Arthur L. Van Vleck* (1844), teacher, deceased Dec. 21, 1863, in Libby Prison, Richmond, Va.

Edmund A. de Schweinitz, left for Europe 1844, pastor of Moravian Church, and President of Moravian College at Bethlehem, Pa.

Constantine L. Rights (1844), teacher, merchant, Salem, N. C.

XII.—Class 1841 (at Bethlehem).

Prof. Emile de Schweinitz.

Matthias T. Huebner, merchant, Litiz, Pa.

Jacob F. Eberman, tinsmith, Bethlehem, Pa.

Gustavus E. Zippel, Secretary Cumberland Coal Co., New York.

James H. Wolle, merchant, Bethlehem, Pa.

Charles Goepp, attorney-at-law, New York.

XIII.—Class 1843 to 1848.

Profs. Dr. Edward Rice, Rev. Chas. A. Van Vleck and Robert de Schweinitz.

Charles Klose (1848), teacher, merchant, Philadelphia.

James N. Beck (1848), teacher, professor of music. Philadelphia.

Bernard de Schweinitz* (1848), teacher, pastor of Moravian Church on Staten Island, deceased July 20. 1854. while on a visit to Salem, N. C.

Max. Goepp (1848), teacher, attorney-at-law, New York.

Charles E. Shober, left 1844, attorney-at-law, Salisbury, N. C.

XIV.—Class 1845 to 1851.

Profs. Ed. H. Reichel (at Nazareth), Dr. Edward Rice and Rev. Her. J. Titze (at Bethlehem).

Lewis R. Huebner (1851), teacher, assistant pastor of Moravian Church at Bethlehem, Pa.

Edward H. Jacobson, left 1849, physician, Bethlehem. Pa.

Lawrence C. Brickenstein, left 1851, attorney-at-law, Baltimore, Md.

John H. Eberman* (1851), teacher (united with Lutheran Church), and deceased September 23, 1868, at Schuylkill Haven, Pa.

Theodore A. Lambert,* left 1851, professor of music, deceased September 1, 1863, at Reading, Pa.

Edward T. Kluge (1852), teacher, pastor of Moravian Church at Litiz, Pa.

Theodore F. Wolle, left 1847, Professor of Music in Young Ladies' Seminary at Bethlehem, Pa.

R. Parmenio Leinbach (1852), teacher, pastor of Moravian Church at Friedberg, N. C.

XV.—Class 1848 to 1853.

PROFS. WM. C. REICHEL, EDMUND DE SCHWEINITZ AND REV. HER. J. TITZE.

Alexander Troeger, left 1849, merchant, Sandwich, Ill.

John P. Kluge, left 1849, physician, Aspinwall, Panama.

Eugene Jacobson,* left 1849, deceased May 9, 1853, at Bethlehem, Pa.

Clement L. Reinke (1853), teacher, pastor of Moravian Church, Chaska, Minn.

Abraham Prince, left 1850, merchant, New York.

Edwin T. Zippel, left 1851, missionary on St. Kitts, W. I.

Herman A. Brickenstein (1853), teacher, editor of the *Moravian*, Bethlehem, Pa.

C. Edward Kummer (1853), teacher; teacher in Moravian Day-school, Bethlehem, Pa.

Eugene Leibert (1853) teacher, Principal of Nazareth Hall.

XVI.—Class 1852 to 1856.

PROFS. L. HUEBNER, REV. ED. RONDTHALER (AT NAZARETH), AND REV. ED. DE SCHWEINITZ (AT PHILADELPHIA).

Henry T. Bachman (1856), teacher, pastor of Moravian Church, Graceham, Md.

Lewis D. Lambert,* left in 1854.

Henry A. Bigler, left 1854, attorney-at-law, New York.

Albert L. Oerter (1856), teacher, pastor of Moravian Church at Salem, N. C.

Samuel Huebner,* deceased January 27, 1856, at Litiz, Pa.

Owen Rice, Jr. (1856), teacher, druggist, Lancaster, Pa.

J. Frederic Frueauff, left 1853, attorney-at-law, Lancaster, Pa.

Robert Spearing, left 1853, attorney-at-law, New Orleans.

Clement T. Paine, left 1852, Troy, Bradford co.. Pa.

Lorenzo Finn, teacher, 1852.

Max Hering,* left 1852.

XVII.—Class 1854 to 1859.

Profs. Ed. T. Kluge, Rev. J. C. Brickenstein (at Nazareth), Rev. Lev. F. Kampman, W. C. Reichel and L. R. Huebner (Bethlehem).

James B. Haman, teacher 1859, pastor of Moravian Church, Gnadenhutten, O.

J. Cennick Harvey, teacher 1859, conveyancer, Brooklyn, N. Y.

Samuel L. Lichtenthaler, teacher 1859, missionary. Barbadoes, W. I.

William H. Bigler, teacher 1859, Professor in Moravian College, Bethlehem, Pa.

Charles B. Shultz (1859), Professor in Moravian College, Bethlehem, Pa.

12 *

XVIII.—Class 1857 to 1862.

Profs. Rev. L. F. Kampman, W. C. Reichel and Lewis R. Huebner.

W. H. Theophilus Haman (1862), teacher, Professor of Music, Ulricsville, O.

Edmund A. Oerter, teacher 1862, pastor of Moravian Church, Lebanon, Pa.

Theophilus J. Zorn (1862), teacher, missionary, Jamaica, W. I.

Edward Rondthaler, left for Europe 1862, pastor of Moravian Church in Brooklyn.

The following students pursued a partial course of classical and theological studies, in connection with Classes XVII. and XVIII., between 1858 and 1862:

Emanuel Ricksecker, music dealer, Bethlehem, Pa.

Philip F. Rommel, pastor of Mission Church, Lake Mills, Wis.

Joseph Romig, teacher, 1861, missionary among Delawares, Kansas.

S. Morgan Smith, pastor of Moravian Church, Canal Dover, O.

Wesley J. Spaugh, Kansas mission.

Herman S. Hoffman (1862), teacher, pastor Second Moravian Church, Philadelphia.

Charles Cooper, Salem, N. C.

The following students were connected with classes XVIII. and XIX. between 1861 and 1864.

Lewis P. Clewell (1864), teacher, pastor of Moravian Church at Gracehill, Iowa.

Francis W. Knauss (1864), teacher, pastor of Moravian Church at Moravia, Iowa.

Edward J. Regennas (1862 to 1864), teacher at Nazareth Hall.

XIX.—Class 1859 to 1864.

PROFS. REV. L. F. KAMPMAN, W. C. REICHEL, L. R. HUEBNER AND WM. H. BIGLER.

Edwin G. Klose (1864), teacher, Professor in Moravian College, Bethlehem, Pa.

Charles Nagel (1865), teacher, pastor of Moravian Church at Hopedale, Pa.

Henry T. Beckler, left 1862, bookkeeper, Lancaster, Pa.

Reuben Oehler, left 1861, bookseller, Columbus. O.

Henry T. Bahnson, left 1861, physician.

Snyder B. Simes, left 1862, Episcopal clergyman.

Henry A. Jacobson (1864), teacher in Nazareth Hall.

Joseph J. Ricksecker (1864), teacher, pastor of Moravian Church, West Salem, Ill.

James T. Borhek, Jr., left 1862, druggist, Bethlehem.

Clarence Kampman, left 1862, deceased June 4, 1865, at Mound City, Ill.

J. Albert Rondthaler (1864), teacher, pastor of English Mission Church, South Bethlehem.

Robert Blickensderfer, left 1862.

XX.—Class 1862 to 1867.

PROFS. REV. L. F. KAMPMAN, L. R. HEUBNER, REV. HERM. A. BRICKENSTEIN AND WILLIAM H. BIGLER.

Jacob D. Siewers, left 1863, 1868 teacher in Nazareth Hall.

Theodore M. Rights (1867), teacher in Nazareth Hall.

John C. Hagen, left 1865, deceased August 7, 1865, at Bethlehem, Pa.

Eugene L. Shaeffer (1867), teacher in Nazareth Hall.

Charles Bishop, left 1862, machinist, Troy. Pa.

William J. Holland.

XXI.—Class 1864.

Profs. Rev. L. R. Huebner, Rev. Wm. H. Bigler, Rev. Fred. S. Hark, J. Theo. Zorn, Rev. Chas. B. Shultz and Rev. Edwin G. Klose.

Adolphus Lichenthaler.

J. Augustus Rice.

Jesse Blickensderfer.

William H. Hoch.

Joseph D. Hillman.

J. Max Hark.

REUNIONS AT NAZARETH HALL.

OF

FORMER PUPILS OF NAZARETH HALL,

June 10, 1854.

(Rev. Edward Rondthaler, Principal.)

THOSE whose youthful days were spent together at some seat of learning rarely meet in after life, without rehearsing the events, the scenes and the pleasures or griefs that checkered its early morn at school. This retrospect is usually of an agreeable character, for the pleasures of youth impress themselves more indelibly upon the mind than its short-lived griefs, which in reality only serve to augment the enjoyment of succeeding happier times. The remembrance of the most trifling incidents and occurrences at school is attended with peculiar emotions, and oftentimes awakens an almost irresistible desire to revisit the scenes in which they transpired long ago. This impulse is as ardent as it is natural.

Feelings of this nature were experienced by two former pupils of Nazareth Hall, Messrs. John Baker and Daniel D. Gassner, of New York, whose conversation, at an accidental meeting in the office of the former, turned upon the Hall and their juvenile associates. They mutually expressed a wish once more to visit the spot where they had spent so many happy days, and to again meet those with whom they had been boys together; and resolved to institute steps for effecting such a reunion.

3

A correspondence was accordingly opened with several former schoolmates, and the idea thus thrown out met with a cordial response.

The 10th of June was designated for the meeting, and invitations were extended to such gentlemen as had been pupils of the Hall during the interval between 1825 and 1830. Fifteen responded to the call, and met at Nazareth on the morning of the appointed day. Many had not seen each other for the space of a quarter of a century.

Those present at this first reunion were:

Ernest F. Bleck, of Bethlehem, a pupil of 1814, and subsequently a tutor at Nazareth Hall. (Most of the others had been under his instruction.)

James Henry (1821), gun manufacturer, Bolton, on Lehietan Creek, Northampton co.

Rev. Edward Rondthaler (1825), Principal of Nazareth Hall.

Daniel D. Gassner (1825), merchant, New York.

John Baker (1826), Secretary Mercantile Fire Insurance Company, New York.

Jacob B. Ritter (1826), merchant, Philadelphia.

Rev. William L. Lennert (1826), pastor of the congregation at Nazareth.

Fanning T. Albert (1827), manufacturer, Saugerties, N. Y.

Hyland B. Penington (1827), attorney-at-law, Philadelphia.

Samuel Penington (1827), farmer, Middletown, Del.

Francis Jordan (1827), merchant, Philadelphia.

Rev. Sylvester Wolle (1827), Principal Female Boarding-school, Bethlehem.

Maurice C. Jones (1828), gentleman, Bethlehem.

Rev. Lewis F. Kampman (1829), pastor of the congregation at Bethlehem.

Henry J. Van Vleck (1832), teacher, Nazareth.

John C. Peters (1835), physician, New York.

Three of the gentlemen were accompanied by their wives.

The morning of the day was spent in rambling over the school-grounds; and in sauntering through the shades of the charming garden, whose devious paths, and trees, and shrubs, and rural seats, and pleasant nooks, and murmuring streamlet had been the almost daily associates of former years. The graveyard above, where loved companions sleep the sleep that knows no waking, next passed in sad review. And then the woods; the trysting-ground of youthful athletes in the foot-race or in games of ball; the scene of hut-building, squirrel-hunting and nutting! Through these, alas! the tide of time had swept relentlessly, making sad havoc among the forest trees which used to lend their grateful shade. The "Bars" and the "Evening Place" were stripped of their glories, and "John Spring," once overarched with foliage, sent forth a slender stream at the foot of a bare and sunburnt hill. Elsewhere fields of grain cover the ground so dear to memory; their waving harvests cheering the husbandman, but saddening the schoolboy's heart as he misses his accustomed haunts. A magnificent panorama of the valley, stretching to the south of Nazareth, has been opened up to the view by the unsparing axe; but this could not compensate for the loss of what those who were met had hoped once more to see.

After a social dinner at the village inn, the former pupils proceeded to organize the meeting by appointing Mr. Ernest F. Bleck, President, and Mr. John Baker, Secretary.

It was declared, as the sense of this meeting, that the first reunion of the former pupils of Nazareth Hall had afforded such gratification to its participants as to excite a lively desire for an annual recurrence of a similar day of enjoyment; and it was therefore,

Resolved, 1. That the President be instructed to take proper measures to effect a second reunion, to transpire in June of 1855;

2. To extend invitations to all former pupils whose addresses could be ascertained;

3. To invite a former pupil to be speaker of the day;

4. To form a programme of exercises for the occasion, calculated to render it one of rational festivity.

With the cheering assurance that the wishes of the company would be abundantly realized in 1855, the meeting separated.

On invitation of Rev. Edward Rondthaler, to meet him at three o'clock in the afternoon, the reunionists repaired to his residence. In front of the Hall they found the pupils and their teachers, who greeted them with cheers such as the warm hearts of the young alone can give. This cordial reception was acknowledged by the President in a short address.

While partaking of Moravian sugar-cake and delicious coffee, the Principal produced the register of the school, and a catalogue of the years 1825 to 1830 was carefully examined. Many an incident, sad, bright, ludicrous, or characteristic, was called forth by active memory and afforded intense gratification. Not a name was read whose owner had not left an impression on the mind of some one present, and whose subsequent history and present state could not be traced. And it was a pleasing result that scarce an instance could be cited reflecting on the training received at Nazareth Hall. An invitation was received to partake of an evening meal with the schoolboys and their teachers in the common refectory,

which, was promised, should be conducted in the manner
and after the discipline of the olden time. The company
adjourned to the teachers' room, and as the clock struck
six the well-known bell announced the evening meal.
The scholars, marshaled by their teachers, passed on the
way to the dining-room ; and the reunionists, headed by
their former instructor, followed in single file, and, to the
no small amusement and wonder of the boys around them,
took their seats at table in due order. As was the custom
formerly, all united in singing a hymn, and the meal began.
The huge loaf was cut by the teachers, and distributed
amid Pythagorean silence. Some of the guests, forgetful
of old-time requirements, opened a conversation ; a rap
on the table by their teacher was respectfully heeded and
at once checked the irregularity.

After tea the President addressed the assembly, directing his remarks more especially to the inmates of the
Hall, stating the circumstances which had led to, and the
import of, the present gathering. He said this was a
beginning of a contemplated series of annual reunions of
former pupils, and that doubtless a large number would
meet next June to revisit the scenes of their youth, to renew the associations and friendships formed at school, to
revive ancient memories, and to learn the subsequent history of those who once were united with them in the pursuit of knowledge in this time-honored and venerable
edifice. He then narrated the manner in which the party
had spent the day, and said that, doubtless, one of the
most interesting incidents for them was the present, when
they met the pupils in the capacity of the " oldest room-
company ;" that while they saw in their young friends
the representatives of what they once were, the present
pupils might justly regard their visitors as the representatives of positions in life they would themselves be called

ere long to fill.   He next dwelt on the importance of a
just appreciation of their present position ; on the necessity and the reward of close and earnest application to
the means afforded them of becoming well qualified for
the active pursuits of life, in whatever station the future
might place them ; and concluded by expressing the
grateful sentiments of his associates for the cordial reception and many marks of kindness and attention extended
them.   The visitors then retired to the teachers' room,
and after an hour of social converse repaired to the
terrace to enjoy the promised beautiful sunset.   In the
evening the Hall was brilliantly illuminated, and a band
of sweet-toned instruments poured forth pleasing melody.
The inhabitants of the village congregated in the square
in front of the Hall to participate in the closing exercises
of a day of unalloyed enjoyment.   The pastor made a
brief address ; an evening hymn, accompanied by a band
of music, was sung, and after the benediction had been
pronounced, the reunionists left for their respective homes.

SECOND REUNION

OF

FORMER PUPILS, June 8, 1855,

(Rev. E. H. Reichel, Principal,)

AND ORGANIZATION OF THE

REUNION SOCIETY OF NAZARETH HALL.

In accordance with the instructions given to its President by the reunion of 1854, he issued the following

"CIRCULAR:

"Bethlehem, Pa., March 3, 1855.

"My dear Sir: On June 10, 1854, a number of the former pupils of Nazareth Hall met at that place by agreement, and spent a day of much enjoyment in visiting the various spots teeming with interesting reminiscences of times long gone by, and in reviving recollections of scenes and events that checkered life's sprightly time of youth, 'when they were boys together.'

"This 'Reunion of Former Pupils of Nazareth Hall' was so gratifying to the participants that it was unanimously resolved to hold similar 'reunions' annually, and to extend invitations to *all* 'former pupils of Nazareth Hall,' and their families, to join in like movements hereafter; and the undersigned, elected President of the Reunion of 1854, was instructed to take such measures as might be requisite to carry out the wish so ardently entertained.

13 *

9

" In accordance with these instructions, the undersigned addresses this circular to 'all former pupils of Nazareth Hall,' whose residence at the present time he may be able to ascertain, inviting them and their families to meet together at Nazareth, on Friday, June 8th next, at ten o'clock A. M.

" Circumstances may render it desirable to know how many may be expected to be present on that occasion; hence, every one receiving this circular will confer a favor by replying thereto before June 1. These replies may be addressed either to the undersigned, at Bethlehem, Pa., or to the Rev. Edward H. Reichel, Principal of Nazareth Hall, Nazareth, Pa.

" Respectfully, etc.,

" E. F. BLECK,
" *President of the ' Reunion of Former Pupils of Nazareth Hall*, 1854.' "

This circular was despatched by the Principal of Nazareth Hall to as many of the former pupils as could be reached. It elicited numerous replies, some announcing the intention of the writers to be present, others expressive of regret at their inability to attend, and all evincing approbation of the initiative about to be taken to render the reunion a permanent institution. These communications were carefully preserved for future reference.

The 8th of June proved a lovely summer's day, although the continuous rains of the previous week had augured no such auspicious change in the state of the weather. Many of the reunionists had reached Nazareth already on the previous day, and when the last arrival from Bethlehem, in a cortege of five carriages, preceded by a band of music, drew up at the village inn, on the morning of the 8th, there ensued a scene of the most pleasurable confusion, which will never be forgotten by those who were present. Principal and tutor and pupil were met on common ground, released from the restraining influences of the distinctions which custom and the laws of the Institution had once sanctioned as inviolable. The children of a common mother were met together to do her homage ; and most cordial were the greetings of older and younger brothers, who had been impelled by the same feeling of reverence to perform this remarkable pilgrimage to the scenes of boyhood's days spent in the old homestead.

The ringing of the village church-bell at 10 o'clock A. M. was the signal for the "former pupils" to fall into line, as the festivities of the day were about to open. Marshaled by the Principal of Nazareth Hall, and headed by the Bethlehem Sixtette (whose pleasing performances added to the enjoyment of the day and evening), they moved through the village, and on entering the green before the venerable building were greeted by its youthful inmates with loud demonstrations of welcome. Master Frederic A. Tilge, of Philadelphia, stepped forward, and in behalf of his companions, bidding the reunionists a hearty welcome, said :

"GENTLEMEN: This day has summoned you once again to ramble among scenes which, no doubt, will vividly recall your school-days, causing you to feel that you were once boys as we now are, *if not to wish that you were now in our stead.* We trust that you will spend a pleasant day, and that its recollection will be a bright spot in your lives. And if our days be prolonged, we hope to be also enabled in after years to meet here, as you do now, in order to live over in a few short hours the school-days spent in Nazareth Hall. We also wish the ladies, who have come to participate in the festivities of the day, a delightful time, and trust they will be favorably impressed by all they hear and see. And now, boys, three more cheers!"

President Bleck replied, in behalf of his associates, to the speaker, expressing their high appreciation of the cordial reception just now extended them. He next referred to the interesting nature of the present occasion, when men whose heads were white with the frosts of many winters—men in the prime of manhood and amid the pursuits of active life—and young men, just entering upon the business and turmoil and cares of an untried world—had left their distant homes to meet former associates, to revisit the scenes of the past, and to spend a day of quiet and refined enjoyment under the shadow of their ancient and venerated Alma Mater. He invited his youthful friends to partake of the pleasures the day would bring, and from them to learn how dear to the human heart are the remembrances of the peaceful times and happy associations of early youth. In conclusion, he expressed the hope that the Institution in which he and his friends had been taught many lessons of worldly wisdom and early piety might continue to flourish, and be the nursery of useful men, ornaments to society, and worthy of citizenship in the great and glorious republic whose proud banner now waved triumphantly, yet calmly, over the stately edifice before them.

The reunionists were now shown to an apartment in the Hall, and proceeded to business. President Bleck took the chair, called the members to order, and, in the absence of the minutes of last year's meeting, gave a brief narrative of what had then transpired. He also suggested the expediency of a regular organization by the adoption of a constitution, and of such measures as would

conspire to ensure the annual repetition of occasions such
as the present. On motion of Hyland B. Penington, Esq.,
of Philadelphia, the President appointed the mover, in connection with Rev. Lewis L. Kampman and Rev. Edward
H. Reichel, a committee to prepare and report a constitution for adoption by the meeting. During its session the
members recorded their names and year of entering the
Hall, in a register prepared for the purpose, as follows:

	A PUPIL OF
J. F. Wolle, Bethlehem	1789.
John S. Haman, Nazareth	1794.
John Beck, Litiz	1799.
Peter Wolle, Bethlehem	1800.
P. S. Michler, Easton	1808.
Ernest F. Bleck, Bethlehem	1814.
John C. Jacobson, Bethlehem (*ex off.*)*	1816.
James Henry, Bolton, Northampton co.	1821.
Joseph Ridgway, New York	1825.
Daniel D. Gassner, New York	1825.
Joseph F. Berg, Philadelphia	1825.
William L. Lennert, Nazareth	1826.
John Baker, New York	1826.
Hyland B. Penington, Philadelphia	1827.
Samuel Penington, Middletown, Del.	1827.
Francis Jordan, Philadelphia	1827.
Maurice C. Jones, Bethlehem	1828.
N. Miller Horton, Wilkesbarré	1830.
John J. Garvin, Philadelphia	1830.
A. G. Kern, Jr., Nazareth	1831.
William H. Butler, Wilkesbarré	1832.
W. J. Romig, Allentown	1832.
Henry J. Van Vleck, Nazareth	1832.
Edward H. Reichel, Nazareth	1833.
Philip A. Cregar, Philadelphia (*ex off.*)	1833.
Isaac L. Ritter, Philadelphia	1834.
William C. Reichel, Bethlehem	1834
Edmund de Schweinitz, Philadelphia	1834.

* Those marked *ex off.* were Teachers, and hence, agreeably to its Constitution,
members of the Reunion.

A PUPIL OF

James Brodrick, Jr., Rockport, Carbon co.................	1838.
Francis Michler, Easton...........................	1838.
James H. Wolle, Bethlehem........................	1838.
Louis R. Huebner, Nazareth Hall..........	1839.
Theodore A. Lambert, Reading.....................	1840.
John Thomas, Catasauqua..........................	1841.
John H. Eberman, Bethlehem......................	1841.
Abraham Prince, Brooklyn.........................	1841.
Bradford Ritter, Philadelphia......................	1841.
James N. Beck, Philadelphia.......................	1841.
William Trucks, Philadelphia......................	1842.
Theodore F. Wolle, Greensboro', N. C...............	1842.
William A. Lilliendahl, New York..................	1844.
Herman A. Brickenstein, Nazareth Hall.............	1844.
Clement L. Reinke, Nazareth Hall.................	1844.
G. Morgan Eldridge, Philadelphia..................	1845.
C. Edward Kummer, Nazareth Hall.................	1845.
George A. Widmayer, Staten Island.................	1845.
George F. Thomae, Jr., Brooklyn..................	1846.
Granville Henry, Bolton, Northampton co............	1846.
Henry H. Wolle, Philadelphia.....................	1846.
Edwin Housel, Easton............................	1846.
Edward T. Kluge, Nazareth Hall..................	1846.
Charles H. Hutchinson, Philadelphia...............	1846.
F. E. Steinle, New York..........................	1847.
Robert Chapman, New York.......................	1847.
Philip S. Pretz, Allentown........................	1847.
Lewis D. Lambert, Hazelton......................	1847.
Henry T. Clark, Easton...........................	1847.
Charles M. Lewis, Philadelphia....................	1847.
David Thomas, Jr., Catasauqua....................	1848.
E. T. Elliott, Towanda...........................	1848.
Eugene M. Leibert, Nazareth Hall.................	1848.
Robert J. McClatchey, Philadelphia................	1849.
Charles L. Bute, Jr., Philadelphia.................	1851.
William H. H. Michler, Easton....................	1852.

The Committee on Constitution reported the following, which was unanimously adopted, namely:

Article I.

This society shall be known by the name of " The Re-Union Society of Nazareth Hall."

Article II.

No person shall be admitted a member unless he has been an inspector, a teacher or a scholar of Nazareth Hall.

Article III.

The officers of this society shall be a President, two Vice-Presidents, a Secretary and an Assistant Secretary.

Article IV.

The President shall preside at all meetings, and the Secretary shall keep accurate minutes in a book to be prepared for that purpose, which said book shall remain in charge of the Inspector of Nazareth Hall.

Article V.

The society shall hold a meeting once a year at Nazareth Hall, in Nazareth. The day of such meeting shall be fixed by the Inspector of Nazareth Hall. The pastor of the congregation of said place shall be *ex officio* a member of this society.

Article VI.

The Secretary of the Society shall always be a resident of Nazareth.

The meeting proceeded to elect the officers required by the Constitution, which election, on motion of Rev. Edmund de Schweinitz, of Philadelphia, was held by acclamation.

The election resulted as follows:

President.

ERNEST F. BLECK, Bethlehem.

Vice-Presidents.

JOHN BECK, Litiz.
G. MORGAN ELDRIDGE, Philadelphia.

Secretary.

REV. WILLIAM L. LENNERT, Nazareth.

Assistant Secretary.

HERMAN A. BRICKENSTEIN, Nazareth.

On motion, it was resolved to hold another meeting for business purposes after tea.

At three P. M. the reunionists repaired to the village church, where a large audience had already assembled, in order to participate in some special exercises. They occupied the front lines of benches, the seats from time immemorial reserved for the pupils of Nazareth Hall. The festivities were opened by an anthem sung by a select choir, sustained by the organ and a band of stringed and wind instruments. The words of this composition are by Mr. C. J. Latrobe, of London, and the music by Rev. Peter Ricksecker, a former teacher of Nazareth Hall, then missionary among the Indians in Kansas. It is No. 566 in the latest edition of the Moravian hymn-book.

Rt. Rev. Peter Wolle having addressed the Throne of Grace in prayer, Rev. Dr. Berg, of Philadelphia, was introduced as speaker of the day, and addressed his audience as follows:

" It is my privilege, in behalf of our venerated Alma Mater, to tender to the alumni of time-honored Nazareth

Hall a cordial welcome to this classic ground, and the warm salutations of all connected with this Institution. A good mother loves her children, and this festive occasion is itself evidence of the affectionate interest with which this Institution regards the health, prosperity and happiness of its former inmates. It exhibits, also, a commendable filial affection on your part, or rather, let me say. on *our* part, for I am not, and I am sure I never shall be. ashamed of my mother. Whatever changes may have passed over us, and around us, and in us—and since some of us were boys together they have been both many and great—they have not affected the love which we must ever feel for the noble old Hall with which our happy childhood is identified. We have come together to talk over old times ; if not, like old soldiers, to fight our battles over again, at least to renew many scenes of youthful toil and conflict. True, we are innocent of all the peculiar sensations with which, as school-boys, we looked up into the face of our preceptors when we were perhaps not as well shod in our preparations as we might have been, and felt, as it were. standing in slippery places, and had visions of post-meridian conning of lessons flitting in prospective. Some of us have long since thrown away our school-books, or, what would be still better evidence of profitable or at least economical discipleship, handed them over to our children. Once here again we are admonished that the march of improvement has rendered them almost as useless as the threadbare coats of our grandfathers. But let the books go ; they may serve as relics to show the next generation the path in which their fathers trod ; how they scribbled in the frontispiece and blotted the pages, and scandalized their preceptors ; and if your son or mine did better in this respect than his father, so be it.

14

" When we visit old localities and scenes familiar to us
in the days of our childhood, we feel all the emotions
with which a generous heart greets the face of a long-
tried friend, from whom he has been separated for many
years. Some of the landmarks have disappeared. In
this utilitarian age the woodman's axe is always sharp.
It would be idle to wish that grindstones had never been
invented, for they are needful in their place, but from my
heart I cannot help wishing that there had been fewer of
them in this good old town. The axe has made sad
havoc. Some of the old trees which we used to climb
are still standing, and lifting their tall heads in prouder
eminence than when seated on them I shook the ripe nuts
from their topmost branches, and sent them pattering
over the dry leaves, cheating the squirrels, and, I grieve
to say, even the pigs, of what righteously belonged to
them. But many of our favorites in those shady groves,
known in days of yore as the guardians of the · First
boys' round place' and the ' Second boys' round place,'
have fallen, like Homer's heroes, with a crash, and their
shady crests, like the plumes of the warrior, have been
soiled and draggled in the dust. Let me not be accused
of pedantry when I say that of every one of those war-
riors old Homer would have said, ' Δούπησεν δε πεσών,
αράβησε δε τεύχε επ' αυτώ,' or, as my dear old preceptor,
Brickenstein, used to say, when reading Voss' matchless
version of the Iliad, at the close of our Greek recitations,
· *Dumpf hin kracht er im Fall, und es klirreten auf
ihm die Waffen.'* The hero of the axe, more terrible
than the lion-hearted Richard in his blows upon the tur-
baned Saracen, more relentless than the redoubtable
Achilles, has slain his thousands, and they are gone—
those noble old trees. Those fences, to men of our generation, are eyesores—our play-grounds had no such en-

cumbrances; we would not have tolerated them, and though the filling grain wears gloriously its green charms in promise of a rich harvest, and the woods have been converted into fertile fields, and all this may be right, still, if we had our way, the woodchopper would have been a thousand miles off in the day when war was declared against the noble old oaks. We rested under them when the sun was high and we were fatigued of our boyish sports. We cannot help sighing, as though it were almost sacrilege to slay those old friends; but the picture still lives. The freshness of youthful impression has imprinted them with all the lifelike vividness of a daguerreotype upon our memories, and we shall carry them, as Queen Mary declared she would take the name of Calais, the last foothold of Britain in France, with us to our graves. 'The Lund Spring' and 'The Bore Spring' are as dear to our memories, and far more really consecrate than the fabled fountains from which the Muses drew their inspiration. Those two old lindens at the gate are still standing—may they live a thousand years, and may their shadows never grow less! My friend tells me they are gone. From my heart I regret it. I remember well the old man who planted them; I can see him yet, standing erect, though the weight of more than fourscore years was upon him. We always venerated that old man. We called him 'Daddy Schæffer.' The boys knew him as 'the man who planted the lindens at the gate,' and we felt like raising our hats when we passed. He is dead, but I could wish that noble monument might still keep his memory green, and that the air were even now loaded with the fragrance of former years, as those boughs wave over his humble grave, their censers filled with the purest incense. Too much sentiment in this matter-of-fact age is, perhaps, out of place; still, before I let the trees go, I must say a word which will perhaps interest the boys. I was a scholar and a teacher in Nazareth Hall, and ten of the happiest years of my life were spent here. I owe more to this Institution than I can ever repay. I deem it a privilege to express my gratitude to God, and to those connected with this venerated Academy, for those ten years of my life; and when these boys shall be men, and shall stand in the place of their fathers, if their hearts are right, they will thank God for the days they spent in Nazareth. When I was a boy, the movable property of the school was marked N. P.—Nazareth Pædagogium; and some of the youngsters from New York and Philadelphia, to whom the restraints of the Hall were rather irksome, used to say that those initials stood for Nazareth Prison. The iron bars at the windows helped them to another idea, and kept up the fanciful analogy. These were the gratings of the dungeon! Now, sober sense would teach you that those bars in the third story were capital contrivances to keep lads, when in a roistering mood, in the absence of the teacher, from throwing themselves away out of the windows; but they thought only of home and the indulgence of a mother, and sometimes mistook the care of the nurse, who was watching them, for the vigilance of a jailer. Now, let me say to you, boys, that if you never get into a worse prison than Nazareth Hall, you will do well, and a great deal better than some who were never trained in the Nazareth Pædagogium. The tendency of all the education you receive here will be to make you useful and honorable members of society. And while I am talking specially to you in this familiar way, let me give you a leaf or two out of my book. I have told you that I was both a scholar and a teacher in the Hall. This gave me some opportunities for observation; and as I have been behind the scenes, I

know all about the ropes, and that boys sometimes will
pull when the teacher is not watching them, or when
they *think* he is not watching them ; and I will tell you
what I have noticed. Those boys that were slovenly in
their recitations, and that cared for nothing except play,
and were anxious only to learn enough to keep them from
being kept in after school-hours, or ' *learning after,*' as
we used to term that especial discipline, so far as I have
been able to trace their subsequent history, have always
been rather of the inefficient, do-little order ; they have
seldom made their mark in the world. This has been
the rule. Exceptions may doubtless be found, but the
rule is, that the most diligent and studious school-boys
have proved the most active and energetic men. You
find them in the halls of legislature and science—you find
them in the pulpit, at the bar, and at the bedside minis-
tering as physicians to the sick and dying—everywhere
active, useful men, leaving the world all the better for
having lived in it. The boy is the type of the man.
Boys are men in miniature, and men are only boys of
larger growth. Your character is forming now, and you
may rely on it, whenever you see a scholar who tries to
cheat his teacher in his recitations—who will, if he can,
sneak out of responsibilities through sloth or indolence—
he is one who will probably prove a profitless pupil ; and
when he has his place in his profession, if you know him,
keep your eye on him, whenever you have dealings with
him, for he will bear watching.

" I promise to let the trees alone, after stating a fact
which belongs to the reminiscences of my experience as
a teacher, and I will give you the story, because it may
be made to point a moral worth remembering. When I
was a teacher, in charge of the second boys' room, we
went out one day in autumn to gather chestnuts. Among

the trees on the play-ground appropriated to boys of that
division, there was a noble chestnut, which was rather
hard to climb, but the nuts were large, and, in short, they
were ripe, and it was time we had them. Among the
boys there was a stout, chubby lad, as lithe and as agile
as a cat, who clenched the tree and scrambled up. Soon
the chestnuts came rattling down, and as the long pole
whipped the branches, the tree was becoming pretty
thoroughly stripped; every bough in the lower part of
the tree had been laid under contribution. John went up,
still making 'excelsior' his motto, until he found himself
swinging in the wind among the topmost branches of
the tree. He became frightened, and called out to me
that he was getting dizzy, and was afraid that he would
fall. I confess, when I looked up and saw him perched
at that height, I felt somewhat of a tremor. I called out
to him, 'If you feel giddy, John, come down!' Very
good advice, but the trouble was that, in order to come
down, he must use his eyes, and so soon as he looked
down, excited as he then was, his brain began to whirl
like a top, and there was danger of coming down in a
kind of extemporaneous, off-hand style that would have
been anything but desirable. Matters were getting serious, for every moment was increasing the boy's agitation.
He cried out again, 'Oh, sir, I am very dizzy, and how
shall I get down? If I look down, I shall fall.' I remember the answer that I gave him. It was, 'Look up,
John, and hold on!' 'Ay, ay, sir, I will,' said he.
Very well, he did so; and forthwith a committee was despatched for one of those long ladders that used to be in
the square near the old market-house; a posse-comitatus
of the citizens was summoned, and a sufficient force was
soon raised for the rescue. We got him down safe and
sound, and he is now perched, I believe, on one of the

topmost branches of the tree whose leaves and fruit bring medicine to the sick; living in New York, respected as an eminent physician. Now, my young friends, when you get out into the world, it is very likely that you may be brought into positions, in your eager pursuits after its pleasures, its riches, its honors or its fruits, in which you may begin to feel dizzy; and if you would be kept from a fall that would break your bones, the soundest advice I can give you, in such circumstances, is to 'Look up and hold on' until you can step down with a clear brain and a sure foot; but still better counsel would be, to 'look up' before you climb, and never to risk your neck for a few chestnuts. This habit of 'looking up,' and keeping your eyes and your heart on the bright heaven above you, and where you and I hope to go when this changing world has done with us and we have done with it, will 'keep your feet from falling, your eyes from tears and your soul from death!'

" It is so natural for us, on an occasion like the present, when houses, fields and gardens, and par excellence *'the garden,'* remind us of the days of our boyhood, to look back upon that period of our youthful history, that I care not to divert my mind from this channel. I seem to be living now in the past. Every foot of that road between Bethlehem and Nazareth, which I so often measured on holidays, when liberty was given me to visit my dear old mother, used to be as familiar to me as the pavement now is before my door. 'The mile-hill,' where my mother used to leave me when the hour for returning to school had come, and I had to march back; 'the four-mile-hill,' on the brow of which, a little to the left, stood an old hovel, occupied by an aged couple, a mother and her daughter—the daughter far advanced in the eighties; Dreisbach's tavern, where we stopped at the pump to

rest and refresh ourselves with the cool water; Dreisbach's hill, on the roadside, famous as the only locality
known in those days to botanists, because noted by the
lamented Schweinitz as the habitat of the *Viola rostrata;*
' The Dry Lands,' with its antiquated stone church, now
displaced by a newer edifice; and the shady patches of
woodland intervening between Hartzell's and that hill
from which the spire of the old Hall beckoned me back
to my books, and which loomed up at times with awful
majesty, as I anticipated a gentle reminder from brother
Brickenstein—always laconic, when needed, and who
would sometimes greet us on our return, if we had lagged,
with a significant *' Etwas spät!'*—the clear ringing of
the Hall-bell, as it would sound out over the hills, and
reach us in the distance with its warnings, making us
quicken our steps;—all these, and a thousand memories
besides, come back like messages from the dreamy past,
whispering with their still small voice of happier days
that are gone, never to return. How often, in the stirring conflict of active life through which we have passed
since we have left the walls of that old Hall, have the
quiet scenes that surround us this day been brought back
to our memories, and proved to our weary spirits the very
balm which was needed to soothe them. In days of per-
plexity and sorrow the pleasant memories of our boyhood have been like the shadow of a rock in a weary
land. The simple lessons of evangelical truth sometimes
addressed to listless hearers were not thrown away. Often
the seed that has long been buried in the dust and covered
with rubbish, germinates, and is found after many days.
It is well to sow beside all waters, and to cast the seed
upon the waters: the flood will not always be high, and
when the seed reaches the moistened soil and the waters
have abated, it springs up and bears fruit an hundred-

fold. The prominence given to religious principles, divested of all polemical or sectarian form, the simple spirit of evangelical purity, which is the very staple of this atmosphere, will be like the small rain upon the tender plant in its influence upon character. Let our youth learn that sincerity and simplicity are the choicest characteristics of genuine piety, and they have learned that which will make them wise for ever.

" Who of us that were denizens of this Institution during the inspectorship of Van Vleck and Herman, can ever forget them? The mild, gentle and paternal earnestness of the one, the cordial, cheerful and generous warmth of the other, endeared them to us all. Both have entered into rest, proving themselves men of God to the last, and dying as soldiers of Christ, with their harness on. I might speak of other excellent men who have since sustained the same relation, but they are still among the living, and some of them are adding to the social enjoyment of this reunion by their presence.

" But I must close. Most earnestly do I desire that Nazareth Hall may long be permitted to exert its influence upon the community, in promoting the best interests of sound education, pure morality and religion undefiled ; and that from these seats of unostentatious but not less solid learning many may go forth who shall stand in the front rank of Christian duty and benevolence, foremost in every good work, with strong hearts and stout hearts, to labor for God, for themselves, their country and the world, until they hear the plaudits of the mighty Judge, ' Well done, good and faithful servant.' Long may the peculiarities of Moravian discipline be here preserved intact and inviolate. Its distinctive character is the very life of this Institution. Let no rash hand of crude reformation be lifted upon it, to mould it into closer resemblance to other schools. That would be to ruin it. Let it rather be like the altar which God chose for His own —built of unhewn stone, '*for if thou lift a tool upon it, thou hast defiled it.*' Let it stand in the quiet dignity of the simplicity and unpretending merit which have heretofore given it character and favor, and it will continue to be a blessing when we and our children shall have yielded the spheres of active duty to other generations."

At the close of the address the Principal announced the programme for the remainder of the day. The following ode was then sung by the choir, with instrumental accompaniment. The words are by the late Rev. G. B. Reichel, of Salem, N. C., and the music by Rt. Rev. Peter Wolle, of Bethlehem, both pupils of 1800:

Come, joyful hallelujahs raise,
The tribute bring of grateful praise !
Exalt, extol the wondrous love
Of Him who lives and reigns above !
His blessings and His mercies all
Our songs and sweetest anthems call ;
The riches of His bounteous hand
Still cheer and crown our favor'd land !

He is our God and our defence,
In danger He our confidence ;
In happiness, our Guard and Guide,
He ever will for us provide.
His matchless goodness He displays
To brighten and to bless our days ;

Then let us join, his name to sing,
And hallowed hymns harmonious bring !
Oh tune thy harp and strike thy lay,
America ! Columbia !

In conclusion, Bishop Wolle pronounced the benediction. The meeting of former pupils and inhabitants of the

village in the square after the exercises was of an interesting character, as the speaker's remarks had recalled scenes
and revived recollections in which both were interested.

At five o'clock the Hall-bell announced tea. A bountiful meal had been spread in the Chapel, and two hundred and eighty-three persons partook of the hospitality
of the Institution. In accordance with the usage of former times, grace-was *sung*, and there was scarce a voice
that failed to join in the familiar stanza :

> " Each crumb thou dost allow us
> With gratitude shall bow us,
> Accounting all for us too good."

The din of knives and forks, and the clatter of plates,
which broke the succeeding silence, were reverberated by
walls and ceiling, and indicated the good-will with which
the company entered upon the duties of the moment. The
room was decorated with vases of flowers ; and as the eye
glanced round the spacious apartment, and took in the
long tables well loaded with wholesome viands, and the
medley of delighted faces, young and old, male and female, in one promiscuous confusion of good-humor, the
scene presented was indeed original and pleasing.

There was much to recall the past. The pupils of the
school sat arranged in classes, with their respective teachers at the head of the tables. The rap of the knife on
the loaf—that well-known signal to the hungry urchin—
had the desired effect, as might be seen from the long line
of upturned hands and fingers that spoke by dumb show
the wants of their owners. The huge tea and coffee cans
were rather less indented than those of former times ; but
the fried potatoes, the cold meat and the doughnuts were
old friends with well-known faces, and welcomed as such.
It required little effort of the fancy to fill up the deficien-

cies of the picture, and to be once again a veritable pupil at an old-time supper-table in Nazareth Hall. Social chat enlivened the meal; and on order being restored, the President communicated several of the letters received from absent former pupils, and among them the following two—the first from Mr. Thomas Horsfield, Librarian of the East India House, London, a pupil of 1785; and the second from Mr. Jacob Kummer, of Bethlehem, a pupil of 1786:

" Library East India House, }
" London, *May* 18, 1855.   }

"The Rev. Edward H. Reichel,
" *Principal of the Moravian Boarding-school, at Nazareth Hall:*

" Dear Sir : I have the pleasure to acknowledge the receipt of your circular, dated Bethlehem, Pa., March 3, 1855, and sent from Nazareth on the 30th of the same month, and to inform you that I have forwarded, by the kind assistance of Mr. William Mallalieu, a small memorial in behalf of my interest in the proposed Reunion, to be held at Nazareth, on the 8th of June next. In this book I have taken the liberty to inscribe my own name, with those of my fellow-pupils who entered the school in 1785. It is intended for the library of your establishment.*

" Allow me briefly to add, that at this period of my life, having just commenced my eighty-third year, I can truly say that I recall with pleasure the three years, from 1785 to 1788, which I spent at Nazareth Hall, under the care and instruction of your venerable grandfather, Charles Gotthold Reichel.

" With best wishes for the prosperity of your establishment, I remain respectfully,
" Yours,
" Thomas Horsfield,
" *Pupil of* 1785."

* A copy of " Plantæ Javanicæ Rariores," *London,* 1853.

"Mr. E. F. Bleck :

"Bethlehem, *June* 5, 1855.

"Dear Sir : Your circular, addressed to all former pupils of Nazareth Hall, inviting them and their families to meet together at Nazareth on Friday, June 8, has been duly received by me ; and although I still feel very much attached to the good old building in which I received instruction, and to 'the various spots in the neighborhood. teeming with interesting reminiscences of times long gone by,' and should be delighted to 'revive recollections of scenes and events that checkered life's sprightly time of youth,' yet I must beg you to take the will for the deed ; and I confidently hope that all the 'former pupils of Nazareth Hall,' assembled this year at the annual celebration, will kindly excuse me, after having heard what I further have to say.

"I believe I am the oldest living scholar of Nazareth Hall. The school, as it is at present, was commenced in 1785, when the Rev. Charles G. Reichel, the grandfather of the present Principal, arrived from Europe, to open a boarding-school for boys at Nazareth Hall, and in 1786 I entered the school, being then only four years of age. I remained ten years as pupil in the school, and in 1803 I again entered the Hall as teacher, and continued in that capacity five years.

"Much as I should like to revive many former recollections, I find in the review, that instead of pleasing incidents, there would be many more of sadness passing before my mind. I would find myself standing solitary and alone, without any of my old school-companions ; and of the various spots in the neighborhood, once so interesting to me, how few would I find as they were formerly ! Now, all are changed, perhaps quite as beauti-

15

ful as they were sixty years ago, but still they are changed, and not the same loved places.

" I remember when the two stately linden trees near the gate leading from the yard to the garden were not thicker than my arm, and one of them, I hear, is no more.*

" Thus I could probably enumerate a hundred and more different things which are not as they were in my time, and which would produce a deep-felt sadness in my mind.

" Even of my former scholars in Nazareth Hall, how few should I find alive if I should go through the list! Besides all this, I feel that at my age it is highly necessary to keep as calm as possible; the excitement of the occasion would be more than I could well bear. And being corpulent, it would certainly take all the breath my lungs could afford to carry me from the Hall to the farther end of the pleasure-garden, and with the greatest difficulty could I get back again; much less could I think of walking along the different roads; and it would be quite out of the question to go up and down the slopes of the pleasant walks. So that, upon the whole, I am sure that my presence in your midst would only be a clog to the enjoyment of all the company. One thing more I must mention—that having always been in good health, I can still enjoy life, perhaps, more than most others of my age, being now in my seventy-fourth year, and that although I am upward of threescore and ten years old, I still have the pleasure and satisfaction of seeing here, at Bethlehem, one of my former teachers, the Right Reverend Andrew Benade.

" Permit me, in conclusion, to wish you and every individual assembled at Nazareth Hall on the occasion

* Both are gone.

much joy and happiness for this and many succeeding days.

"In spirit I shall be with you.

"Yours, truly, etc.,

"JACOB KUMMER,

"*Pupil of* 1786

The society having been called to order for business, the following resolutions were adopted :

Resolved, That the letters received from former pupils of Nazareth Hall be put on file, and be the property of this association.

Resolved, That it is the sense of this society that no more of the trees within an area of two square miles about the village be cut down ; and that Rev. E. H. Reichel, Principal, and Rev. W. L. Lennert, pastor, be requested to exert their influence to have this resolution carried into effect.

Resolved, That the thanks of the meeting be tendered to Rev. Dr. Berg for his address, and that a copy of the same be requested for publication.

Resolved, That the historical sketch of Nazareth Hall, written and furnished by Rev. L. T. Reichel, of Salem, N. C., be printed with the above address, in connection with the proceedings of the day.

Mr. John Beck, of Litiz (a pupil of 1799), now rose and said : "He was at a loss for words with which to express the happiness he experienced throughout the day and felt at the present moment. Fifty-six years ago, this very day, he had been brought here to school. Born and raised beyond the Blue Mountain, he remembered well with what astonishment he looked upon the huge building into which he was about to be entered. St. Peter's at Rome could not have awakened ideas of the sublime

more forcibly than did the Hall as it first rose up in
majesty before his wondering gaze. That he was none
of the brightest when he arrived here from his rustic
home, he well knew. There could not be much expected
of him, yet he had been trained and taught to some purpose in this Institution of learning. The practical education he had received within its walls had served him well,
as all who were acquainted with him knew. On this
very floor, and almost on the very spot on which he
stood, he had made his first essays as a juvenile orator.
Here, too, he had received indelible impressions of the
great truths of religion. He thanked the teacher who
had first turned his attention to the concerns of his soul;
and, though he was long since gone to a better world, yet
most sacredly did he revere his memory. To-day he felt
himself a schoolboy again. A host of incidents crowded
on his recollection. The comic and the serious strove for
the mastery. How could he ever forget the holiday-feast
down at Danke's, where they had gingerbread and small
beer? In those days the scholars were mulcted a farthing
for talking at meals, a ha'penny for falling on the floor,
onepence for tearing a leaf out of a book, twopence for
telling a lie, and threepence for an oath; and whenever
the treasury was filled, it was turned to advantage in an
excursion to Danke's, where gingerbread and small beer
were to be had. It was a most delicious treat—*it tasted
good yet!* When seated at the tea-table this evening, he
noticed the march of improvement, and oh how different
from the times when boys fared, mornings and evenings,
on milk and brown bread! Cups were a rarity in those
days, and milk was dipped up from pewter plates with
pewter spoons. How the softness of the metal tempted
the busy, mischievous fingers of the schoolboy, at all
times itching to cut, carve and devise. Many were the

circles nicely drawn with the fork (used as a pair of dividers on the broad surface of the useful dish) until the metal gave way and the perforated plate rendered but imperfect service. The wholesome beverage, true to the laws of hydraulics, issued forth, saturating the white table-cloth beneath; but well-moulded plugs of plastic bread effectually stopped the wasteful leakage."

The speaker proceeded to narrate incidents of a similar character, in a style ludicrously graphic, and which called forth repeated plaudits from his delighted hearers. Among others, the circumstances which resulted in the introduction of coffee for breakfast were amusingly detailed.

" When on a visit," said he, " to Nazareth a few years ago, in company with a gentleman who had also been educated here, as they entered into the 'square,' they stood on the walk below and admired their Alma Mater in her noble simplicity. He then remarked, and would repeat the observation now, that Nazareth Hall had turned out more practically-trained men than any other school. Though the Institute had seen many ups and downs, he felt confident that he would be borne out in the assertion, that on this day the ' Old Hall' had reason to feel proud—that it stood pre-eminent among the schools of the day, with a staunch and highly respectable patronage, an enviable reputation, and the prospect of a bright and prosperous future; and no doubt the prayers of its pious founders, uttered a century ago, were now being answered by the smiles of a gracious Providence."

The speaker was repeatedly interrupted by manifestations of assent; and when he sat down rounds of hearty applause rewarded his effort.

Mr. Philip A. Cregar proposed the following sentiment :
" *Our Alma Mater*"—God bless her ! May she ever
15 *

continue to exert her hallowed influence in training future generations for usefulness both in Church and State."

Rev. Edmund de Schweinitz, of Philadelphia, alluded very feelingly to the death of Rev. Edward Rondthaler, who had been a deeply-interested participant of the festivities of the day last year.   He said :

" Mr. President : ' There is a time to laugh,' and a time to be serious ; and if I now speak words of seriousness, they will, I trust, not be considered out of place.

" I rise, sir, by request, to fulfill a duty, a sacred duty, which this society owes to the memory of a departed associate.

" When the gentlemen of last year's reunion came to this place and into this house, they were most cordially welcomed to the scenes of their boyhood's days by one who had once been their fellow-scholar, but who was then the Inspector of Nazareth Hall.   And although he was dwelling at the time in a desolate home, stricken in mind and in body, near, very near, to the valley of the shadow of death, yet so vividly were the recollections of former years awakened, and so freely were the fountains of his feelings opened, that, as I have been informed by one of the gentlemen present, he repeatedly declared it to be the happiest day of his life.

" Mr. President, I look around this chapel, but I do not see our friend.   He is gone—gone that road which all of us must go ; but I can lead you to a spot where you will hear of him.   At Bethlehem there is a beautiful cemetery— God's acre, we love to call it in Moravian language—and on that acre there is a lowly mound and simple slab upon it bearing this inscription : ' *In memory of Edward Rondthaler.*'

" I see before me former teachers and former companions of our departed associate, but many more who were his scholars. I, amongst the rest, belong to the latter, and I rejoice in being able, on this occasion, to bring a feeble tribute to his memory, for I owe him much.

"Mr. President: Edward Rondthaler was no ordinary, but, in the fullest sense, an extraordinary man—a genius. Had he chosen, he might have gone the way of earthly fame, and might have employed his many and wonderful talents in the acquisition of glory and renown amongst men. But he did not. He went another road and sought out another career, even the service of a Master who is Divine. Called to preach the gospel of Jesus Christ, he obeyed; and as a Christian minister devoted all his intellectual powers, and all his profound knowledge, to the furtherance of the highest and most momentous interests of his fellow-men; laboring in so glorious a cause with an enthusiastic fervor of spirit not often to be found. And it was here, in this venerable building, that he acquired much of his knowledge; it was here that his scholars daily saw him poring over his books, as he sat at his teacher's table in one of the upper rooms. Those ever memorable books! I saw some of those identical volumes this afternoon in the library of the Theological Seminary. How forcibly they reminded me of by-gone days! The image of my departed teacher rose anew upon my memory, bending over his dictionaries and grammars, while piles of dusty tomes fairly besieged him on all sides. But with this image came also the reflection that he had well done his work on earth; that, although his years were few and his life but a span, he had yet, as teacher, as minister of the gospel, and as Principal of this Institution, accomplished much for the good of his fellow-men and for the glory of his Redeemer and his God.

" Happy shall we, the former teachers, companions and scholars of Edward Rondthaler, be if the same shall come to be said of us !

" Mr. President, I am not about to preach, although preaching is my most sacred duty ; yet, in view of the fact that we have to-day to mourn a departed associate—and such an associate !—I cannot refrain from turning to the gentlemen who composed the reunion company of last year, with the solemn words of my Master, 'Be ye also ready !' Yea, I cannot refrain from turning unto all who are now here assembled, in order to remind them that good, and great, and glorious as this reunion has been to-day, there is another and an eternal one at hand ; and that is infinitely better, infinitely greater and more glorious. Oh that all of us, from the youngest former scholar even to the eldest, could but have a share therein, and meet again before ' the throne of God and of the Lamb :' "

Mr. Charles M. Lewis, of Philadelphia, alluded with much originality to his past career as a scholar at Nazareth Hall, expressed regret for what he had done amiss or left undone, and concluded with observing that the incidents of the day, the familiar scenes and objects around and in the vicinity, had so completely carried him into the past that he found it extremely difficult to refrain from engaging in those manifestations of exuberance which had earned for him some notoriety while at school.

G. Morgan Eldridge, Esq., of Philadelphia, now rose and said :

" I have been much pleased, Mr. President, to hear. from the various gentlemen who have so ably and agreeably entertained us this afternoon, of the pleasurable reminiscences which occupy their minds in recalling their schoolboy days spent within its venerable walls ; but it

appears to me that it were well that we should view the
subject in another light.

" It seems to me, sir, that we might with profit consider
what disposition we had made of the very important
period of our lives that has elapsed between the time
when we, like our young successors here beside us, were
wondering what kind of a thing life would be, and the
present, plunged as we are headlong into the strife and
struggle of the busy world.

" It is a question of grave importance to each of us,
whether, during that period, we have properly used and
fully improved our advantages and opportunities. for so
many of which we are indebted to the fostering care of this
our Alma Mater ; and I apprehend that it would much
tend to the improvement of such of us as have not (and
they will comprise a large majority of our number), if,
whenever our minds revert to the pleasures of to-day's reunion, we ask ourselves whether we have, to the utmost
of our ability, availed ourselves of those advantages, and
made the best use in our power of the time since we were
boys together.

" If the question meets a negative answer, let us, in duty
bound, resolve that, though the past cannot return. still,
as the future is ours, we will make such better use of it
that, when we meet here from time to time hereafter, we
may look back to this day as the commencement of a
new course, and the first dawn of the brighter prospects
which will assuredly ensue from the steadfast carrying out
of such better resolves. And let us determine so to keep
such resolution that, when we have run our race here below and are gathered to our fathers, we may deserve
such a remembrance from our surviving friends, when
they gather around this board, as we have had in the eloquent tribute paid to the late Edward Rondthaler. Let

us do this, and we will find so great advantage arising from it that we will never hereafter fail to make an annual pilgrimage to the old Hall; and whenever it may lie in our power we will give our successors an opportunity of going the same road that we have traveled before them, with a well-assured confidence that it will be as beneficial to them as it has been to us."

Mr. James N. Beck proposed the following sentiment: " The ' Bethlehem Sextette.'—May they ever be bound to us by the ' *common chord*' of friendship; may their ' *unisons*' always be those of good-fellowship and perfect ' *harmony;*' their ' *dominant*' a ruling passion to excel; their ' *tonic*' rarely, if ever, anything stronger than tea or coffee; and all their ' *rests*' spent in the unalloyed pleasures of domestic felicity."

Rt. Rev. John C. Jacobson, a trustee of the Insti- tion, dwelt forcibly and at large on the system of edu- cation pursued by the Moravians in their schools —a system which makes no pretensions to superficial display and the rapid attainment of so-called accomplish- ments, but which strives patiently and laboriously to plough up the stubborn soil, to lay deep and firm the foun- dation for the future building; to analyze the ground that is to receive the seed, to adapt the seed to the ground, to sow in the name of God and to the glory of God, and to look to him in patience and in hope for the fruits of the future harvest.

The Principal, in conclusion, made a few remarks ex- pressive of his gratification at the occurrences of the day, and the meeting adjourned.

In the evening the Hall was illuminated. A transpa- rency, with the word " Reunion" in large characters, was displayed in front of the building, and the belfry was fan- cifully decorated. To add to the pleasures of the entertainment, Mr. Wm. A. Lilliendahl, of New York, had furnished a selection of elaborate fireworks, which were exhibited under his superintendence.

A rotary globe, the "diamond and cross," and " Reunion." were conspicuous for brilliancy of effect. The evening was lovely, and the square was crowded with spectators. At the close of the exhibition the village pastor invited the assembly to join in singing a hymn of praise, and thus the pleasing exercises of this interesting day were concluded.

THIRD REUNION

OF

FORMER PUPILS, June 6, 1856,

(Rev. E. H. Reichel, Principal.)

The day appointed by the President, in his circular of
March 14, for the third reunion, dawned unpropitiously,
for the sky was overcast, and a chilly east wind, with occasional showers of rain, rendered the air raw and damp.
Altogether it augured ill for a Nazareth Hall boys' hol-
iday. But when did clouds or rain or wind ever inter-
fere with schoolboys bent on enjoying themselves?

Alone and in carriage loads the old scholars arrived at
the village inn. The joyful recognition of schoolmates
who had never met since they had bidden each other
good-bye on that eventful day which closed what seemed
a year of weary imprisonment—the meeting of teachers
and inspector with former scholars and with each other—
combined to render the scene one of real interest and unaffected feeling.

But the "three-quarter bell" has been ringing for some
time. The voice of Mr. Ernest F. Bleck, once their
teacher, now their President, disperses the happy knots
gathered here and there within and without the inn ; two
by two, as of old, they are marshaled into procession,
and, preceded by a band of musicians from Bethlehem,
move toward the Hall. Arrived in the square, the present boys and teachers are seen collected on and about the

40

stoop. As the procession nears, and the sound of music has ceased, a shout of hurrahs greets the old scholars, who form themselves into a line facing their venerable Alma Mater. Master James I. Grafton,* of Boston, a member of the first-room company, then stepped forward and addressed them as follows :

" Gentlemen of the Reunion Society, in behalf of the boys of Nazareth Hall, I bid you welcome to our common mother. In spite of clouds and rain, never has her time-worn face beamed with kindlier smiles than to-day, as she beholds so many of her children gather around her. It is with joy and pride she sees her boys have not forgotten her, and she greets them most heartily. We hope the day, about to be spent amid scenes consecrated by a thousand recollections of boyhood, may prove a pleasant and memorable one to you all. We also welcome the guests who are come to participate in the festivities, and may it be to them and us a season of unalloyed and sanctified enjoyment."

The President of the association briefly responded, after which the Principal announced the programme for the day, and the society proceeded to business in the chapel.

After dinner a drizzling rain set in, seemingly precluding the possibility of rambling and indulging in outdoor amusements. Some of the Reunionists, however, with a traditional disregard of wet feet and damp clothes, set out for the woods, bent upon once more at least *seeing* their former playgrounds. The greater part, however, were to be found within the Hall, roaming from room to room and from floor to floor. All the minutiæ of indoor Hall-life were reviewed, and a thousand associations connected with the school-rooms, the " chambers, " the dining-room,

---

* Killed in battle at Averysboro', March 16, 1865.

16

the sleeping-halls, the sick-room, the chapel and the garrets were vividly brought to mind. Here was a group standing around, or, contrary to rules, seated on the tables, comparing the recollections of incidents that had there transpired. The names of comrades were passed in review, and as far as was possible the subsequent history of each individual traced or recounted. And it was found that some were dead, and that some, alas! were living lives of ignominy, recreant to their faithful mother's teachings. There was another group gathered around a teacher, recalling both pleasant and unpleasant incidents that had occurred in years gone by. Acts of kindness and severity on the one hand, of willfulness and disobedience on the other, were severally rehearsed. Many an old grudge was here confessed, and confessed to be forgiven and forgotten for ever. It was grateful to the teacher to learn how small acts of kindness on his part, or words of earnest admonition from his lips, were still affectionately remembered and recognized as having been of lasting benefit; and the pupil now first learned how much solicitude had been expended on his behalf, and how he had misconstrued or misapprehended the words and acts of his conscientious preceptor. Here again were two friends pacing the long halls, busy in comparing biographical notes since they had last parted. It was with a mixed feeling of pleasure and sadness that they recalled the sweet dreams of happiness and ambitious hopes in which they indulged while inmates of the Hall, and from which the experiences of their present manhood so widely differed. Each felt strengthened to return to the active duties of life, cheered by the lessons which the retrospect into the past had taught him so impressively.

At three o'clock the Reunionists repaired to the village church to participate in the stated exercises of the day.

The Rev. Samuel Reinke, class of 1799, having opened with prayer, the President introduced Max. Goepp, Esq., class of 1841, who addressed the audience in an oration which was replete with vigorous and philosophical reflection and scholarly illustrations.

At five o'clock the bell rang for supper. An array of happy faces was soon disposed around four tables extending the length of the chapel, and loaded with all the well-remembered dishes of several "Hall" suppers. After the buzz of conversation had been hushed by a rap on the table from the President, grace was *sung* according to old-time custom, and each one addressed himself to the pleasing task of doing "Hall-boy" justice to the many good things before him. Impartiality as a historian compels the writer to here charge the "old boys" with having deported themselves to a man very unbecomingly; for they laughed and talked aloud, they held up their fingers for "more" at the wrong time, and some even suggested the propriety of "hooking" doughnuts. The young boys over the way caught the infection, and enjoyed themselves perfectly as they followed the indecorous example set them.

The reading of letters from absent former pupils was now in order, and among these the following were communicated:

"BETHLEHEM, June 4, 1856.

"Your circular of the 14th of March last, addressed to all former inspectors, teachers and pupils of Nazareth Hall, informing them that the annual meeting of its Reunion Society will convene on June 6 next, was duly received. I regret that it will again not be convenient for me to be present on that interesting occasion, and therefore would beg to be permitted instead to address the association in writing through this letter, which I would request you to communicate. Meetings of this kind, of which two have already been held, are in my opinion highly creditable both to the Hall and to those of its former pupils who are pleased, in this wise, to express their grateful acknowledgment of the benefits derived from spending more or less of the time of their youth at that well-known and well-reputed Institution.

"It was in November, 1795, that I entered Nazareth Hall in the capacity of teacher, and the reminiscences which I retain of my four years' residence there are mostly agreeable ones. The Rev. Charles G. Reichel, whose kindness I shall never forget, was Inspector at that time. With my fellow-teachers I had the satisfaction of being on good and friendly terms. To the pupils, more especially to those whom I had to instruct and to supervise, I became much attached ; and am happy to say that most of them, by their diligence, progress and dutiful deportment, rendered the performance of my duties an easy and pleasant one. The beauties of nature, which the environs of Nazareth offer, I greatly enjoyed ; and the acquaintance I made with some worthy and intelligent citizens of the town was also a source of pleasure.

"But many of those who then were known and dear to me in the Hall and in the town have departed this life, while I have lived to be a very aged man of fourscore and seven years. Still, I have great reason to be thankful for the measure of health with which I have been blessed. Thus I have been enabled to employ myself in my retirement chiefly with reading and studying that Book which is the inexhaustible source of divine wisdom and knowledge, and whose pages teach that godliness which is profitable unto all things, having promise of the life that now is and of that which is to come.

"With my best respects to yourself and to the highly

esteemed friends who with you will participate in this year's Reunion at Nazareth Hall, and with sincere wishes for your and their temporal welfare and eternal happiness,

"I remain, dear sir, yours.

"ANDREW BENADE.

"*Tutor* 1795–1800."

"SENATE CHAMBER, March 14, 1856.

"MY DEAR OLD FRIEND AND TEACHER: I have delayed a reply for a day or two to your letter of the 7th inst., conveying to me an invitation to address the Reunion Society of Nazareth Hall on the 6th of June next, in the hope that I might be able to accept it. Such a proposition, and coming as it does from you, not only awakened the pleasantest possible of all memories, but held out a prospect of so much pure enjoyment that I hesitated long, and declined only from the conviction that public duties here cannot be arranged as to permit me to act so far in advance. I must therefore decline the invitation, but with heartfelt thanks, be assured, for the kindness and honor it conveyed to me. Nevertheless, my dear sir, I shall endeavor to steal away from here, and join you on that day, if possible, with my family, to indulge my heart's yearning for its first love.

"STEPHEN R. MALLORY,

"*Pupil of* 1826."

"NEW YORK, October 19, 1855.

"I cannot tell you what pleasure I derived from the receipt and perusal of the History of Nazareth Hall,* and

* Then just published.

16 *

of the account of the Reunions of old scholars. I read them to my children, and talked over my schoolboy days around our evening table, much to their delight ; and the only thing that marred the enjoyment I experienced in reviving hallowed associations was the fact that I had not participated in those festive gatherings. As I read how the former pupils partook of a repast after the custom of olden days, I could see us all again seated around the board, with our pewter plates, a large dish of boiled beef, or sour-crout, or apple pie, or wheaten pap, sprinkled with brown sugar, set before us ; and I could see the large loaf in the tutor's hand, and each hungry boy gesticulating with fingers the state of his appetite. Then the 'week-holders' province !' For the emptying of slops and bringing of water they were entitled to the remnants of the teachers' portion at the evening meal ! How forcibly, too, was Brother Schmidt brought before me ! Dear me ! I have a most vivid recollection of the air and gait with which he came into recitations, with a round of buttered bread in his hand, munching away for dear life !

" But, withal, it was a melancholy thought that many of my comrades have gone the way of all the earth. I marked the names in the catalogue I knew I should have missed, and prominent among these was that of my intimate schoolmate, John Schropp, with whom, in school parlance, I ' *went joints*' in all matters involving expenditure for our mutual comfort—such as vespers, etc., etc. I naturally recur to many things which have ever endeared his memory to me ; among the rest to a box he gave me when I left the Hall, in which are preserved my youthful correspondence and German and English school-books. His memory I shall ever cherish ; and as I believe hereafter we shall ' see as we are seen and know as we are known,' I may hope to meet him in that great Sanctuary, where we shall know neither sorrow nor sighing, but shall be as the angels of God.

" HENRY SMITH,
" *Pupil of* 1814."

"OCKBROOK, England, May 14, 1856.

" The receipt of your circular of March 14 afforded me much pleasure, and was calculated to awaken recollections of days gone by which I delight to cherish. Though my personal attendance at your annual meeting is out of the question, I am not the less sensible of your kindness ; and I beg to assure you, and those who may be around you on that occasion, that I will not be unmindful of your gathering on the 6th of June next. More than half a century has passed since I left the place where you propose to hold your Reunion ; nevertheless, I remember Nazareth Hall and its environs well, and often have I longed to revisit my native land and the abode of my infancy and early youth. Great, no doubt, are the alterations and improvements that have taken place in the Hall ; still, I fancy I should find no difficulty in recognizing the stately edifice, with its gardens, walks and meadows ; as well as the distant hills, brooks, rivers, woods and villages. Lively also are my recollections of those who were engaged as teachers, and of not a few of my fellow-pupils. But how many of them are gone—or, I should rather say, *how few of them are left!* And though I might for a little while imagine myself again young, as I was when for the last time my eyes were fixed upon the house of my birth, I should soon be aroused from the dream of my youth by the mournful fact that the majority of those to whom I then bid farewell are now sleeping in the silent grave ; and that the few whose memory goes as far back as mine must shortly follow them. Nor are reflections such as these confined to the aged, such as I am ; each meeting of your society must tend to remind its members of the rapid flight of time and the steady approach of eternity. And if these gatherings are, on the one hand, calculated to foster kindly feelings among those who have enjoyed a common early instruction, and to keep alive their interest in the Institution they frequented as boys, they have, on the other hand, a powerful tendency to remind the young of the necessity of redeeming the time given them, and of preparing for the eternity that is before them.

" Not many of those whom you will meet at Nazareth Hall on the day named in your circular, or who have for a longer or shorter period resided within its walls, can feel a deeper interest in its prosperity than I do. And I can say that, as the prospect of my visiting the place of my birth decreases, my remembrance of it, and my interest in its welfare, increase ; nor shall I cease to pray that it may be set for a blessing to many—not only by leading the young to the acquirement of what is useful and praiseworthy, but also, and especially, by directing them to the path of life, and making them acquainted with their God and Saviour. With these sentiments, however imperfectly expressed,

" I am, very sincerely, yours,
" SAMUEL R. REICHEL,
" *Pupil of* 1800."

After the reading of these letters, Mr. Lebbeus Chapman, Jr., of New York, pupil of 1838, was vociferously called for ; in obedience to which summons he rose, and for half an hour kept the audience in alternate bursts of laughter and pauses of deep-felt emotion. The descrip-

tion he gave of his schoolboy experiences was as amusing
as a tribute he paid to the patient instructions of one of
his teachers was touching and unaffected. Other gentlemen were called on to address the meeting, but no one
seemed willing to follow Mr. Chapman.

It was now growing late, and the company adjourned
to the square, there to participate in the day's closing exercises. The Hall was illuminated; and a transparency
in front, inscribed with " 100," and the words " *Te Deum
Laudamus*," commemorated the fact that the venerable
pile, dedicated to the service of God in the year 1756,
had, under His protecting care, reached its centenary.

Owing to the chilliness of the night air and the damp-
ness under foot, prudence forbade prolonging the enjoy-
ments of the evening; the visitors left the ground at an
early hour, and the festivities of the Reunion were pre-
maturely closed.

At the society's business meeting, held in the chapel
after supper, Articles I., III. and V. of the Constitution
were amended so as to read:

ARTICLE I. This society shall be known by the name
of the " *Reunion* Society of Nazareth Hall."

ARTICLE III. The officers of this society shall be a
President, *four* Vice-Presidents, a Secretary, and an *Assistant Secretary*, who shall be elected at each annual
meeting, and serve until the election of their successors.

ARTICLE V. The society shall hold a meeting once a
year in Nazareth Hall, at Nazareth, on the second Friday
in June. The pastor of the congregation shall be *ex
officio* a member of the society.

The following committees were appointed: one " on
communications," one " on arrangements," and a third
" on engaging the speaker of the day."

Upward of twenty letters had been received responding to the circular of March 14, and twelve of these were communicated. A copy of " Plantæ Javanicæ Rariores," *London*, 1853, presented to Nazareth Hall by Thomas Horsfield, M. D., was also submitted for inspection.

Pursuant to a resolution adopted, to wit, " that a historian of the society shall be appointed at each annual meeting, whose duty it shall be to prepare a narrative of the acts of the society, and of the events and festivities of its meetings, with a view to publication, so as to form a continuous history and a sequel to the " History of Nazareth Hall," published in the course of last year,

Mr. Herman A. Brickenstein was appointed Historian by the chair.

The election of officers resulted as follows :

President.

Ernest F. Bleck, of Bethlehem, Pa.

Vice-Presidents.

Rev. John C. Jacobson, do.

Rev. Philip H. Goepp, do.

Daniel D. Gassner, New York.

Samuel Penington, Delaware.

Secretary.

Rev. Wm. L. Lennert, Nazareth, Pa.

Assistant Secretary.

Herman A. Brickenstein, do.

FOURTH REUNION

OF

FORMER PUPILS, June 5, 1857.

(Rev. E. H. Reichel, Principal.)

The forenoon business meeting of the society was called to order by the chair at eleven o'clock A. M., in the Hall chapel, and Rev. F. F. Hagen, of York, opened with prayer.

After the election of sundry committees, the one "on nominations" reported as follows:

President.

Ernest F. Bleck, of Bethlehem.

Vice Presidents.

Rev. John C. Jacobson, do.

Rev. Philip H. Goepp, do.

Henry Smith, of New York.

Francis Jordan, of Philadelphia.

Secretary.

Rev. William L. Lennert, of Nazareth;

Assistant Secretary.

Herman A. Brickenstein, do. ;

which report was adopted as a whole by acclamation, and the gentlemen named, declared unanimously elected.

On motion of Mr. John Baker, Reunion appointed Philip A. Cregar, of Philadelphia, Speaker for the next year's festival; and on motion of John C. Gunther, H. A. Brickenstein was appointed Historian of the current year.

The Principal proposed the planting of two lindens, presented by Mr. John Beitel, of Nazareth, near where the " Two Brothers" formerly stood ; the same to be planted by the oldest four of former pupils present, in the course of the afternoon. Christian Brunner, of Bethlehem (day-scholar in 1785), John S. Haman, of Nazareth (1794), G. Charles Schneller, of Bethlehem (1800), and George Frick, M.D., of Baltimore (1803), were ascertained to be the four.

In the evening session, on motion of Mr. Henry Smith, H. B. Penington and Lebbeus Chapman, Jr., in conjunction with the mover, were appointed a committee to take into consideration the expediency of procuring a marble tablet, to be inscribed with the names of the Principals of the Hall ; said committee to report at the next annual meeting.

In conclusion, a vote of thanks was tendered to the Messrs. Lilliendahl, of New York, for a display of fireworks, presented by them for the closing festivities of the present reunion.

Master Thomas Van Beuren, of the IV. Room, spoke greeting to the Reunionists, as the procession was drawn up in line before the Hall: " Gentlemen of the Reunion Society," said the young Demosthenes, " in the name of my comrades I bid you welcome, for this day is a great one for us Nazareth Hall boys ; and we are inclined to believe it will be as great a one for you ! And now, boys, three cheers for the ' old scholars !' "

The compliment having been acknowledged in behalf of his associates by the President, the society proceeded to business ; after which lunch was served in the " Round Place" woods. This was an agreeable variation of the

usual programme. The sun had long since dispelled the
gloom and threatening clouds of the early morning. It
proved a lovely summer's day; and amid the songs of
birds and the lisping of leaves, all " under the greenwood
tree," the sylvan feasters indulged in good cheer and
mirth, and talked over battles lost and won; and the
fountains of memory then opened, flowed, I ween, thro'
emerald meads on which the noonday's scorching sun had
never beat. A game of ball, too, was in progress at the
" First boys' round-place;" but the hours were short, and
the summons " Home! home!" broke in rudely upon the
exciting sport, for the time was come to meet in the village church.

The exercises here having been opened with singing
and prayer, Rev. Ambrose Rondthaler, of York, addressed his audience in these words:

" It is **not with** feelings of a stranger unacquainted
with Nazareth Hall, and indifferent to the interests of this
time-honored Institution, that I appear before you, this
afternoon, respected friends, to speak a little of bygone
days. While the pulse of life beats gratefully to my God
and Saviour, I deem it a privilege, after a lapse of twenty-
two years, to come forward in order to add my humble
testimonial of the esteem in which I hold Nazareth Hall.

" We meet as children of the same mother; and, as
such, we mutually tender, on this happy Reunion-day,
our sincere, our warm and our cordial salutations. Nor
do we, by any means, consider ourselves guests hospitably
admitted, and then left to wander at our pleasure in a
strange place. No; *we have come home!* And here, at
home, after a longer or a shorter absence, we find much
that is still unchanged. We find the scenery around our
Alma Mater still presenting all the features of beauty and

variety and loveliness which it wore when we first beheld it: and even the little brooks and rills in the neighborhood, with which we first formed our acquaintance when sporting with child-like playfulness upon their banks, are yet flowing in the same current in which we then saw them flow; and though a great change may have come over some of the more frail and fragile things with which we are surrounded—though some of the trees which once waved in all stateliness may be withered or may have been cut down—still we *are*, and feel ourselves *to be, at home!* Again, we visit some of the beautiful and romantic valleys of our home, and climb the hills we so often climbed, and enjoy the luxury of once again looking upon the enchanting prospect. And while we stand and ponder on periods long, long ago gone, the joy of other years glides by us, and we seem to live in the atmosphere of former days. And while thought does its part, almost sacred are the associations and recollections which enshrine the memory of many once familiar places—the memory of our round-places—the memory of the sylvan scenery of the Lund Spring—the memory of once lovely spots carpeted with smoothest and brightest verdure. We recall to our minds many a sweet summer's morning, so calm, so gentle, as if this world were no tumultuous scene, as if there were no storms, nor tempests, nor hurricanes of life—many a sweet morning on which we strolled through the ' *Kinder-Garten,*' while the odor of flowers, rising up from the scented earth, added a new charm to the scenery. We walk again the streets of dear Nazareth, and almost everywhere we recognize old and familiar buildings; we tread again the floors of old Nazareth Hall; we visit its ancient rooms, changed by the hand of improvement; we linger here, we linger there; we walk into the chapel, the old meeting-place, the old church of the dear Nazareth congregation. And here—pardon my egotism—I think of my sainted parents. Yes, pardon me, my dear friends, and I know you will, for those educated in Nazareth Hall have hearts to feel; pardon me, then, if a tear of filial recollection gathers in my eye and saddens my heart. I think of my father! I picture him to myself, in our simple children's meeting, giving out, with his German accent, the sweet and beautiful hymn,

'Dearest Jesus, come to me;'

and that German accent is sweet music to *my* ear, and I can never forget it. And thinking of my parents sweetly sleeping in Jesus on yonder hill, I cannot help thinking of the many well-known villagers who worshiped here, and are now old and grayheaded (and may God, their Saviour, not forsake them!), and of others who, since our time, have been borne to the lonely tomb, there to rest until the resurrection of the just, when the dead in Christ shall be raised incorruptible. And, as we think of these, we think of others whom long, long ago we followed to the grave; and again we hear the sweet music of trombones accompanying the beautiful German words:

'Ei wie so selig schläfest du
Nach manchem schweren Stand,
Und liegst nun da in süsser Ruh
In deines Heiland's Hand.'

We stand again around the old dead-house—but no! it has disappeared, and its disappearance reminds us of one of the sweetest and most consolatory words of Holy Writ:

'There shall be no more death!'

" And then, hallelujah! *reunion for ever!*

" And, while thinking of my parents, I cannot but associate with them a certain brother, who crossed the ocean with my father upward of half a century ago, and who for eight years was Principal of this Institution, now a venerable father in Israel. And perhaps this venerable father, our aged brother Seidel, is this day looking back through the long vista of almost seventy-nine years; and while thinking of this one and of that one—and of his own dear Henry, once a scholar and teacher in Nazareth Hall, who is resting at the roots of the old trees near Hopedale—is erecting an Ebenezer unto God in his heart, as he says:

'Hitherto the Lord hath helped us !'

And surely on a day like this we cannot forget Father Benade, one of the first teachers in this Institution, and now almost ninety-three years of age. Perhaps this patriarch, while thinking of Charles Gotthold Reichel, the first Inspector, and during whose term he entered as teacher, and running over in his mind the term of the next Principal, Jacob Van Vleck, and so down the stream of time to the present Inspector, a grandson of the first, through a long period of seventy-two years, is saying in his heart, 'Lord, thou hast been our dwelling-place in all generations!' And thinking of our aged Brother Benade, we recall one of his old pupils—one of the first admitted into Nazareth Hall—two years ago, one year ago (with the exception of the aged Thomas Horsfield, residing in London), the oldest living pupil of this Institution. I mean the venerable Jacob Kummer, who lived in yon building ten years as scholar, and five in the capacity of teacher. But a few weeks ago, on the fifth of last month, he fell asleep in Jesus. And what must the feelings of such venerable men have been, or still be, on a day like this? Methinks they must feel like Moses of old, that faithful servant of the Lord—like Moses, who, after having led the children of Israel through many scenes, and directed their wanderings in the desert for forty years, once more, before ascending Mount Nebo, and its highest summit Pisgah, where he died, gathered the congregation of Israel together. A new generation born in the wilderness stood before him. Where was Aaron, his brother, who had shared his joys and griefs? Gone! He had died on Mount Hor, and the children of Israel had mourned for him thirty days. Where was Miriam, his sister? Gone! She had died in the encampment in Kadesh, in the wilderness of Sin. Where the many who, standing on the shores of the Red Sea, had sung a song of triumph unto Jehovah, their deliverer? Gone! They had died in the wilderness. And when our Moseses look back and think of the many changes which have taken place around them since their youthful days, well may they ask, deeply affected, where are many of those with whom we were boys together? Where so many of our former pupils, our colleagues, our companions? Where those faithful servants of God, John Frederic Frueauff, Abraham Luckenbach, with their younger brother Lewis de Schweinitz?—all of them former inmates of the 'Hall?' They are sleeping in their graves at Bethlehem. Where those self-denying men, Nathaniel Brown and Benjamin Mortimer? While one of them rests on Staten Island, the other hears no more the din and bustle of a mighty city. And while our Moseses thus look back, others who, in all human probability, have finished more than half, perhaps more than three-fourths, of their journey, may put the same question with regard to their former comrades. Where, such may ask—lost in deep thought—where is Ernest L. Hazelius, in after times a bright and shining light in the Lutheran Church? Where those

17 *

humble but true evangelists of the New Testament, Adam Haman, Samuel R. Huebner, George Hartman, Charles A. Van Vleck—all of them former teachers, and the latter a Principal of Nazareth Hall? Where John G. Kummer, who for many a long year so faithfully superintended the Litiz and Bethlehem Female Seminaries? They are resting until the return of Christ from heaven?

"And may not we, who are yet in the prime of life, although liable to be called hence to-morrow or even to-day—may not we ask the same question with regard to others? Whilst I, for example, know that four of my first teachers, whom I love and esteem, are still in the land of the living, where is kind-hearted Lewis Benzien, who dried my tears on the very first night I slept in Nazareth Hall? Where dear Christian R. Schropp? Well do I remember the day of his funeral thirty-six years ago, and well do I know the very spot where he is buried; and not far from him reposes an aged missionary, Sebastian Oppelt, who, in his old age, once more descended to the humble and arduous but noble task of instructing the young. And where are some of my teachers of later times? While I know that one of them, who became a faithful Principal of this Institution, is filling a responsible post in Europe, where is kind-hearted Jacob Zorn? He sleeps beneath a tropical sun. Where my faithful professors, Charles A. Bleck and Christian Dober? While the one rests at Gnadenhutten, Ohio, the other sleeps at Bethlehem. And where the worthy Principals of my time? While the first, after many years of faithful service in America, Russia and Holland, is living in retirement at Herrnhut, paternal William H. Van Vleck and kind and cheerful John G. Herman have entered into their rest. Where are two of those who were colleagues with me—John Rickert, the esteemed mathematician, and the amiable Daniel Steinhauer? Asleep in Jesus. 'waiting for the adoption ; to wit, the redemption of the body.'

" And where are some of those who were boys with me ? Where my brothers Emanuel and Edward, both of them former pupils and teachers and professors, the latter once a principal of this Institution? They sleep not far from each other in the graveyard at Bethlehem ; while one of their former pupils, and in later times a teacher here, Bernard de Schweinitz, rests at Salem. And are these all? Is my memory so frail as not to think of others? No ; as long as Memory holds her seat I cannot forget four mothers—the four sick nurses during my time. While two of them are now tottering on the brink of the grave, Mother Kummer and Mother Sievers will wake up in that land where the inhabitants no more say, ' I am sick.'

" Yes, most of us may ask, Where are some of the teachers who disciplined and instructed us in our tender years? Where many who guided us amid the frowardness of youth? Where are many of those venerable for age and wisdom and experience, upon whom we were taught to look with respect and reverence? Where are many who set out with us in the path of life?

" But shall we remember only those who are dead and gone, and shall we forget the living? No ; courtesy, friendship, respect and gratitude compel me to allude to others.

" We cannot forget, on a day like this, two venerable men, who, with the lamented William H. Van Vleck, once formed a lovely trio, and who, after having left their Alma Mater, went wherever God and truth and duty called them ; and, while we remember these, we cannot but associate with them one of their former school-companions, who has been eminently successful as an in-

structor of youth, and who is honorably known as the
'Old Schoolmaster.' And while we remember one
who in after times served for many years as a missionary,
and who is now, in his declining years, teaching a school
of Indian children in the Far West, we cannot forget the
kind-hearted brother who served as teacher and professor
of Theology for ten years, and for five as inspector; and
his six, and in later time seven, theological students, most
of whom were my teachers for a longer or a shorter period
—all of whom I respect and love. We know where
these eight have pitched their tents; those who once
thought together—acted together—wrote together. May
they be lovely in their lives, and in their death may they
not be divided! And we must not forget the respected
brother who superintended two theological classes, and
who, together with one of his sons, is again engaged in
Nazareth Hall. And we are not permitted to forget his
two classes of students, many of whom were teachers in
this institution, and all, excepting Dr. Edward Rice, still
on earth, and either actively engaged in the Church of
Christ, or taking the liveliest interest in the dissemination
of knowledge, of truth and of pure religion. I cannot
forget my fellow-students, three of whom are yet in the
land of the living, and one the beloved pastor of the Nazareth congregation. I cannot forget my colleagues, the
one known as the antiquary of the Moravian Church,
who in after times was Principal of Nazareth Hall; the
second, a dear brother, who for almost a quarter of a
century has been engaged in teaching in the metropolis of
this State; the third now residing in retirement in the
West; the fourth a missionary in Canada; the fifth and
sixth who left the very month I did, and whom I have
followed with a brother's eye—the one well known as a
champion of Protestantism, and the other as a faithful

missionary, who, after years of hard service, resides again in the bosom of this congregation. And let us not forget one who served as missionary in Surinam, and who has, as a well-known physician, dwelt for years under the shadow of the old ' Hall.'

" And now, having mentioned or alluded to all the Principals of Nazareth Hall, and to many of its former teachers, I would have it distinctly understood that I must refrain. Twenty-two years ago I left this place, and therefore am not as well versed in the modern history of the ' Hall' as I am in its middle ages and its ancient history. However, one class of students with their professors I would not forget, since most of them entered as teachers immediately after I left. One of them resides in the borough where my tent is pitched at present. With him I am on the most friendly footing, and together we often live over Nazareth Hall times. But, though I cannot mention all, I would love to see every former inmate of that old building who is still on earth. Oh how I should love to shake hands with every one of them, and, laying off all reserve, call my old schoolmates and my former pupils by their Christian names—John, Michael, Reuben, Moses, Thomas, William ! Yes, I would love to see them all. Deep is the interest I take in the welfare of each, even of those whom I do not know. I look upon such either as older brothers, who had left before my time, or as younger brothers, born while my companions and myself had already set out on the tempestuous voyage of life.

" And deep, too, is the interest which I take in the future progress and success of the ' Hall.' And why ? Not only because I was educated here—not only because an orphan son of my brother's is here—not only because my own son is here—not only because the sons of many whom I esteem are here—but also because the sons of others, who, as well as we, and we as well as they, have been redeemed, not with gold and silver, or any such corruptible thing, but with the precious bleeding and dying of our Lord Jesus Christ—are here. I wish the 'Hall' success—I do, I do indeed—success from the bottom of my heart. A school where not only the head is educated but the heart, ought and is deserving of our best wishes. It will and must continue to prosper. The blessing of the Lord will abide upon it. Amen!

" Present pupils of Nazareth Hall, where are you? Oh I see some of you in the rear of the church. Perhaps my address hitherto has been as 'stale' and uninteresting to you as chronological tables, with nothing but dates and names, were in times of yore to me. But bear with me a little longer. Be diligent! Be up and doing! Study, and study laboriously. Never be dismayed by difficulties with which you may meet in your studies. Let your motto be '*Nil desperandum!*' 'Never despair!' Remember, my boys, it is not genius, it is not talent, but perseverance that is a mighty conqueror. Be docile, but at the same time dare to think for yourselves, and thus the whole tone of your thinking will become manly and powerful. Cultivate urbanity of manners, kindliness of feeling and loveliness of disposition toward all with whom you associate. But let not this be all. If this be all, and remain all, then all your knowledge, and whatever benefit may result from it in after life, will prove at last a thorn to your pillow—a dagger to your breast—a millstone round your neck. If this be all then, 'Vanity of vanities, all is vanity!' Oh, my dear boys, let your prayer to-day be this, let it be your prayer while kneeling this night on the bare floor of your bedside:

'To thee, Almighty God, Almighty Saviour, to thee,
  Ourselves we now resign :
  'Twill please us to look back and see
  We were in childhood thine !'

" Former pupils of Nazareth Hall, and my own heart, do you hear the echo or do you not—

'We were in childhood thine ?'

" Present teachers of Nazareth Hall, love your profession. Endeavor to give life to the intelligence of your pupils, sharpness to their penetration, and ardor to their attempts in the pursuit of knowledge and wisdom. And so rule, govern, watch in your rooms and in your classes, and at the table and at the plays of your pupils, that they may feel and know that there is in their midst a God of love, of mercy, of compassion, of justice, of truth, who is angry not with the dull, not with the ignorant, not with the weak, but only with the wicked, and that every day.

" Present Principal of Nazareth Hall, suffer a few words of brotherly exhortation. Responsible, and well you know it, is the office which you fill. May the Lord continue to be with you. May he enable you to exercise a watchful and parental care over those entrusted to you. And while you superintend their literary education, you will continue to attend to their moral and religious culture. While you dwell but little upon the peculiar tenets of our Church, show them the whole apparatus of Redemption ! Daily, every morning and every evening, often throughout the day, commend them prayerfully to the gracious care and guidance of the great Principal of us all. Yes, dear brother, so continue to superintend this Institution that those committed to your care may once rise up and call you blessed.

" One word more, and I have done. Dearly beloved,

one and all, as we meet to-day, in all probability we shall never again meet on earth. But, though we meet thus no more on earth, may we all once meet around the throne of God. There may we meet to celebrate a happy, never-ending reunion; there where

' Sorrow and pain and every care,
And discord, all shall cease ;
And perfect joy and love sincere
Adorn the realms of peace !'

AMEN."

Perhaps the most pleasing of the day's transactions was the one witnessed immediately after the close of the exercises in the church. This was the planting of two lindens at the gateway, through which the walk leads into the pleasure-grounds and up " Garden-hill." Here the " Two Brothers" had stood, saplings from the Lund Spring woods, set out by Frederic Schaeffer, in the days of Charles G. Reichel ; and here, side by side, they had been fostered by the same dews from heaven, and shoulder to shoulder had borne up against the same winds and storms, until, after having outlived many generations of boys at school, and in the summer of 1830 witnessed the funeral obsequies of the old man who had planted them, their allotted time was accomplished in 1854, and they ceased to be warders at the gate. And now the representatives of those who had known them when not thicker than an arm, of those who had marked their growth, who had passed and repassed under their spreading canopy to sports in the woods above, into the garden or to the cemetery on the hill, and of others who had seen them in all the glory of multitudinous leaves and sweet-smelling blossoms, were met to perpetuate their stately presence within the precincts of old Nazareth Hall. For the young lindens, it was hoped, would grow up to be the

"Two Brothers" for future generations of boys and men.

Rt. Rev. Peter Wolle prefaced the ceremonies of the occasion by some appropriate remarks, and the gentlemen designated in the morning proceeded to plant the trees—Messrs. Brunner and Schneller the one to the right, and Messrs. Haman and Frick the one to the left of the gate.

Supper was served in the Chapel at half-past five P. M. to almost three hundred guests.

Some business details, postponed from the morning, having been despatched, Messrs. Henry Smith, Lebbeus Chapman, Jr., and Max Goepp in conclusion, addressed the meeting.

FIFTH REUNION,

OF

FORMER PUPILS, June 11, 1858,

(Rev. H. H. Reichel, Principal.)

The erection of a mural tablet (the workmanship of
George A. Krause, of Bethlehem), inscribed with the
names of the Principals, in the rear of the pulpit in the
Hall-chapel, was the most interesting feature of this
Reunion. The officers elected to serve for the ensuing
year were:

President.

Henry Smith, New York.

Vice Presidents.

John Beck, Litiz.

Francis Jordan, Philadelphia.

Ernest F. Bleck, Bethlehem.

George Frick, M. D., Baltimore.

Secretary.

Rev. William L. Lennert, Nazareth.

Assistant Secretary.

Henry T. Bachman,   do.

Herman A. Brickenstein was continued Historian.

At three P. M. Professor Philip A. Cregar pronounced
the annual oration before the members of the society, in
the village church.

Having been introduced, the Speaker said:

"MY FRIENDS: We have met here to-day to roll back the curtain of time, and live over again our youthful days.

"Ever since we entered the precincts of this place this morning, we have been Nazareth Hall boys. Those who accompanied us here and thought us men, and as such looked up to us for support, have been obliged to bear with our boyish demeanor. The cheering welcome of the present residents and foster-children of our old Alma Mater waked up our youthful blood and sent it circling through our veins as rapidly as our hats circulated round our heads, and as vigorously as our voices made the welkin ring, in answer to their greetings. Every spot that we have visited, every turn to the right or the left that we have made, has renewed our youth, brought up old faces and new incidents as vividly to our recollection as if they were the actors in present transpiring scenes. Some of the grave and reverend seniors, and the matured and manly figures that now surround us, are seen to-day in no other form than the ruddy youth and flaxen-haired boys they were years ago. In fact, we are all boys to-day, and will be so for some days to come, in spite of the occasional glimpse that toilet-glasses will give of wrinkled brows and silvery hairs. We need not wish that we were boys again, for who does not now feel himself such? The same generous and noble emotions that filled our bosoms in boyhood swell our hearts to-day; and no incident of schoolboy days which could darken our brows or arouse one sullen feeling dare make its mark upon the tablet of our memory.

"Although boys in feeling, the experience which we have acquired in our minglings with the world gives a somewhat different coloring to many of the recollections that crowd themselves on our minds. The trials of our

schoolboy lives that we then viewed as insufferable hardships are now looked upon as necessary training for the
battles we have since fought. The tasks that sent our
weary heads with aching throbs to our restless pillows
are now looked upon as breaking up fallow ground that
would otherwise have remained parched and unfruitful.
Those who imposed them, and who were construed into
the most cruel tyrants by our impatience of restraint, are
now remembered and greeted as our best friends. Every
unheeded admonition, every disregarded counsel and
every neglected lesson stands before us as a sceptre of
some murdered opportunity of improvement. How
gladly would we live over again those school-days, that
we might testify our gratitude to those whom we now
know were working to promote our welfare alone! How
cheerfully would we perform every task, however laborious! with what alacrity would we carry out every in-
junction, and how meekly receive every admonition!

    " To you, my young friends, who occupy our old places,
I would say there is no mortification, no remorse like that
which proceeds from a consciousness of misfortunes
brought on by our own faults or neglect. If wealth accu-
mulated by years of patient industry is destroyed in a
moment by the devouring element; if by dearth or flood
our fields are laid waste; if our nearest and dearest friends
are struck down by 'the pestilence that walketh in darkness and wasteth at noonday',—in all these we may see the
hand of an overruling Providence, and bow submissively
to Him that doeth all things well; but when surrounded
by difficulties that our own hands have made, and en-
tangled in the meshes of nets which our own fingers have
woven, where shall we find relief? There will be nothing
to soothe our anguish or save us from the scorpion lashes
of a tormenting conscience. Improve, then, every op-

portunity which this Institution affords, and your future will not be filled with vain and fruitless regrets. Boys, the life you now live—your school life, I mean—unimportant as you may think it, is a part of your never-ending existence, and must and will affect your whole future course. You look upon your days and years spent here as unnecessary restraints on your liberty, and long for the time, the happy time, of deliverance. In looking forward on a year which you are to spend here, you mark its tedious length by three hundred and sixty-five slowly moving days; and if the design of your parents or guardians should lead you to anticipate a residence here for three or four of these same long years, you see almost an unending period of time before you, and wonder if it will ever terminate. I represent those who filled your places twenty-four years ago, and there are others around us who were pupils here more than forty years ago ; and we all look back on the whole period since our residence here as but a very short time. Our recollections of what transpired when we were the residents of this Institution are such as to make the whole intervening period appear as but yesterday, or, in the language of Scripture, as a tale that is told. If we could only realize in our youth the fact that *now* is the only part of our existence which is really our own, how different would our lives be ! Every opportunity would be improved in its turn, and the most made of it. Nor would so many of us in after life be found wounded and bleeding amid the ruins of our own air-built castles, whose baseless fabrics had scarcely been reared till their fragments were scattered in desolation at our feet. This living without a present purpose, contracted in our youth, is apt to follow us through life.

" My old companions and old scholars will forgive me

o

for playing the schoolmaster, and bear with me while I address a few more words to the present pupils.

"My young friends, labor is the price of happiness. Although part of the curse that succeeded man's fall was that he should earn his bread by the sweat of his brow, yet our first parents were not, in their innocence, idle inhabitants of Paradise, but the dawning day and fading eve found them training and cultivating the beautiful flowers by which they were surrounded. Our very nature calls for activity; and he who uses his ability most will reap the most abundant harvest of enjoyment. But labor without a purpose is useless. Every one of you should early fix some point toward which all your labor should tend. There is no calling in life, however humble, if you find yourself fitted for it, in which you cannot become eminent and useful. Nor is there any profession, however thronged its ranks may be, where you may not find place for distinction if you mark it out as the great object and aim of your life. The great Webster once remarked that there was plenty of room in the most crowded professions for first-class men. Now, boys, the only way to become first-class men in any pursuit is early to determine your calling, and pursue it steadily with your whole ability. There is nothing, however noble and lofty, that man has ever achieved that you cannot attain by the necessary effort and application.

"My friends, indebted to you for the kindness with which you have borne the digression into which my teaching habits have led me, I again turn to you. You, who meet us here for the first time after the lapse of years, will be struck with the change marked on almost everything around us. The old Hall, which you undoubtedly expected to see in its pristine glory, has had its fair face of nature disguised with a *modern something*—certainly

not improvement. I may be more sensitive on this point
than the rest of you, for it robs me of a figure in which I
once represented the superiority of this school over most
other boarding-schools. I described the course of studies
in many other schools as that of a mere showy character,
as the smooth mastic coat of a modern building, which
would soon scale off and show its want of depth and
solidity; while that of Nazareth Hall as of a sub-
stantial nature, like the native rock of its own walls,
which, while it might present more corners and rough
places, would stand the test of time, and weather out the
stormy blast unscathed.

" Our assembling here to-day may be attributed to the
solid character of the education received in this Institution. Whatever reverence for true morality and for all
that really dignifies and exalts the human character we
possess, we owe to our early impressions received within
these walls; and the desire to show our gratitude and re-
kindle the fraternal love we learned to cherish here has
brought us together again. Those who planned the studies
of the ' Hall' were not afraid nor ashamed to take the Bible
as the basis of the morality taught here. Here we were instructed that the domestic altar should be dedicated to the
living God, and that that nation was alone blessed whose
God is the Lord. Imbued with these sentiments, the
pupils of Nazareth Hall must become the centres of
happy firesides, and such citizens as the nation might
confidently rely on in her dark hour of trial. So much is
suggested by the change in the Hall itself. But wherever
we have been to-day we have traced the finger of time in
the changes that have marked its touch. Our play-
grounds and wood-secluded walks have yielded to the
ploughshare, and fields ripening for the harvest take their

places. Standing on these spots so altered, which in other days we knew and loved so well, and calling for the companions that then stood beside us, how painfully conscious do we become that we too have changed! We represent a large number of classes, but how thin their ranks! We have been busily inquiring during the day for all our classmates who are absent. But where are they? It has been our pleasure to hear of many of them holding distinguished positions in the various callings and professions which they have selected. But we have been called upon to shed the tear of sorrow over the memory of many a loved one. Of those who labored with me as teachers, three have passed to their rest; and the Inspector, whose cheerful countenance radiated pleasure wherever he moved, has also closed his career of usefulness. Although it will continue to afford gratification to meet our old companions here year after year, it will be our melancholy task on all these occasions to miss some familiar face, and find that he has been gathered to his fathers.

"Our ceremonies to-day are marked with a deserved tribute of respect in the erection of a tablet to the memory of those worthies who have presided over this Institution, and whose virtues will thus be commemorated by all succeeding generations of Nazareth Hall pupils. Of this list, it has been my pleasure to have a personal acquaintance with all except the first two. Of these, four have changed this scene of trial and conflict for one of triumph and victory, two having served the Church in the capacity of bishops, and have left us examples well worthy our imitation. Of the remainder, two were my colleagues as teachers, and one my pupil. Some of those who remain are resting from active service, and waiting the call of the Master that shall summon them to their eternal rest. I know I shall find a hearty response in every breast when I express the wish that a long and peaceful life may be the portion of all those who are still with us, and that, having *lived* the life of the righteous, their end may be like his."

SIXTH REUNION

OF

FORMER PUPILS, June 10, 1859,

(Rev. E. H. Reichel, Principal.)

In the forenoon business meeting, the following officers were elected:

President.

HENRY SMITH, New York.

Vice Presidents.

JOHN BECK, Litiz.

FRANCIS JORDAN, Philadelphia.

JOHN F. WOLLE, Bethlehem.

WILLIAM J. ALBERT, Baltimore.

Secretary.

HENRY T. BACHMAN.

Assistant Secretary.

JAMES B. HAMAN.

Treasurer.

REV. E. H. REICHEL.

Historian.

ALBERT L. OERTER.

The annual address in the village church was pronounced by Lebbeus Chapman, Jr., of New York.

After supper, remarks were made by Messrs. George W. Perkin, Henry Smith, Rev. Joseph D. Philip, Rev. Edmund de Schweinitz and Rt. Rev. John C. Jacobson.

74

SEVENTH REUNION

OF

FORMER PUPILS, June 3, 1864.

(Rev. E. H. Reichel, Principal.)

A business meeting of the society was held in "The Cottage" during the afternoon, at which Professor Philip A. Cregar presided. Comparatively few of the members had responded to the call, and, excepting routine business, nothing of special interest transpired. The following is the result of the annual election:

President.
Henry Smith, New York.

Vice-Presidents.
Francis Jordan, Philadelphia.
Lebbeus Chapman, Jr., New York.
Rev. Sylvester Wolle, Bethlehem.
Rev. Edmund de Schweinitz, Litiz.

Secretary and Historian.
Edward Rondthaler.

Assistant Secretary.
J. Theophilus Zorn.

Treasurer.
Henry J. Van Vleck.

EIGHTH REUNION

OF

FORMER PUPILS, June 8, 1866.

(Rev. Edward H. Reichel, Principal.)

The following members were present:

1800—Peter Wolle, Bethlehem.
1814—Henry Smith, New York.
1815—Elihu L. Mix, New York.
1816—John C. Jacobson, *ex-off.*, Bethlehem.
1821—James Henry, Bolton, Pa.
1823—Seth W. Paine, Troy, Pa.
1827—Francis Jordan, Philadelphia.
1828—Thomas Sparks, Philadelphia.
1828—Maurice C. Jones, Bethlehem.
1831—N. S. Wolle, Litiz.
1832—Henry J. Van Vleck, Bethlehem.
1832—Charles C. Paine, Troy, Pa.
1832—George A. Kohler, Philadelphia.
1833—Philip A. Cregar, *ex-off.*, Philadelphia.
1833—Edward H. Reichel, Nazareth Hall.
1834—Edmund de Schweinitz, Bethlehem.
1835—Samuel C. Wolle, Catasauqua.
1838—James H. Wolle, Bethlehem.
1839—Francis Wolle, *ex-off.*, Bethlehem.
1842—Theodore F. Wolle, Bethlehem.
1843—Amos C. Clauder, Bethlehem.
1844—Herman A. Brickenstein, Bethlehem.
1846—Granville Henry, Bolton, Pa.
1846—E. T. Kluge, Nazareth.

1847—Obadiah T. Huebner, Nazareth.
1852—J. T. Zorn,   do.
1853—John R. Jones, Montgomery co., Pa.
1853—Joseph John Ricksecker, Nazareth.
1853—E. T. Lichtenthaler,   do.
1853—William H. Jordan, Philadelphia.
1853—William H. Nixon,   do.
1854—Edwin G. Klosè, Nazareth.
1854—Charles Nagle,   do.
1855—Frank H. Ellis, Philadelphia.
1856—Samuel R. Colladay, do.
1856—Harding Williams,   do.
1859—Ferdinand C. Mayer, Brooklyn.
1859—S. C. Chitty, Nazareth.
1859—William H. Vogler, Bethlehem.
1862—George T. Coyne, Staten Island.

The Committee on Nominations reported the following officers for the ensuing year, which report was adopted; to wit:

President.

HENRY SMITH, New York.

Vice Presidents.

ELIHU L. MIX, New York.
SETH W. PAINE, Troy, Pa.
THOMAS SPARKS, Philadelphia.
REV. EDWARD H. REICHEL, Nazareth.

Committee of Arrangements.

REV. ROBERT DE SCHWEINITZ, Salem, N. C.
WILLIAM H. JORDAN, Philadelphia.
GEORGE A. KOHLER,   do.
LAZARUS D. SHOEMAKER, Wilkesbarre.
MAURICE C. JONES, Bethlehem.
RICHARD R. TSCHUDY, Litiz.
JOHN C. GUNTHER, New York.
CHARLES W. HELD,   do.

19

Secretary and Historian.

EDWIN G. KLOSE, Nazareth.

Assistant Secretary.

CHARLES NAGLE,   do.

Treasurer.

MAURICE C. JONES, Bethlehem.

A vote of thanks was passed to the retiring Principal, who had provided for the entertainment of former pupils, met at seven of the eight Reunions celebrated up to this time.

It was finally resolved that Mr. William H. Jordan, of class 1853, be appointed a Recorder to collect the names of such pupils of Nazareth Hall as had fallen during the war.

OF

FORMER PUPILS, June 11, 1868,

And Inauguration of a Memorial in honor of such Alumni as fell in defence of their Country during the war of the Rebellion.

(Rev. Eugene Leibert, Principal.)

The reunion of 1866 appointed Mr. William H. Jordan, of Philadelphia, a Recorder to ascertain the names of such former pupils of the Hall as had fallen in the civil contest which the surrender at Appomattox terminated in the triumph of constitutional liberty. This commission was conducted with untiring labor, and resulted in the accumulation of facts from which a record of the military career and fate of most of the alumni who served in one or the other of the contending armies was subsequently compiled. It attests, almost unexceptionally, to the gallantry, devotion, endurance and patient suffering of those whose names appear upon its pages. Upward of two hundred pupils, representatives of almost every successive class of students at the Hall, men past the prime of life, men in the vigor of manhood, young men and mere boys, were found to have participated in the war of the late rebellion. And while such as had thought, had acted, had learned together at school, oftentimes stood side by side in the battle-field, comrades, too, were found arrayed against comrades, and brother against brother. Hence the feelings awakened by a perusal of this record of members of a common household were of mingled sorrow and regret—of sorrow for the untimely loss of good and patriot men who had contended for right, and of regret that men as brave should have been deluded by the mad ambition of wicked leaders to venture even their lives in the cause of an unprovoked rebellion.

A wish to perpetuate the memory of such patriotism by a tribute other than is rendered by the common instincts of humanity in the hearts of all good men was expressed by the Recorder to those whom he consulted in prosecuting his labors. It was this wish, thus intimated and gradually defined by the interchange of views and sentiments between former pupils of the Hall, which impelled the movement whose extraordinary ceremonies rendered the 11th of June, 1868, an eventful day in the history of the quiet town of Nazareth. At first there was marked indecision as to the propriety of excluding from participation in the intended honor such pupils as had fallen in the so-called Confederate service. With some, this originated in sympathy for comrades; with others, in sympathy for the cause they had espoused. But it was resolved to sacrifice the former, to disregard the latter, and yet, "with malice toward none," to render honor to those only who had stood up for the defence of their entire country and its constituted laws. Any other course, it was rightly reasoned, would in the sequel detract from the character and worth of the memorial, which was intended not to gratify the impassioned feelings of men of the present day, not to compromise truth and error by a double record, but to hand down to men of future generations the names of such only as had felt themselves moved to defend the liberties of their fore-fathers against the assaults of an internal foe.

The erection of a monument or cenotaph within the precincts of the Institution at which the heroic dead had learned their early lessons of love of country, was unhesitatingly accepted as the most appropriate mode of testifying gratitude and respect to their memories.

In October of 1867 the following circular apprised the former pupils of the Hall of the nature of the initiatory steps taken, with a view to consummate what had been foreshadowed by the resolution of June, 1866:

IN MEMORIAM.

TO THE FORMER PUPILS OF NAZARETH HALL.
1785–1867.

AMONG the teachings of this Moravian Institution, the " Amor Patriæ" has ever been pre-eminently inculcated. Its youth are brought up in the pride of Liberty and Independence, as an undoubted birth-right, but this pride is always tempered by the supreme obligations of Law.

It was therefore but the result of the discipline of our venerable " Alma Mater" that upward of two hundred and fifty of our former companions, during the gloomy days of the late rebellion, promptly responded to the call of our Country, and imperiled their lives in doing battle with the Spirit of Sedition, and that twenty-six sealed their patriotic devotion with their blood, thus confirming the assertion which has been frequently made, that from no class of men in this Republic did the response of patriotism come more readily and surely than from its cul-

19 *

tivated class, who threw themselves heartily into the war both from solid conviction and absolute rule of conscience.

Nazareth Hall is distinctively a Christian Institution, bestowing the benefits of its training and culture on youth from all parts of our common land.

We, the undersigned, therefore, who were its inmates at periods more or less remote, and who cherish its associations with warm affection, in proposing to perpetuate the memory of our martyred brethren, while desiring to avoid every appearance of vindictiveness or of triumph over the vanquished, can only feel that we would thereby erect a shrine to the high religious purpose of love of country and love of law.

It is designed to place a Cenotaph, with a shaft of thirty-five feet in height, within the " Green " fronting the ancient " Hall," the grounds of which will be appropriately embellished by its authorities and by the inhabitants of the village.

The monument, the cost of which is estimated at three thousand dollars, will be executed by Mr. Wm. Struthers, of Philadelphia ; and we earnestly solicit you to co-operate with us to the extent of your ability in providing the means for its erection.

All communications and contributions should be addressed, at as early a period as possible before November 15 next, so that the memorial services may be held on Thursday, the 11th June, 1868,

To WILLIAM H. JORDAN, *Treasurer,*
No. 209 North Third street, Philadelphia.

1814.   HENRY SMITH,
Pres. Reunion Society of Nazareth Hall.

CLASS.

1822—ANDREW A. HUMPHREYS, Maj.-Gen. U. S. A.
1837—JOHN BAILLIE MCINTOSH, Brev. Maj.-Gen. U. S. A.
1836—NATHANIEL MICHLER, Brev. Brig.-Gen. U. S. A.
1836—GEORGE P. IHRIE, Brev. Brig.-Gen. U. S. A.
1823—Joseph H. Hildeburn, Philadelphia.
1827—Francis Jordan,　　　do.
1828—Thomas Sparks,　　　do.
1830—Philip A. Cregar,　　　do.
1832—Charles Lafourcade,　　　do.
1855—Richard M. Shoemaker, Jr., do.
1814—Ernest F. Bleck, Bethlehem, Pa.
1818—Charles Aug. Luckenbach, Bethlehem, Pa.
1830—Rev. Robert de Schweinitz,　　do.
1844—Rev. Herman A. Brickenstein, do.
1841—John Thomas, Catasauqua, Pa.
1838—Francis Michler, Easton, Pa.
1855—L. H. Forman,　　do.
1831—Nathaniel S. Wolle, Litiz, Pa.
1855—Haydn H. Tschudy,　do.
1849—Henry H. Huntzinger, Pottsville, Pa.
1831—L. D. Shoemaker, Wilkesbarre, Pa.
1858—George C. Lewis,　　do.
1817—Edward Minturn, New York.
1825—Arthur Gillender,　do.
1830—Rev. A. A. Reinke, do.
1831—Andrew G. Bininger, do.
1838—Lebbeus Chapman, Jr., New York.
1855—Charles Erben,　　do.
1810—Major Giles Porter, U. S. A., Albany, N. Y.
1852—Charles V. Henry,　　do.
1854—Garret P. Bergen, Brooklyn, N. Y.
1835—Dr. James G. Clark, Staten Island, N. Y.
1855—Cornelius A. Simonson,　do.
1829—William J. Albert, Baltimore.
1821—WILLIAM BEITEL, Nazareth, Pa. ⎫
　—J. C. LEIBFRIED,　　do.　⎬ *Executive Com.*
1848—Rev. EUGENE LEIBERT, do.　⎭

PHILADELPHIA, October 1st, 1867.

Encouraged by the assurances of a hearty co-operation

which this call drew, even from such on whom there
rested no especial claim for sympathy in the movement,
the committee pushed its work vigorously.   The Rev.
Edmund de Schweinitz (1834) was appointed Orator of
the day, and on the first of June, 1868, committee made
the following announcement :

IN MEMORIAM.

THE Committee of the Alumni of Nazareth Hall, appointed under the terms of the circular dated October
1st, 1867, have the pleasure of announcing the completion of the Cenotaph in memory of their brethren who
fell in defence of the Union and Liberty during the war
of the late Rebellion.

The dedicatory exercises will be held in the village of
Nazareth at 9½ o'clock on the morning of *Thursday,
June* 11, *next.*

The Alumni and their friends proceeding from Philadelphia can obtain excursion tickets of the North Pennsylvania Railroad Company (Berks Street Station) for
two dollars to Bethlehem, and those from New York at
the station of the New Jersey Central Railroad Company
for three dollars to Easton, on exhibition of this circular.

It is recommended that all should assemble on the evening of Wednesday, the 10th, at Bethlehem, Pa., "where
carriages are provided to convey them to the Hall" at
7 A. M. on the memorial day.

On behalf of the committee.

WILLIAM H. JORDAN,
Treasurer.

PHILADELPHIA, June 1, 1868.

NOTICE.

The Reunion Society of Nazareth Hall will meet on Thursday, June 11, 1868, at the usual place.

By order of the President,

HENRY SMITH.

BURLINGTON, N. J., June 1, 1868.

On the 27th of May the monument stones, together with truck and tackle for their overland transportation, were loaded on three cars at the freight depôt of the North Pennsylvania Railroad in Philadelphia. They reached Bath, on the line of the Lehigh and Lackawana Railroad, on the 29th. Here men and horses were in waiting to receive and convey the ponderous freight five miles across the country. The horses had been volunteered by farmers in the neighborhood of Nazareth, and Mr. Samuel Knecht, of that borough, was entrusted with the general management of the novel transportation. In the absence of necessary appliances, great difficulty was experienced in handling the large stones, and it was late in the afternoon of the 29th when the first consignment was despatched by the "Lower Bath road" to Nazareth. This was the granite base, weighing six and a half tons, suspended by tackling from a four-wheeled marble truck of five tons additional weight, drawn by seventeen horses, two abreast. Owing to previous rains, the condition of the road was unusually bad for the time of year, so that, after proceeding but a short distance, it was found necessary to attach two more horses. The wheels, notwithstanding, several times stuck so deep in the mud that the horses came to a stand-still, broke the chain-traces in their endeavors to extricate the ponderous load, and the men almost despaired of ever accomplishing the task they had

P

undertaken. On several occasions, also, an upset was imminent : and while crossing the stone bridge over the brook at Christian Spring the truck collided with the masonry on one side, tearing it completely away. At Bath crowds of farmers and quarrymen had collected to witness the arrival of the train ; and at intervals along the route the rustic population in groups watched the laborious progress of the " big wagon" with deepest interest. Before attempting the ascent of the hill near Nazareth, four fresh horses were impressed, and at last, at eight P. M., the imposing and unprecedented equestrian display reached its destination amid the acclamations of upward of fifteen hundred spectators, who had assembled in the course of the afternoon.

The carriage of the remaining portions of the structure was attended with less difficulty, and before the evening of the third day all of them had been deposited uninjured near the site of the monument. The aggregate bulk of the material was three hundred and nine cubic feet, equivalent to a weight of twenty-two tons.

The open square in front of the Hall, which from time immemorial has been the campus of its students in their lighter pastimes, and where under Lombardy poplars* and lindens they were wont to rest from the toil of boyish sports, had been selected as the site of the " empty stone" whose shaft should bear the names of fallen ones who slept in distant or unknown graves. As the liberality of citizens of Nazareth had provided for the grading and general improvement of the plot, and a foundation for the structure had been laid in November of the previous year, there was no delay in its erection, and the work was

---

* The Lombardy poplars, which formerly lined three sides of the Square, were planted by Mr. John Jacob Schmidt, tutor, about 1804, and were cut down when ground was broken for the church of 1841.

finished on the 4th of June. The monument was at once veiled with white muslin.

The majority of former pupils and specially invited guests, among whom were Major Generals Andrew A. Humphreys and John Baillie McIntosh, Brigadier General Nathaniel Michler and ex-Governor Curtin, had rendezvoused at Bethlehem on the evening preceding the eventful day. They met at the Sun Hotel, and till late into the night the apartments of the old inn were alive with the mirth and joyousness of comrades met once again after long years of absence to rehearse the experiences of schoolboy days; and when they separated it was with bright anticipations of a glorious morrow.

The 11th of June, however, proved a most unfavorable day, for it rained without intermission from early dawn till nightfall. Eight four-horse omnibuses and twenty two-horse carriages had been engaged at Bethlehem, Nazareth, Allentown, Newburg and Belfast by the Committee of Arrangements for the transportation of the Reunionists and their guests. Messrs. Joseph B. Jones, C. A. Luckenbach, B. C. Webster, Tinsley Jeter, Lewis A. Gerlach, John Fritz, Samuel Adams and Mrs. George Myers, of Bethlehem, and Mr. Samuel Thomas, of Hokendauqua, had volunteered their carriages for the occasion. The imposing cortege set out from Bethlehem at eight A. M., and after a two hours' drive, in a cold, pelting rain and through heavy roads, reached Nazareth. The consequent delay, as well as the inclemency of the weather, rendered a change in the programme of exercises as announced by the Committee of Arrangements unavoidable. One hundred and thirty-three members of the Reunion Society had responded by their presence to the President's circular of June 1. Special invitations to participate in the extraordinary ceremonies of the day had been extended to Mrs. John Fream, of Tivoli, N. Y., to Mr. H. W. Ryerson, of New York, and to other parents of Alumni who had fallen in the Union service. Also to General U. S. Grant, Governor John W. Geary, ex-Governor Andrew G. Curtin, General W. E. Doster, Easton, Pa.; General Alexander S. Webb, New York; General Robert McAllister, Allentown; General W. H. Emory, Washington; General James L. Selfridge, Bethlehem; Generals George H. Crossman, A. J. Pleasanton and Colonel Samuel Wetherill, Philadelphia; Henry Coppée, President Lehigh University; Rev. E. N. Potter, South Bethlehem, Pa.; Hon. Simon Cameron, Harrisburg; Hon. John N. Conyngham, Wilkesbarre; Hon. Henry D. Maxwell, Easton; Hon. Wm. S. Pierce and others.

General Grant replied as follows:

> HEADQUARTERS ARMY OF THE UNITED STATES, }
> WASHINGTON, D. C., June 8, 1868. }

MR. WILLIAM H. JORDAN—

SIR: General Grant directs me to express his thanks for your invitation of the 4th instant to be present at the dedicatory exercises of the Nazareth Hall Monument on the 11th instant, and his regret that previous engagements will prevent his availing himself of your courtesy.

He directs me also to convey to you the assurance of his profound sympathy with every undertaking whose object is to honor the memory of those "who fell in defence of the Union and Liberty during the war of the late rebellion."

I am, sir, very respectfully,
Your obedient servant,
ADAM BADEAU,
Brevet Brig. Gen. and A. D. C.

Pupils Present at the Ninth Reunion.

Those marked * were day-scholars.

1788—John Beitel,* Nazareth.
1795—Christian D. Busse,* do.
1798—Andrew G. Kern,*   do.
1800—George C. Schneller, Bethlehem.
1802—William Henry, Wyoming.
1807—Charles F. Kluge, Nazareth.
1814—Henry Smith, Burlington, N. J.
1814—Ernest F. Bleck, Bethlehem.
1814—Arthur Cernea, Buckingham, Bucks co., Pa.
1815—John Jordan,* Jr., Philadelphia.
1816—John C. Jacobson, *ex-off.*, Bethlehem.
1816—Joseph J. Albright,* Scranton.
1817—Josiah O. Beitel, Nazareth.
1817—Henry A. Shultz,   do.
1821—Sidney A. Clewell, Philadelphia.
1821—James Henry, Bolton, Northampton co., Pa.
1821—Richard Christ,* Nazareth.
1821—William Beitel,*   do.
1822—Andrew A. Humphreys, Washington.
1823—Seth W. Paine, Troy, Pa.
1824—David Bigler, Lancaster.
1824—John F. Kohler, Philadelphia.
1824—John C. Brickenstein, *ex-off.*, Nazareth.
1827—Levin A. Miksch,* Bethlehem.
1827—Edward O. Smith,* Philadelphia.
1827—Comenius Senseman,* Nazareth.
1827—Francis Jordan, Philadelphia.
1828—Thomas Sparks,   do.
1828—Sylvester Wolle, Bethlehem.
1828—Maurice C. Jones,   do.
1829—Lewis F. Kampman, do.
1830—Robert de Schweinitz, do.
1830—Reuben A. Henry, Scranton.
1830—Amadeus A. Reinke, New York.
1831—Nathaniel S. Wolle, Litiz.
1831—Lazarus D. Shoemaker, Wilkesbarre.
1832—George A. Kohler, Philadelphia.
1832—James Lee, Jr., Boston.

1832—Henry J. Van Vleck, Bethlehem.
1832—William H. Butler, Wilkesbarre.
1832—Thomas Brodrick,   do.
1833—Edward H. Reichel, Nazareth.
1833—Philip A. Cregar, *ex-off.*, Philadelphia.
1833—John C. Philip, Brooklyn.
1834—Edmund de Schweinitz, Bethlehem.
1835—Samuel C. Wolle, Hokendauqua.
1835—William Higgins, New York.
1836—Nathaniel Michler, Washington.
1837—John Baillie McIntosh, do.
1837—Horace W. Smith, Philadelphia.
1837—Eugene T. Henry, Oxford, N. J.
1837—Joseph Dean Philip, Brooklyn.
1838—James H. Wolle, Bethlehem.
1839—Francis Wolle, *ex-off.*, do.
1839—Lewis R. Huebner,   do.
1839—Robert S. Hall, Philadelphia.
1842—Theodore F. Wolle, Bethlehem.
1843—Edward H. Jacobson,   do.
1843—Thomas Overington, Frankford.
1845—C. Edward Kummer, Bethlehem.
1846—Henry H. Wolle, Philadelphia.
1846—Granville Henry, Bolton, Northampton co., Pa.
1847—Frederic K. Womrath, Philadelphia.
1848—Eugene Leibert, Nazareth Hall.
1848—Peter A. Keyser, Philadelphia.
1848—Obadiah T. Huebner, Litiz.
1849—James E. Audenried, Philadelphia.
1849—Frank C. Stout,* Bethlehem.
1849—Philip S. P. Walter,* Nazareth.
1851—William H. Loyd, Philadelphia.
1852—Charles B. Shultz, Bethlehem.
1852—J. Theophilus Zorn, Nazareth Hall.
1853—William H. Bigler, Bethlehem.
1853—John David Wolle,*   do.
1853—William H. Jordan, Philadelphia.
1853—Francis Jordan, Jr.,   do.
1853—Edward Rondthaler, Brooklyn.
1853—Edward E. Hoeber,* Nazareth.
1854—Joseph R. Kenney, Philadelphia.

CLASS.

1854—Edwin G. Klosè, Bethlehem.

1854—Charles Gilsey, New York.

1854—Peter Gilsey,   do.

1854—Garret P. Bergen, Brooklyn.

1855—J. Albert Rondthaler, Bethlehem.

1855—Edward J. Regennas, Nazareth Hall.

1855—Philip H. Kutzmeyer, New York.

1855—Thomas M. Gilchrist, Wilkesbarre.

1855—Lawrence H. Forman, Easton.

1856—Richard M. Shoemaker, Jr., Philadelphia.

1856—Harding Williams,   do.

1856—Frank H. Ellis,   do.

1856—Samuel P. Wetherill,   do.

1856—George Sellers, Washington.

1856—Edward M. Knox, New York.

1856—Jay Jarvis, New York.

1856—Edward T. Henry, Bolton.

1856—William W. Yohe, Bethlehem.

1856—Henry A. Jacobson, Nazareth Hall.

1857—George C. Lewis, Wilkesbarre.

1857—Frank S. Rowland, Philadelphia.

1857—Adolphus Lichtenthaler, Bethlehem.

1858—Ewing Jordan, Philadelphia.

1858—Charles H. Landenberger, Philadelphia.

1858—David F. Rank, New York.

1859—Norman J. Mayer, do.

1859—Ferdinand C. Mayer, do.

1859—Joseph W. Longmire, Philadelphia.

1859—William A. Meurer,   do.

1859—Theodor C. Engel,   do.

1859—Benjamin P. Whitney, Pottsville.

1859—Joseph R. Siewers, Nazareth Hall.

1859—Joseph H. Kampman, Bethlehem.

1859—Herbert W. Wolle,*   do.

1859—Theodore M. Rights,   do.

1860—Silas L. Early, Palmyra.

1860—John F. Beitel, Nazareth.

1861—George T. Coyne, Staten Island.

1861—Frederic J. Grote, New York.

1861—Franklin B. Evans, Philadelphia.

CLASS.

1861—Joseph S. Rowland, Philadelphia.
1862—George W. Landenberger, do.
1862—Clement F. Oehler, Bethlehem.
1863—J. Max. Hark,* Nazareth.
1863—Samuel S. Yohe, Bethlehem.
1863—Robert McC. Turner, Philadelphia.
1863—Alfred M. Berg, do.
1863—Clarence A. Wolle, Bethlehem.
1863—Francis L. Wolle, do.
1863—Edward Barnes, New York.
1863—Albert Barnes, do.
1863—Samuel M. Skirving, Philadelphia.
1863—John James Skirving, do.
1864—William A. Himes, New Oxford.

The following is the programme of exercises published by the Committee of Arrangements:

MEMORIAL DAY, NAZARETH HALL.
June 11, 1868.

The Alumni will assemble at the Nazareth Hotel at 9½ A. M., and move in procession at a quarter of 10 precisely, in the following order:

THE NAZARETH BAND.

Chief Marshal.
PROF. PHILIP A. CREGAR.

Assistant Marshals.
JOHN THOMAS,
ROBERT J. McCLATCHEY, M. D.,
FRANCIS JORDAN, JR.

The President of the Reunion Society and the Orator of of the Day.

The Bishops of the Moravian Church.

The General and other Officers of the U. S. Army and Navy.

The Trustees of Nazareth Hall and the Rev. Clergy.

The Invited Guests and Strangers.

The Alumni.

The Citizens.

On arrival at the "Green," they will be received by the pupils of the Hall with an address, and after a reply from the President, the divisions will take their places in order around the platform.

PRAYER—BY THE RIGHT REV. HENRY A. SHULTZ.

MUSIC—BY THE TROMBONES.

ADDRESS—BY THE REV. EDMUND DE SCHWEINITZ.

UNVEILING OF THE CENOTAPH.

HYMN—THE RIGHT REV. DAVID BIGLER OFFICIATING.

BENEDICTION—BY THE RIGHT REV. PETER WOLLE.

THE DOXOLOGY, WITH MUSIC BY THE TROMBONES.

Immediately afterward, the meeting of the Reunion Society will be held in the Chapel of the Hall, which the Alumni are urgently requested to attend, in order that their names may be recorded on the minutes.

At 4 P. M. they will reassemble in the Hall for " Coffee and Moravian Cake," when the Military and Naval Reports will be read.

COMMITTEE OF ARRANGEMENTS.

Washington, D. C.	*Philadelphia.*
CLASS.	CLASS.
1822—Andrew A. Humphreys, Maj.-Gen. U. S. A.	1823—Joseph H. Hildeburn.
	1827—Francis Jordan.
1836—Nathaniel Michler, Brev. Brig.-Gen. U. S. A.	1828—Thomas Sparks.
	1830—Philip A. Cregar.
1837—John Baillie McIntosh, Brev. Maj.-Gen. U. S. A.	1831—Sidney J. Solms.
	1841—Edwin T. Eisenbrey.

20 *

Bethlehem, Pa.

CLASS
1814—Ernest F. Bleck.
1828—Maurice C. Jones.
1828—Rev. Sylvester Wolle.
1844—Rev. Herman A. Brickenstein.

Hokendauqua, Pa.

1841—John Thomas.

Easton, Pa.

1816—Theodore R. Sitgreaves.
1855—Lawrence H. Forman.

Nazareth, Pa.

1821—William Beitel.
—J. C. Leibfried.
1846—Granville Henry.
1848—Eugene Leibert.

Lititz, Pa.

1799—John Beck.
1831—Nathaniel S. Wolle.
1855—Haydn H. Tschudy.

Pottsville, Pa.

1849—Henry H. Huntzinger.

Wilkesbarre, Pa.

1831—L. D. Shoemaker.
1858—George C. Lewis.

New York.

CLASS
1817—Edward Minturn.
1825—Arthur Gillender.
1831—Andrew G. Bininger.
1837—George W. Day.
1838—Lebbeus Chapman, Jr.
1854—Herman Uhl.

Brooklyn, N. Y.

1837—Rev. Joseph Dean Philip.
1854—Garret P. Bergen.

Staten Island, N. Y.

1855—Cornelius A. Simonson.

Burlington, N. J.

1814—Henry Smith.

Albany, N. Y.

1810—Giles Porter, Major U.S.A.
1852—Charles V. Henry.

Baltimore.

1829—William J. Albert.

Boston.

1832—James Lee, Jr.

Kalamazoo, Mich.

1833—Charles E. Smith, Brev. Brig. Gen. U. S. Vols.

All business communications to be addressed to

WILLIAM H. JORDAN, *Treasurer*,

No. 209 North Third Street, Philadelphia.

The above order of proceedings was observed, as far as the inclement day would permit. At 10½ A. M. the procession formed at the hotel, and, marshaled by Professor P. A. Cregar and his aids, moved to the Chapel of the Moravian parochial school, where the inaugural ceremonies were conducted. The distinguished visitors and the reverend clergy occupied the platform. At a quarter to 11 the Nazareth Hall Cadets, to the number of one hundred, in neat gray uniform, entered the crowded Hall, and took a position in four lines in front of the stand. Master Willie St. Clair Gibbs, of Hyde Park, stepped forward, and, in behalf of his schoolmates, said: "My friends, and former pupils of Nazareth Hall: To me is given the honor of welcoming you back to your old home, again to spend a day amid the scenes of your boyhood. In the name of my companions, I extend you a hearty welcome. Although part of the exercises of the day may be fraught with painful recollections, yet we hope your visit may also yield you much enjoyment. Again wishing you a hearty welcome, I propose three cheers for the ' old boys' of Nazareth Hall."

These having been given with a will, the President responded on the part of the Society, and concluded by calling for three cheers for Nazareth Hall. Prayer was then offered by Rt. Rev. Henry A. Shultz, of Nazareth. After a general invocation to the throne of grace, which was full of patriotic fervor, he closed with the words of the Lord's Prayer, in which the audience devoutly joined. A funeral chorale was now performed by the Nazareth trombonists. Hereupon, Rev. Edmund de Schweinitz, of Bethlehem, the Orator of the day, was introduced, and proceeded to speak as follows:

" On ground rich in the associations of our boyhood, in the first days of opening summer, that used to be more

fragrant than their full-blown roses, under all circumstances of wind and weather—let them have been bright
and serene, as we hoped to-day would prove, or dark and
stormy, as it has turned out to be—because they brought
us the 'examination holidays,' we are met, alumni of
Nazareth Hall to celebrate another Reunion. For more
than twelve years such gatherings, with occasional interruptions, have taken place, and have been times of unalloyed pleasure, when we forgot the cares of life, laid
aside its burdens, and were boys again. To-day, however, we come not merely with this purpose. We have
a mission to fulfill, a work of love to do. As those of our
associates, whose decease was reported at former Reunions, won a tribute of respect from the lips of some
friend, so, on the present occasion, we all unite in perpetuating the names, and embalming the memory, of a
number of our fellow-alumni, who, whether we were
personally acquainted with them or not, had us all for
their friends, because they died for our common country,
and belonged to the ranks of those whom the God of our
fathers summoned to its rescue, in the hour of its direst
peril, when its glorious union of Commonwealths was
broken, and its history as a world-power seemed drawing
to an end.

"To honor such men is an intuitive impulse of the
heart, a prerogative of free citizenship, an evidence of
true patriotism. It has been done wherever the people
governed since the days of Sparta and Athens. While
monarchies exalt the conqueror, republics pay reverence
to their defenders. While Alexander the Great erected
twelve towers on the banks of the distant Hyphasis, to
mark his irresistible advance into the kingdoms of India,
the pillars at Marathon bore the names of heroes who, on
that immortal field, rolled back the tide of Persian inva-

sion and saved Greece from a despot's heel. While the
Triumphal Arch at Paris blazons those battles of Napoleon
that laid Europe in glittering chains, Bunker Hill is
crowned with a monument which tells of deeds that gave
to Liberty, both in her civil and religious manifestations,
a home such as she never had before, and made this
Western buttress of the world a refuge for the oppressed
of every land.

" For us, however, as a body of alumni, and at a Reunion in these never-to-be-forgotten precincts, to offer
such a tribute is to exalt not only the memory of fellow-
pupils, but also the name of our Alma Mater, whose
teachings first produced in them a tendency and an aim,
whose instructions helped to shape our course through
life. That block of stone proclaims as well what an
American citizen will sacrifice for the sake of Liberty and
the Union, as what one of the oldest educational institutions of America can accomplish in making a citizen.

" It is from this point of view that I wish to address
you. I cannot consistently occupy any other. The war
in which our brethren fell is over. Who does not devoutly thank God for that? The mighty armies of
which they formed a part have melted away as suddenly,
I might almost say as miraculously, as they sprang into
existence, and have given back to the family, to the pursuits of business and to the Church elements of manly
activity and well-tried strength. The stormy events of
the conflict, the news of battles won or lost, the daily
bulletins from the camp or the field, and all that made
that time a period of unparalleled excitement, belong to
the past. And so do the groans of the wounded, the
wails of the dying, the tears of the bereaved and the
broken-hearted. Peace smiles upon us and our children.
The summer's grain covers the ensanguined fields of An-

tietam and Gettysburg. The broad highways of travel
are no longer obstructed; the great arteries of trade no
more refuse to pulsate. On the waters of the Mississippi,
commerce is joyfully doing its work; the railroads of
Pennsylvania and Virginia are again in friendly harmony—
avenues of legitimate barter, means of union for friend
and friend. The righteous indignation of the hour is
soothed; the bitter animosities of the strife are allayed.
Hence, although we are not here in order to call evil
good and good evil, in order to put darkness for light
and light for darkness, we do not come to say what would
have been proper amidst the experiences of the Rebellion itself, while its issues were still doubtful, while plain
truths and strong words were necessary to vindicate our
cause. We have no enemies to denounce. God has or-
dained that the people of America, whether in the North
or the South, should be one and remain indivisible.
That, however, which we are not to forget, and which
we can magnify 'with charity for all and malice to
none,' is *the principle* which led our brethren to yield
their lives—a principle setting them before us, first, as
scholars of the 'good old Hall,' and then as soldiers of
the grand army of the Union.

 "Nazareth Hall has a twofold mission—namely, to
train the mind and to mould the character. In pursuing
the latter, the fundamental rule which it imparts is *faithfulness to duty.* This is the groundwork of its peculiar
system of discipline, the substance of all those lessons
and the life of all those plastic exercises that are to form
the man. This gives tone to its social relations, and con-
stitutes the element in which its teachers and scholars
move. It brings this tenet of Moral Philosophy down
from the region of theory and makes it a power in the
boy for practical life. By this law, which rings out in the

early watches of the morning, when the bell sounds the signal for rising, and which then guides whatever is done through the day, in the hours of study or recitation, in the house or on the play-ground, until the word is spoken, at bed-time, that hushes the room-company into absolute silence, Nazareth Hall has performed wonders, coerced, without an effort, many an ungovernable lad, saved him from ruin and sent him forth to usefulness and prosperity. Other schools may do more in the way of a brilliant show of knowledge, but none surpass it in building character upon this solid corner-stone.

" Now the object of the late war, on the part of the loyal States, was not ambition or conquest, or glory for its own sake merely. It was resistance against the most gigantic and causeless rebellion ever originated, and, consequently, a necessary act of self-preservation, an in- alienable right to hold fast that which the Almighty Ruler of the world had himself bestowed upon our fathers in their struggle for independence, and which had crowned us with the richest benefactions. Or, rather, to state the case in the words of that man for the crisis whom the Lord of hosts raised up and treason struck down, who sleeps, a martyr, in his Western grave, and has the prai- rie-winds to sing his requiem throughout all generations —words as transparent as his life, and as noble as his work—it was ' that the nation should, under God, have a new birth of freedom, and the government of the people, by the people, and for the people, should not perish from the earth.' This was the call which stirred the hearts of millions, this was the solemn obligation of the hour.

" And therefore the response came, literally, from every avocation of life. Men left the anvil and the plough, the counting-house and the workshop, the professional office and the college ; and armies were marshaled which formed the bone and sinew of the people, represented its intelligence and wealth, and were animated by a lofty purpose and a high resolve. On the same scale such a result was never accomplished before in any nation. Hosts gathered unprecedented in point of numbers since the times of Xerxes, and yet, for the most part, they were hosts of freemen, of citizens who voluntarily seized the musket with the same hands that deposited the ballot by which they govern themselves. A greater contrast cannot be imagined than that between our soldiers and those who, from year to year, in war and peace, make of Europe one vast camp. The former were conscious embodiments of a principle—the latter are unconscious machines, set in motion by a royal cabinet and working under the strain of inexorable discipline. The enthusiasm of the one was the natural emotion of a patriotic heart, clinging to its national birth-right, a thing of life, stirring the depths of their being—the enthusiasm of the other is drilled into them, like the use of the needle-gun, and does not soar higher than a constrained regard for glory as an abstraction.

" Of a call that produced such an 'uprising of a great people,' the alumni of Nazareth Hall were not unmindful. With honest pride, let it be proclaimed to-day, that two hundred and thirty 'Hall boys' arrayed themselves under the flag of their country, helped to save it from dismemberment, aided to bring on a new era in the history of Liberty, and to send her rejoicing and blessing over the earth. It is as honorable a record as any one can wish for, as genuine a satisfaction as any achievement in life will confer, as rich a legacy as can be left to children and children's children. The time is coming when the descendants of the Union soldiers in the War of the Rebellion will be not less proud of them than men now are of their

Revolutionary sires, when the musket that was carried to the bloody field of the Wilderness, and the sword that flashed in the morning's sun of the assaults upon Vicksburg, will be heir-looms as sacred as the present generation esteems like relics from Lexington or Yorktown.

"But what was it that induced so large a proportion of former pupils to leave their business and forsake their homes, in order to enlist as soldiers? I turn to look upon the 'old Hall,' I remember its class-rooms and Chapel, I recall its lessons and life, and, with that deep conviction which experience gains, I answer: It was the grand principle laid as the foundation of their character when they were boys in this School—it was faithfulness to duty here taught and learned. They paid what they owed their country.

"This principle found its most perfect type in those of their number whose memory we signalize to-day, for they carried it out to the end, and, in the strength of it, gave all that a man has, even their lives.

"Ere I proceed to illustrate this, it is fitting that I should read the roll of our honored dead. It is as follows:

"DAVID BAKER, the oldest on the list, of the class of 1822.

"CHARLES M. BERG, of the class of 1829.

"FRANK POTT, of the class of 1830.

"ARTHUR L. VAN VLECK, of the class of 1835.

"CHARLES M. STOUT, of the class of 1841.

"EUGENE F. CLEWELL, of the class of 1843.

"HERMAN L. BEITEL, of the class of 1845.

"CHARLES M. SMEIDLE, of the class of 1847.

"ASHER GAYLORD, of the class of 1848.

"JOSEPH P. BACHMAN, of the class of 1849.

"DAVID T. LATIMER, the first who fell, and one of the first Union soldiers killed; CHRISTIAN F. SMITH, EDMUND

21   Q

A. Shouse, John F. Wood and Van Brunt M. Bergen, all of the class of 1853.

"John A. Witmer, Horace C. Bennet, Daniel H. Fasig and James I. Grafton, of the class of 1854.

"George L. Fream, Benjamin F. Landell and Charles Ryerson, of the class of 1855.

"Clarence Kampman, John C. Hagen and William W. Ladd, the youngest on the list, but sixteen years of age, all of the class of 1858.

"Edwin A. Skirving, of the class of 1860.

"Pliny A. Jewett, Jr., of the class of 1861.

"Twenty-seven in all, who were either killed in battle or died of disease contracted while in the service.

"Ten of them were sent out by Pennsylvania, four by Ohio, three by New York, two by New Jersey, one by Massachusetts, one by Connecticut, one by Illinois, one by Iowa, one by Kentucky. Three belonged to the Navy; and the fields of Great Bethel and Harper's Ferry, of Averysborough and Pocotalico, of Chattanooga and Vicksburg, of Antietam, Williamsburg and Hatcher's Run, together with the blood-stained deck of the Frigate Cumberland—that would not yield even to the iron monster which attacked her, but was engulphed by the waters of Chesapeake Bay, with her colors flying—make up the places where our brethren, in the appropriate language of the monument, 'died that their country might be healed and live.' It thus appears that in the regiments of nine of the loyal States, as well as in that puissant navy which filled the maritime powers of the world with astonishment, and in battles fought along the border, in the West, and in the South, from one of the earliest to one of the latest, the alumni of Nazareth Hall were represented by these their comrades in everything that was true, brave and faithful.

" Without going into all the details of their service, which will be given at another time in the course of the exercises of this day, I will adduce but a few facts to establish the position I have taken.

" One of the fallen was my own classmate. I knew him well, both in the Hall and afterward in the Theological Seminary. He was the most innocent of boys and the most guileless of men. Diffident, shrinking even from play as soon as it grew boisterous, an obscure corner his retreat and a book his friend, kind-hearted, too, never resenting an injury, and bearing the banter of his companions with unruffled patience, I would sooner have believed anything most strange, when we sat together in our class-room and construed that Latin line which says, ' It is sweet and becoming to die for one's country,' than that the poet's sentiment would, in his case, grow into a personal experience. And yet this honored companion won a medal for bravery at the battle of Chancellorsville, bore himself, under all circumstances, with unvarying gallantry as a soldier, and with true heroism as a Christian, until his heartstrings cracked amidst the nameless horrors of Libby Prison. Nothing under heaven but a deep sense of duty and a lofty determination to be faithful could have induced him to enter the army and expose himself to the associations of the camp and the other experiences of military life, which, in themselves considered, were as foreign to his nature as they were repulsive to his feelings.

" And touching the rest whom I have named, it will stir your hearts, my friends, as it did mine, when you will hear their records. It is impossible to read the letters, written by those who knew them in the army, without gaining a vivid consciousness of the operations of that principle of power which Nazareth Hall taught them. In every instance in which the diligent search, deserving of all praise, made by the Treasurer of the Monument Association, for the incidents of their military history, was rewarded with success, something true and honorable, something to be proud of, has been brought out.

"Of one his captain says, 'He met his fate with a manliness never excelled;' and of another, 'He presented, in an eminent degree, the qualities of a soldier and a gentleman,' while the surgeon, who witnessed his death-struggle, calls him a 'manly and noble boy.' A third receives this testimony: 'He was a brave and fearless soldier, respected by all the men and officers.' A fourth, who was mortally wounded while leading a desperate charge at Vicksburg, stood so high in his company that, with one accord, the survivors sent to his mourning family a tribute of respect in memory of his virtues. Several were promoted from the ranks for bravery in the field. Around the body of an officer brought to Hilton Head for burial, who had marched at the head of his men across a cornfield swept by a terrific fire as coolly as if he were drilling them, and who was shot later in the action, there gathered persons high in rank, that had been acquainted with him, exclaiming, 'Brave man! Brave man!' Another officer, to use the words of his own colonel, 'in everything he said and did was always manly, honorable and noble.' General Slocum held him in such esteem that he reported his death to Governor Andrew, of Massachusetts, designating him as 'one of the best officers under his command,' while General Sherman himself lamented his loss, and seemed to feel it as though it were a personal bereavement. Still another, who, after filling various positions of trust, was finally made Ordnance Officer of the Middle Military District, labored so inces-

santly in the discharge of his arduous duties that his
health failed. But he would not relinquish them until
peremptorily ordered home to recruit. He obeyed, taking
with him, however, the papers of the Department, and
resuming his work under the parental roof. At last he
could write no more. Then he employed amanuenses,
and dictated to these until the very day of his death, on
which his father sent all his returns completed to Washington. Even the youngest on the roll, that lad of sixteen summers, who went forth from a happy home of ease
and wealth, is not without a record; even of him it is
said, ' He was faithful as a soldier, and much loved by
his company.'

" It is unnecessary to bring forward more facts in order
to substantiate my argument. The testimony now given
by officers of their men, and by superiors of their officers,
has a clear ring, and tells us unmistakably that faithfulness to duty was the distinctive trait of the sons of Nazareth Hall who fell in defence of their country; that as
their character was moulded in the days of their boyhood,
so it came out in well-marked lines of beauty under circumstances which, more than any other, try men and
show the stuff that they are made of. Who, then, is
there here who will not glory in our Alma Mater? She
did her part in the most momentous struggle of this age.
Other schools performed theirs; all honor be to them!
She, however, caused her influence to be felt in her own
peculiar way, as an institution which had drawn its life
for eighty years not merely from human philosophy, but
also from the depths of that knowledge which reveals the
Eternal Son of God as a teacher and a Lawgiver and a
Redeemer to the world.

" Therefore, we, the Alumni of Nazareth Hall, gathered
to-day from all quarters of the land, and counting among
21 *

our number representatives of nearly every class back to the closing year of the last century, now dedicate this cenotaph, with sincere respect, to the memory of our brethren, and, with filial reverence, to the honor of the School, and adopt, as an appropriate formula, one of the sentences graven on the stone: 'The Academy is the nursing-mother of patriots, rearing her children in the ways of truth and freedom.'

"Long may this monument stand to show the present generation of pupils, and other generations that will come after them, what those patriots did whose names it bears, what this Academy can perform through the sons whom it educates, and what the Lord God Omnipotent wrought for the salvation of our country!

"It will not be a sectional landmark; for, although it is perhaps too early to expect such a thing now, yet, eventually, those who preserved the Federal Union from disintegration, and thus gave a new impulse to the development of our popular institutions, and originated the new relations by which the same is conditioned, will become the common heroes of the whole country. This is a truth established beyond all cavil by the results of the war of the Revolution. There were thousands of Tories then who labored with heart and soul for the triumph of Great Britain; but there is not one American now who does not glorify the men through whose devotion and sufferings and blood the United States were made free.

"But, in a higher sense, this cenotaph will be more than even a national memorial. That is a contracted vision which fails to see in the events of the Rebellion an issue for the entire brotherhood of man. That is a dwarfish philosophy which is unable to grasp a divine plan in history;

' For I doubt not thro' all ages one increasing purpose runs,
And the thoughts of men are widen'd with the process of the suns.'

" This purpose is ripening fast. Nations rise against nations, and peoples are divided against themselves. But ' hast thou not known, hast thou not heard, that the ever-lasting God, the Lord, the Creator of the ends of the earth, fainteth not, neither is weary?' Like the throne upon which He sits, His design stands fast, as it ever did from the beginning; and in order to its consummation ' the nations are as a drop of a bucket, and are counted as the small dust of the balance.' Above all their wars and tumults and shouts of conquest sounds the voice of the Everlasting Counsel, saying, ' The Lord reigneth, let the earth rejoice!' Yes, let the earth rejoice, for the morning's red of a new time is breaking. We live in the grandest epoch the world has yet seen. It is a glorious thing to have one's being in such an age, to be a factor in its development, to belong to a people that has been or-dained, I reverently believe, to lead the van in subduing our globe to the sway of that liberty which is perfect be-cause Christ is its Author, and of that glory which is eter-nal because it flows from universal righteousness and peace.

" In this exalted sense, my friends, let us, as we are gathered here in the shadow of our Alma Mater, and in the presence of yonder cenotaph, learn anew the lessons of our boyhood. We will go back to our several spheres of labor faithful to duty—duty to our fellow-men, our country and our God."

The " select choir" of the Hall next sang a requiem, be-ginning with the words, " Oh weep for the brave who are gone to their graves," to the accompaniment of brass instruments. Right Rev. David Bigler, of Lancaster, announced the concluding hymn, and the services in the

Chapel closed with the benediction, pronounced by Right
Rev. John C. Jacobson, of Bethlehem.

The company now repaired to the Square to witness
the unveiling of the monument, although the storm had
not abated in the least. The alumni were drawn up on
the sidewalk and the Cadets stood in front, uncovered, in
the driving rain. To General Humphreys, the senior of
his fellow-officers present, had been awarded the honor of
conducting this impressive ceremony; and as the white
covering slowly fell to the ground, the saddened feeling
which had pervaded the audience during the earlier exercises was exchanged for one of intense enthusiasm; for
before them stood the tribute of their affection and reverence for lost companions and fallen patriots, which,
though an "empty stone," was yet graven with the names
of cherished ones. The band struck up a dead march,
and the inaugural services closed.

The memorial is a composite structure of stone and
marble, rising from a grassy mound in the centre of the
green to the height of thirty-five feet. Its base is a block
of granite, six and a half feet square. On this rests the
pedestal, consisting of slabs of Connecticut sandstone,
supporting a solid block of New Brunswick drabstone,
into whose southern face is cut the national coat of arms.
The pedestal is surmounted by a square die of Italian
white marble, on which are inscribed appropriate legends
and the names of the fallen alumni. The obelisk itself is
composed of blocks of Cleveland drabstone alternating
with slabs of Connecticut brownstone. The south face
of the marble die bears the following inscription:

"To commemorate the memory of sons of Nazareth Hall, who died that their country might be
healed and live, this stone is erected by the

IN MEMORIAM, JUNE 11, 1868.

"Hence it is that the fathers of these men, and themselves too, being nurtured in all freedom and well born, have shown before all men deeds many and glorious in public and private, deeming it their duty to fight for freedom and their country, even against their countrymen."

ALUMNI OF THE INSTITUTION IN THE YEAR OF GRACE, 1868."

On the east face are inscribed the following names:

DAVID BAKER, VAN BRUNT M. BERGEN, HERMAN L. BEITEL, CHARLES M. BERG, EUGENE FER'D CLEWELL, GEORGE LORILLARD FREAM, DANIEL H. FASIG, JOSEPH P. BACHMAN, HORACE C. BENNETT,

and below the comforting words of Scripture:

"THEY SHALL HUNGER NO MORE, NEITHER THIRST ANY MORE; NEITHER SHALL THE SUN LIGHT ON THEM, NOR ANY HEAT. FOR THE LAMB WHICH IS IN THE MIDST OF THEM SHALL FEED THEM, AND SHALL LEAD THEM UNTO LIVING FOUNTAINS OF WATERS; AND GOD SHALL WIPE AWAY ALL TEARS FROM THEIR EYES."

The north side bears the names of

ASHER GAYLORD, JAMES J. GRAFTON, JOHN C. HAGEN, PLINY A. JEWETT, JR., CLARENCE KAMPMAN, WILLIAM W. LADD, DAVID T. LATIMER, BENJAMIN F. LANDELL, FRANK POTT,

and the legend,

"THE ACADEMY IS THE NURSING-MOTHER OF PATRIOTS, REARING HER CHILDREN IN THE WAYS OF TRUTH AND FREEDOM."

On the west face the record is completed with the names of

CHARLES RYERSON, EDMUND A. SHOUSE, EDWIN H. SKIRVING, CHARLES L. SMEIDLE, CHRISTIAN F. SMITH, CHARLES M. STOUT, ARTHUR L. VAN VLECK, JOHN A. WITMER, JOHN F. WOOD.

and underneath the words of Plato:

"HENCE IT IS THAT THE FATHERS OF THESE MEN,

AND THEMSELVES TOO, BEING NURTURED IN ALL FREEDOM
AND WELL BORN, HAVE SHOWN BEFORE ALL MEN DEEDS
MANY AND GLORIOUS IN PUBLIC AND PRIVATE, DEEMING
IT THEIR DUTY TO FIGHT FOR FREEDOM AND THEIR
COUNTRY, EVEN AGAINST THEIR COUNTRYMEN."

At three o'clock in the afternoon, an hour earlier than
had been fixed, the Society members and their guests
(among whom were a number of ladies), together with
the pupils of the Institution, sat down to an old-fashioned
supper in the Hall Chapel. Six tables, each extending
the length of the large apartment, and profusely laden
with wholesome meats and cakes, were surrounded with
an array of happy faces indulging without restraint in
the good cheer and social pleasures of the occasion.
Upward of three hundred and fifty persons shared the
bountiful repast.

After supper the President called the meeting to order,
and, having made a few introductory remarks, proposed
as a sentiment "The Keystone State," to which ex-Governor Curtin, having been called for, rose amid enthusiastic cheering and responded :

"I congratulate you on the pleasure—*I may say pleasure*—of this occasion. I congratulate you on having
assembled to pay homage to the memories and to extol
the virtues of those of your brethren who so faithfully
served and died in the service of their country. I thank
you for erecting this monument to their memory. I thank
you, because that, while Chief Magistrate of this Commonwealth, I made promises which are thus in part
fulfilled. It is an example which, let us trust, will be
imitated all over our State. The proportion killed of
those who entered the service was nearly ten per cent.,
or about three hundred thousand of the whole—half the

population of Philadelphia, the second city in the Union
and the fourth in the world. Our country was saved at
the cost of three thousand millions of treasure, but our
country was worth it all. We living know that the
country they died to save was worth it all, and more.
It is now no time to inquire into the causes of the gigantic
rebellion. History will record that eight millions of people suddenly struck at the rights and institutions of twenty
millions, as well as their own. The government was at
last saved. It has filled our land with widows and orphans, and with named and unnamed graves. It has
also left in our midst numberless maimed, decrepid and
diseased soldiers, who are left to grind organs at the corners of streets and to beg their way from door to door.
This should not be. It is our duty to provide for them
at all times, and to provide asylums for them, not as a
charity, but as something they may demand as a right.
While the monarchies of Europe always make provision
for their disabled soldiers, ours are living monuments of
broken pledges and ingratitude. We engaged them to
enter the service, and made promises which have not
been redeemed. Let us take them from the highways
and the byways, and place them in positions of ease and
comfort which they so richly deserve. I, as Chief Magistrate of this Commonwealth, had a right to make such
pledges, and demand that the present authorities fulfil
them. I thank you for the opportunity afforded me of
speaking on this subject, and of asking that, while we remember the dead, our living heroes may also have their
due and just reward. I commend them for what they
have done. I will say these things wherever I go, and
wage war in their behalf until their claims are recognized
and satisfied also by those whose duty it is to take counsel
for their welfare. I had much to do with the men who

entered our military organizations during the rebellion,
and I feel a personal interest in this matter ; and though
on this occasion I might have dwelt upon a more agreeable subject, I could not have enforced a higher duty.
Honor the living as you honor the dead.   If your blessings on the latter were flowers, their graves would be
clad in perpetual bloom ; and why should not the flowers
of gratitude perfume the path of the former through life?"

The speaker sat down amid a storm of applause, and
the band struck up Hail Columbia.

President Smith having proposed "The Army of the
United States," Major General Humphreys, in acknow-
ledging the sentiment, said :

" MR. PRESIDENT, LADIES AND GENTLEMEN: I feel
most happy in meeting you here to-day, though the object of our assembling brings up before the mind many
sad reflections.   There is, however, a melancholy pleasure
in perpetuating the memory of the deeds of our brave
and patriotic schoolmates, as we do this day by the erection of this beautiful and fitting monument.   It is now
forty years since I was last here as a school-boy, and the
recollections of those days are of a most pleasing character.   The mild and parental discipline, the wholesome
moral and religious influence that this Institution has ever
thrown around its pupils gave a bent to my mind and
character for which I am very thankful.   If I have
achieved any success in life, or have been enabled to
render any service to my country or to my fellow-men, I
attribute all to the advantages which I received in this
Institution.   A review of my life, which I have made
here to-day, binds my affections very strongly to Nazareth Hall.   Permit me, Mr. President, in conclusion, to
thank the Committee of Arrangements for the very great
pleasure I have enjoyed in meeting so many of my friends

here to-day, and also for the personal kindness which I have received at their hands."

Major General McIntosh was now called for, and, in response to the demonstrative summons, spoke as follows:

"MR. PRESIDENT AND FRIENDS: Although I feel much pleasure in meeting you under the present circumstances, yet when you call on me to make a speech, you call me out of my usual line; but anticipating that I might be expected to say something, I shall fall behind my masked battery, where I have a shot in reserve."

(Drawing out his notes from the breast of his coat, amid general and hearty applause, he continued:)

"Mr. President, this is my first visit to Nazareth after an absence of thirty years, and I am highly gratified that it should be on an occasion like the present, notwithstanding memories of a mixed character cluster around it.

"For those of our classmates who gave their lives in defence of their country we do but pay a fitting tribute to their memories in the beautiful monument which we have this day dedicated. To old Nazareth Hall they owed much of that self-discipline and that spirit of faithfulness to the claims of duty which called them to the nation's defence and enabled them to do their duty as soldiers. We must also be reminded to-day of others of our former companions who strayed away from their allegiance and were hurried by prejudice or passion into the adoption of the heresy of secession; over the memory of those let us spread the broad mantle of charity. Many of them also perished; but as we cannot perpetuate their names in marble, let us who were the victors in that terrible struggle cherish in our hearts a loving and beautiful charity for their memories. In conclusion, ladies and gentlemen, I shall write down this day as one of the memorable days of my life."

22

Brigadier General Michler, being next called for, arose and said :

"Mr. President: The Army of the United States, to which I have the honor to belong, has been so well represented by my brother officers, Generals Humphreys and McIntosh, that I feel there is nothing left for me to say.

"You will permit me, however, to express my gratification at being present on this occasion, and accept my thanks for the hospitality extended to us with so lavish a hand."

General James L. Selfridge, of Bethlehem, in response to a call to speak, remarked that he did not know what to say after what had already been said ; that he had not been educated at the Hall, but sincerely wished he had been ; and would call upon Major Samuel Wetherill, of Philadelphia, to speak for the volunteer service.

Colonel Wetherill said that he came to hear and not to be heard. In the late rebellion the volunteers did to the best of their ability what they could. In some cases he knew they had failed, but they always did the best, and endeavored to serve their country faithfully. In conclusion, he remarked he had "a crow to pick" with General Selfridge for calling him before the audience.

Mr. Seth W. Paine, of Troy, Pa., proposed "The Moravian Institutions of Learning." The sentiment was seconded by the Rev. E. N. Potter, of the Lehigh University, who, in the course of his remarks, referred to the successful work of the Moravian Church in the department of education ; congratulated Nazareth Hall upon its record in the past, presented greeting from the Lehigh University, and expressed the hope that success might attend the efforts of both Institutions in the noble work they had undertaken for all the future.

Governor Curtin being about to retire, the audience rose to their feet and once more testified their esteem of the patriotic Governor by enthusiastic cheers.

The military record of Nazareth Hall was now communicated. Of the two hundred and sixty-two names of former pupils enrolled on its pages, two hundred and thirty-four enlisted in the Union, and twenty-eight in the so-called Confederate Army. Twenty-seven of the former were killed in battle or died of disease contracted in the service; one, Clarence E. Siewers, is missing, and five rose to the rank of General. Of those who fought under the latter flag, five were killed and three rose to the rank of General.

It was moved and seconded that the above report be preserved among the archives of the Society.

Prof. Philip A. Cregar hereupon offered the following sentiment: "Our patriotic dead associates—May their memory not only be perpetuated by the monument which we have this day dedicated, but may it be cherished in our hearts and embalmed in our memories." In response to this the audience rose to their feet.

Mr. James Lee, Jr., of Boston, and Mr. E. F. Bleck, of Bethlehem, were then called for. The latter proposed a resolution of thanks on the part of the Society to Rev. Edmund de Schweinitz for his eloquent address, requesting a copy of the same for publication and distribution among former pupils of the Hall.

Rev. Joseph D. Philip, Brooklyn; Rev. A. A. Reinke, New York; Rev. Edward Rondthaler, Brooklyn; Rev. E. H. Reichel, Nazareth, and Rev. L. R. Huebner, Bethlehem, responded at greater or less length to the calls made upon them.

The Committee on Nominations proposed the following officers of the Reunion Society for the ensuing year:

President.

HENRY SMITH, Burlington, N.J.

Vice Presidents.

ELIHU L. MIX, New Haven.
SETH W. PAINE, Troy, Pa.
THOMAS SPARKS, Philadelphia.
MAJ.-GEN. ANDREW A. HUMPHREYS, U.S.A.

Committee of Arrangements.

REV. ROBERT DE SCHWEINITZ, Bethlehem.
REV. EUGENE LEIBERT, Nazareth.
WILLIAM H. JORDAN, Philadelphia.
RICHARD R. TSCHUDY, Litiz.
MAURICE C. JONES, Bethlehem.
GEORGE A. KOHLER, Philadelphia.
LEBBEUS CHAPMAN, JR., New York.
LAZARUS D. SHOEMAKER, Wilkesbarre.
MAJ.-GEN. JOHN B. MCINTOSH, U. S. A.
BRIG.-GEN. NATHANIEL MICHLER, U. S. A.

Secretary and Historian.

EUGENE L. SHAEFER.

Assistant Secretary.

THEODORE M. RIGHTS.

Treasurer.

MAURICE C. JONES.

Before the question of their adoption was put to the vote, President Smith begged leave to observe that he thought it was time some other " Old Boy" take his place. He felt so young to-day he refused being considered one of that class any longer. Rotation in office was a law without exception. Professor Cregar hereupon expressed the unanimous sense of the Society in declaring that the only rotation in office in the present case it could tolerate was a fresh rotation of Mr. Smith into the position he had so long and acceptably filled. The nominations, unchanged, were accordingly accepted.

A resolution of thanks to Mr. William H. Jordan, for his untiring labors in the work which on this day had been happily consummated, was proposed by Prof. Cregar, and most cordially adopted.

In conclusion, a vote of thanks was passed to the Principal of Nazareth Hall for his warm reception and hospitable entertainment of the members of the Society and guests of the day.

The long-metre doxology,

"Praise God from whom all blessings flow,"

was then sung, and the meeting dissolved.

The sympathy with the movement which resulted in the erection of the Nazareth Memorial was not confined to those who were immediately interested—to parents and friends of the fallen, or to comrades by whom the project has been conceived, and by whose energy it was successfully completed. Its expression by communities and the public, in different and distant parts of the country, was an evidence that the object harmonized with the common impulse of our nature, which instinctively seeks to award the meed of honor to the good and the brave. Early aware of this, the Society's officer who managed the perplexing details of the project to its realization was encouraged in the disinterested labor of love he had undertaken; for, with but few exceptions, his call for aid and assistance met with a generous response. The names of those who contributed toward liquidating the expense of the beautiful Cenotaph appear elsewhere in this volume. An acknowledgment here of the courtesy of Messrs. Edward Armstrong and Robert H. Sayre, of the North Pennsylvania and Lehigh Valley Railroads; to Messrs. Wm. J. & S. H. Horstmann, of Philadelphia, for the presentation of an American flag for use on the memorial day, and to Professor Philip A. Cregar and Mr. Maurice C. Jones for special services rendered, is thought to be only just and eminently proper.

THE

MILITARY AND NAVAL RECORD

OF

A L U M N I

WHO WERE ENROLLED IN THE SERVICE OF THE
UNITED STATES.

MILITARY AND NAVAL RECORD.

CLASS OF 1822.

DAVID BAKER, killed March 8, 1862, on board the frigate Cumberland, during the engagement with the iron-clad steamer Merrimac. Fifteen minutes after being struck on her larboard side, the Cumberland went down with all on board, her tops only remaining above water, and the American flag flying at the peak. In that sunken ship lie the mortal remains of David Baker.

CLASS OF 1829.

CHARLES M. BERG, Acting Assistant Surgeon of an Ohio regiment, killed accidentally October 13, 1864, by the discharge of his own pistol, the contents of which entered his head, inflicting a mortal wound.

CLASS OF 1830.

FRANK POTT, Captain 27th Pennsylvania Volunteers, June 19, 1863, died December 17, 1867, of disease induced by excessive exposure while in the service.

3

CLASS OF 1835.

ARTHUR L. VAN VLECK, Private 126th Ohio Volunteers, died, as is supposed, in Libby Prison, December 21, 1863. The 126th distinguished itself as a regiment *especially* at Chancellorsville, and its members were presented with medals for bravery and meritorious conduct displayed on that hard-fought field. Mr. Van Vleck's medal was forwarded by him to his mother and sisters at Salem, N. C., through a friend who visited him while a prisoner on Belle Isle.

The subject of this memoir, a scholar and graduate of the Moravian Theological Seminary, exhibited already in childhood the love of country in a marked degree; impelled by which, he exchanged his peaceful walk in life for the din and tumult of the camp, there to learn how to fight for the country he so dearly loved, sensitive as a woman, and physically frail as he was. Beneath a quiet and undemonstrative exterior, there was, as his intimate associates unhesitatingly testify, a depth of feeling and a fixed determination of purpose to adhere to that mode of action which the principles of religion and the dictates of conscience pointed out to him as right. No wonder, then, such being the man, that the whilom divinity student enlisted in defence of his country in the summer of 1862, and, as a private of the 126th Ohio Volunteers, endured the hardships of a soldier's life, cheerfully and patiently, in the spirit of a true soldier of the cross. "*Ever*," as his comrades testify, "*was he true to duty;*" on all occasions manifesting friendly solicitude for their spiritual welfare, encouraging such as were professors of religion to "be not weary in well-doing" and to approve themselves faithful followers of the Captain of their salvation, and recommending the blessed cause of his heavenly

Master to the indifferent, the heedless and the profane; and thus his record is a double one, for he fought for his country and for his God.

On October 14, 1863, he was taken prisoner at Bristow Station, conveyed to Richmond and placed on Belle Isle. The trials and privations he had previously undergone had so weakened his delicate frame that disease found him an easy victim; and far away from the peaceful associations of his former life, with neither mother nor sisters to smooth his dying pillow—and yet we believe in the full enjoyment of an apocalypse as heavenly as was that granted to the patriarch of old, who saw angels ascending and angels descending—the Christian soldier breathed his last on the 21st of December, 1863, exchanging the horrors of a prison for the celestial Paradise.

Mr. Van Vleck's family never learned the full particulars of his death; but they knew that he was always looking for the summons to that land where there is no war nor rumors of war; and being assured that death to him at any time would be but the portal to everlasting bliss, they mourn not as those who have no hope.

Class of 1841.

CHARLES M. STOUT, Lieutenant 36th Pennsylvania Volunteers, August 1, 1862. Adjutant, December 1, 1862. Discharged November 13, 1863. Joined the Western army, and served again in Virginia, participating in the battle of the Wilderness, since which time he has never been seen or heard of by his comrades and relatives.

Class of 1843.

EUGENE FERD. CLEWELL, Private 19th Iowa Volunteers, enlisted November 16, 1863; died of chronic dysentery in hospital at New Orleans, September 5, 1864.

CLASS OF 1845.

HERMAN L. BEITEL, Private 165th Ohio Volunteers, enlisted October 5, 1861; killed September 7, 1863, in the battle of Chattanooga.

CLASS OF 1847.

CHARLES L. SMEIDLE, Second Lieutenant 21st Illinois Volunteers (Gen. U. S. Grant's regiment), April, 1861. Appointed First Lieutenant for meritorious conduct in the battle of Murfreesboro', Tenn., December 31, 1862. Also, on the same occasion, promoted Judge Advocate on the staff of General J. C. Davis, and transferred successively to Generals Stanley's and Mitchell's staffs. At the close of the trial of the "Anderson Troop" he was attacked with pneumonia, and died April 27, 1863.

Numerous commendatory notices of Mr. Smeidle's services as officer and Judge Advocate, eliciting from Generals Rosencranz, Davis, Stanley and Mitchell frequent and open praise, are preserved on record.

CLASS OF 1848.

ASHER GAYLORD, Captain 143d Pennsylvania Volunteers. November 3, 1862. Wounded severely in the battles at Gettysburg and in the Wilderness. While still suffering from the effects of his wounds, he again volunteered, against the advice of his family and superior officers, and was killed in the battle at Hatcher's Run, February 7, 1865.

The brigade in which he fought on that occasion, encountering a strong body of the enemy in the woods, was hard pressed and obliged to retreat, and thus his company was unable to bear off the dead body of their captain, which they saw lying on the field. No information has been received regarding its disposition. Mr. Gaylord left a widow and two children to mourn his death.

CLASS OF 1849.

JOSEPH P. BACHMAN, First Lieutenant, and Assistant Surgeon 4th Kentucky Cavalry, enlisted November 21, 1863. Superintendent of hospital at Calhoun, Ga. Resigned December 9, 1864, on account of sickness, which occasioned his decease, at Hope, Ind., April 4, 1865.

CLASS OF 1853.

HORACE C. BENNETT, Captain 55th Pennsylvania Volunteers, killed October 22, 1862, in the battle of Pocotaligo, S. C., having been wounded in the groin by a minie ball, which severed an artery, causing death in fifteen minutes, without apparent suffering. A correspondent writes : " I never saw Captain Bennett more pleased than on the fatal day, as he started with his company on the double quick for the woods in front of the Confederate battery. When stopping at one of the frequent halts, he said to me, who was next to him on his right, 'I think I will be one of the first to fall on the field this day.' I made answer, advising him to dispel all such ideas from his mind. He replied, 'You know I am not afraid, but my mind tells me so.'

" When in line of battle he went through his men, giving them every encouragement, taking a position in front of his company, about two paces from where I stood. In a few moments after he received the fatal bullet. I thought he was only wounded, as he grasped his thigh with both hands, exclaiming, ' Boys, I am shot,' which were the last words I heard him say. A number of his comrades at once went to his assistance, and carried him off the field.   Captain Bennett had entered the service from motives of purest patriotism, was a brave young officer, and beloved by all who knew him for his many estimable qualities of mind and heart.   He died as a true soldier, at his post."

EDMUND A. SHOUSE, Private 1st Pennsylvania Volunteers, died August 20, 1863, at Easton, Pa., from typhoid fever contracted in the service.

JOHN F. WOOD, Second Lieutenant 58th Pennsylvania Volunteers, March 16, 1863.   Captain, September 30, 1864.   Died of disease at Richmond, Va., November 25, 1865.

DAVID TEFORD LATIMER, the first of the alumni who fell in defence of the Union.   Private 5th New York Volunteers (Duryea's Zouaves).   Killed in the battle of Big Bethel, June 10, 1861.

Captain Bradagee writes: "On the march the company to which David belonged was deployed as skirmishers, and while thus engaged with the enemy he received a rifle bullet in the shoulder.   He fell; but bleeding and in agony, his brave heart buoyed him up, and he rose to his knees as if to be his own avenger.   An officer told him to lie down, and even as he spoke another bullet crashed through his brain, and he fell dead."

The officer named above, who stood by David when he fell, had his pistol knocked from his belt and his sword broken by balls, and the soldier next to him, on the other side, was killed.

"A brave man and an honest soldier; his friends, while they deeply mourn his early death, can but feel a swelling pride to think how glorious was his fall."

VAN BRUNT M. BERGEN.—At the outbreak of the war, Mr. Bergen was following the pursuit of an artist, and in response to the first call for troops, in 1861, joined the 13th New York Volunteers, with whom he served four months in Virginia. On the second call he volunteered in the same regiment, and while belonging to it was offered and accepted the position of First Lieutenant 131st New York Volunteers, August 28, 1862. The 131st, after a short campaign in Virginia, was transferred to Banks' expedition, participating in the capture of Port Hudson, and in the Red River campaign. During the latter, Lieutenant Bergen was assigned, and filled with great satisfaction, the several positions of Assistant Inspector General of the 19th Army Corps, Post Adjutant of Brasher City and Ordnance Officer of Lafourche Middle District.

In the summer of 1862 his regiment and corps were ordered to join Sheridan in the Shenandoah Valley. He arrived at Harper's Ferry on the eve of the battle of Winchester, and while hastening to join his regiment was surprised by an order from General Stephenson (by command of General Sheridan), assigning him to the position of Ordnance Officer of the Middle Military District, which included all of Sheridan's army.

It was in the performance of the arduous duties of this position at an exciting period that he contracted a cold which, unattended, settled upon his lungs. Nevertheless he labored day and night until December of 1864, when he was ordered home by his superiors to recruit his health. He obeyed reluctantly; took his official papers with him in order to work them up, which he did personally, until failing health compelled him to employ an amanuensis. Thus, with harness on him, the resolute young officer died in Brooklyn, June 8, 1865, in the 27th year

of his age, on the very day on which his returns complete
were forwarded to Washington.

CLASS OF 1854.

JOHN A. WITMER, Orderly Sergeant 83d Ohio Volunteers, July 28, 1862, killed May 22, 1863, in the desperate charge on the enemy's works in the rear of Vicksburg.

Though only Sergeant at the time, he was in command
of his company, leading them up under a heavy cross-fire;
and, exposing himself fearlessly to the enemy's sharpshooters, he was wounded by three distinct shots, all
taking effect in the head. His comrades at once carried
him to the rear. He lingered four days, during which
time he suffered intense agony. His last words on the
battle-field, after receiving the order to charge, and while
springing from the ground where he and his men had
lain on their faces, were, "Boys, for God's sake stick to
me now!"

A few months after his death his family were presented
with a tribute of respect testifying to his excellence of
character—to the bravery he displayed at the battles
of Chickasaw Bluffs, Arkansas Post, Greenville, Port
Gibson, Black River—and how nobly he fell at Champion Hills. This testimonial is signed by Generals S.
G. Burbridge and R. Conover, of the 1st Brigade,
Colonel F. W. Moore and officers of the 83d Ohio Volunteers.

CHRISTIAN F. SMITH, Private 12th Pennsylvania Volunteers, April 25, 1861. A few months later transferred
to the Signal Corps, accompanying General Sherman's
expedition to South Carolina. Contracted diphtheria, and

died June 14, 1862, at the Legareville Hospital, St. John's Island, S. C.

JAMES INGERSOLL GRAFTON, youngest son of Major Joseph Grafton, U. S. A., who served in the war of 1812. Second Lieutenant 2d Massachusetts Volunteers, November 1, 1861. First Lieutenant 2d Massachusetts Volunteers, July 21, 1862. Captain 2d Massachusetts Volunteers, November 9, 1862. Killed in the battle of Averysborough, N. C., March 16, 1865.

He served faithfully with his regiment through all its hard service, declining a colonelcy on one occasion, from unwillingness to leave it. He was badly wounded in the head in the battle of Cedar Mountain, and severely in the leg at Chancellorsville, in consequence of which he was on both occasions off duty for several months.

In the autumn of 1863 the 2d Massachusetts was ordered to the West, and took part in Sherman's famous march. At Averysborough, N. C., they first encountered the enemy in force, and the action that followed is thus described by an eye-witness:

"At seven o'clock A. M., on the 16th, our brigade, with skirmishers in front, advanced over the works, and had proceeded but a short distance when we met the enemy's skirmish line. It was on our skirmish line, but a short distance in advance, that Captain Grafton was killed. He had command of his company and another, and worked hard with them, against heavy odds, until he was struck in the leg. He started to the rear, but, in his anxiety to do his whole duty, turned back to give some last instructions to his men, and received a mortal wound in the neck. He was seen staggering back, and was helped to the rear, but he never spoke, and died in a few minutes."

23 *

Major-General E. Slocum mentioned the circumstances of his fall in a letter to Governor Andrew of Massachusetts, stating Captain Grafton to have been one of the best officers under his command.

Lieutenant-Colonel Morse, commanding the regiment, wrote as follows to Captain Grafton's brother :

"JAMAICA PLAINS, May 1, 1865.

" Please, sir, to accept my sincere sympathy for the loss you have sustained by the death of your noble brother.   Although I never knew him before he joined the regiment, I have since that time been on terms of intimate friendship with him, and during the last three years have learned to love and respect him more than almost any man I ever knew.

" In everything he said and did he was always manly, honorable and noble ; he attracted respect and attention wherever he served, both from superiors and inferiors. We had a review a few days before the battle.   As the regiment passed the reviewing officer, General E. Slocum pointed out Captain Grafton to General Sherman, telling him what a fine officer he was.

" On the night of the battle some one told General Sherman that he had been killed that morning.   The General said, 'What, that splendid fellow that Slocum pointed out?'—and seemed to feel his death as a personal loss.

" I have seen and noticed the faces of a great many men as they stood up to meet death, but I have never seen on any of them such an expression of fearless gallantry as was on Captain Grafton's when I gave him his last order.   I was quite near him when I gave it ; he looked me full in the face to catch every word, then, fully understanding what I wanted, he turned and gave the necessary orders.   I shall never forget that face ; so cheer-

ful, so handsome, and yet so full of stern determination
to do or die.

" The records of our regiment can show the name of
no better man or better officer.

> " I am,
>> " Very truly, yours.
>>> " C. F. Morse."

Class of 1855.

George Lorillard Fream, Private 9th New York
State Militia, November 11, 1861, and clerk in Adjutant
General's Office. Killed at Front Royal, Va., June 18,
1862.

The sad story of his sufferings may best be gathered
from the following letter, received by your Recorder, under
date of February 23, 1863:

" Dear Sir: I have just been informed by Major-
General McDowell of your inquiries relative to George
L. Fream, of the 9th N. Y. S. M., and late clerk in my
office.

" It is with pain and regret that I have to convey the
intelligence of his death. We were *en route* from Front
Royal to Manassas by railroad. As the train started, he
attempted to jump into a freight car from the ground, as
there was no platform at the station. Endeavoring to
throw his leg in, in order to raise himself, and his strength
being unequal to the strain, he gradually relaxed his
grasp, sliding under, until his nerve failed him, when,
falling with both legs on the track, he was run over and
mangled in a most melancholy manner.

" He was taken to the General Hospital at Front Royal,
where every care and attention were taken to save his life.
Amputation was performed, but the shock to the system

had been so great that he died soon after. He had endeared himself to all with whom he had been connected, and his untimely fate will be mourned for many years to come. Your obedient servant,

"George B. Drake,

"Capt. and A. D. C., U. S. Army."

Surgeon Jesse W. Brock writes: "He suffered more than tongue can express, but was not heard to murmur at any time. The operation was performed about five o'clock P. M. on the 17th. He lived until the 18th, at 11 o'clock A. M. He was very patient amid all his sufferings, and only complained because *his was an accidental wound*, instead of one received on the field of battle. He was perfectly rational until within an hour of his death, and knew full well that his wound was fatal, and often spoke of you as his kind father and dear and affectionate mother."

Colonel J. W. Stiles, of 9th New York Regiment, writes: "It gives me pleasure to testify to the character of Mr. George L. Fream, who presented in an eminent degree the qualities of a soldier and a gentleman; and believe me when I say no one can miss him more than myself."

His remains are interred in a retired spot in the beautiful cemetery at Saugerties, N. Y., overlooking the Hudson, amid the scenes of his early childhood. The last letter received by his family, prior to his decease, is engraved upon his tombstone. It is briefly this:

"Dear Parents: The expected word has come. We move. I am perfectly resigned, and will do my duty. Your affectionate son,

"George."

Above these words are inscribed the legend, " *Our all for our Country*," and the name "*George*."

Mr. Fream was an only child of John and Adah Fream, and in his nineteenth year when he died.

DANIEL H. FASIG, Private 6th Pennsylvania Cavalry, August 8, 1861. Wounded at Gettysburg. Died August 30. 1863. at Camp Stoneman, near Washington, of disease contracted in the service.

CHARLES RYERSON, Private 1st Regiment, Excelsior Brigade, June 19, 1861. Killed in the battle of Williamsburg, Va., May 5, 1862, while in the act of loading his piece.

The following extracts from his letters exhibit the spirit and motive by which he was actuated, particularly when the news reached him of the disastrous rout of Bull Run. He writes :

" The regiment leaves to-night for the seat of war at only one hour's notice, so that we leave immediately. I just got my appointment as General Sickles' orderly this morning. but as soon as I heard that we were going to leave, I threw it up at once and joined my regiment. So good-bye ; think of me often. If I fall, remember it was in the cause of my country."

Again : " Soldiering is a very hard life, and I will be glad when the war is over, but I won't come home until it is. You may make up your minds that if we ever get into action I will win an honorable position, no matter at what cost, for I am determined never to return (God sparing my life) until I do win one."

In this spirit he went forth until he met the enemy at Williamsburg. The result we must let his friend Cary describe in a letter dated May 7, 1862 :

" Before this reaches you, you will see from the papers the horrible slaughter our regiment met with. Among the killed in our company is my friend Charley, your son. After the battle my first thought was about Charley. I found his body, but alas! he had gone to his long, silent home of death. I got a soldier to assist me, and we carried him from the battle-field, buried him and erected a soldier's monument inscribed with his name and regiment. I found his Bible, which he carried in his pocket through his entire service, lying by his side."

His captain and chaplain both testify to his being a true soldier and a fine young man.

CLASS OF 1856.

BENJAMIN F. LANDELL, Private 88th Pennsylvania Volunteers, August 29, 1861. Killed by a musket ball in the battle of Antietam, September 17, 1862.

CLARENCE KAMPMAN, October 25, 1864, appointed Captain's Clerk by Admiral S. P. Lee, commanding Mississippi Squadron. Died at Mound City, Ills., June 4, 1865.

"FLAGSHIP TEMPEST, June 5, 1865.

"MY DEAR SIR: I regret to announce to you the death of our amiable and excellent friend, Clarence Kampman, who died last evening of acute dysentery on board the Hospital Ship 'Red Rover.' He was under the care of Fleet Surgeons Pinkney and Bradley, two accomplished medical officers of this squadron, and received every care and attention.

" He had previously had an attack of jaundice, followed some time after by erysipelas, for which he had been under treatment on board the hospital ship for some time, and had just recovered from it, when he was attacked with dysentery on Tuesday last. He was buried this evening at the Naval Burying-ground, near Mound City Naval Station. Such of his effects as were not burnt with the 'Black Hawk' will be packed up and held subject to the order of his family, to whom the surgeon of the 'Red Rover' announced his death. His accounts will be transferred to the Fourth Auditor.

> "Respectfully and truly yours,
> "S. P. LEE,
> "A. R. Admiral.

"MR. DELANO, Washington, D. C."

CLASS OF 1858.

WILLIAM W. LADD, Private 2d New Jersey Cavalry, enlisted July 15, 1863, in the sixteenth year of his age.

He was taken sick in camp at Columbus, Kentucky, and died in a negro cabin of disease contracted in the army, December 15, 1863, after a service of nearly six months.

He was a bright, intelligent boy, of manly address, and left a home of ease and affluence, with the prospect of fortune, although young and delicate, to serve the government and to help defeat the Rebellion. He was faithful as a soldier, and much loved by his comrades.

JOHN C. HAGEN, Private 2d Pennsylvania Cavalry, February 6, 1865. Contracted typhoid fever while encamped at Cloud's Mills, near Alexandria, Va., and discharged from the service in consequence, July 13, 1865. Brought home to Bethlehem, Pa., and died August 7, 1865.

CLASS OF 1860.

PLINY A. JEWETT, JR., Private 1st Connecticut Cavalry; enlisted March 11, 1863, and killed at Harper's Farm, Va., April 6, 1865.

At the time of his decease he held the position of Quartermaster Sergeant, and had received the day before a recommendation from his colonel for promotion as lieutenant for bravery.

Was taken prisoner near Harper's Ferry, and confined six weeks on Belle Isle. He participated with his regiment in General Sheridan's raid around Richmond, Va.

CLASS OF 1861.

EDWIN H. SKIRVING, at the time of General Early's raid upon Washington, was studying engineering at the Washington Navy Yard, and volunteered with other employés in defence of the city.

His company camped around Fort Lincoln, performing guard duty. At night they were obliged to lie upon the ground outside of the fortification, without any shelter, not even a blanket being provided for them.

He remained exposed in this way for three days and three nights, and returned home in ill health. In a few days he took his bed, and died on July 25, 1864.

* What errors occur in the Military and Naval Record, and in the dates of entrance of the Alumni present at the Reunion of June 11, 1868, the Recorder begs to state, are in consequence of incorrect information furnished at the time of compilation, and discovered too late for correction.

ROLL OF ALUMNI WHO SERVED IN THE UNITED STATES ARMY OR NAVY.

CLASS OF 1810.

GILES PORTER was graduated at West Point, July 24, 1818, and promoted Second Lieutenant corps of artillery U. S. Army. Captain, September 30, 1833, and Major 4th Artillery, February 16, 1847. Served in the Florida war against the Seminole Indians, 1836, '37, '38. Retired September 31, 1861, after more than forty consecutive years of service.

CLASS OF 1822.

ANDREW A. HUMPHREYS was graduated at West Point, July 1, 1831, and promoted Second Lieutenant 2d Artillery U. S. Army. First Lieutenant August 16, 1836, serving in the Florida war. First Lieutenant Corps of Topographical Engineers, July 7, 1838. Captain, May 31, 1848. Major, August 6, 1861. Colonel of Staff, March 5, 1862. Lieutenant-Colonel Engineers, March 3, 1863. Brevet Brigadier-General, March 13, 1865. Brevet Major-General U. S. A., March 13, 1865. Brigadier-General Volunteers, April 28, 1862. Major-General Volunteers, July 8, 1863. Served throughout the war in Virginia, participating in the numerous battles and engagements of the Army of the Potomac. Appointed Chief Topographical Engineer Army of the Potomac under Major-General George B. McClellan, and Chief of Staff under Major-General George G. Meade. Commanded 3d Division 5th Corps, and 2d Division 3d Corps. Commanded 2d Army Corps. Distinguished himself (particularly) in the battles of Gettysburg and Fredericksburg. At the latter place he had two horses killed under him,

24

all his staff but one dismounted, three of them wounded, and for one hour was exposed to a deadly fire, within one hundred yards of the stone wall held by the enemy, while he vainly endeavored to retrieve the fortunes of the day, being deliberately shot at by sharpshooters whenever the heavy musketry and artillery fire abated. Had a horse killed under him at Gettysburg. Never wounded, and had many miraculous escapes from death. August 8, 1866, Brigadier-General and Chief of Engineers U. S. A., in command of the Corps of Engineers, headquarters Washington, D. C. Still in the service.

Class of 1827.

Samuel Penington, Captain 5th Delaware Volunteers. November 6, 1862. Served in Maryland. Mustered out of service August 6, 1863.

Class of 1828.

Thomas Sparks, largely instrumental in organizing and equipping 1st Regiment Pennsylvania Gray Reserves. Commissioned Lieutenant Company A, April 19, 1861. Displayed great ability, when detached and stationed at Philadelphia, as Chief Recruiting Officer and Commissary of Supplies during the invasions. Lieutenant Pennsylvania Minute Men. April 19, 1862, presented with an elegant testimonial by the officers of the Gray Reserves, for efficient services rendered the regiment while in service. Received two other testimonials at a later period of the war.

Class of 1829.

William P. Levy, Private Pennsylvania Volunteers.

Class of 1830.

John J. Garvin, Captain U. S. steam transport Union,

Quartermaster General's Department, September, 1861. Ordered to carry supplies for General Sherman's expedition against Port Royal, S. C., October 29, 1861. Encountered a fearful gale, and to save his crew was compelled to run the vessel on the beach at Bogue Island, N. C., as it was barely possible to keep her afloat. Fell into the enemy's hands, and was a prisoner eight months at Fort Macon, Raleigh, Salisbury, N. C., and Libby Prisons. Exchanged, August 17, 1862. Reappointed Captain of steam transport John Rice. Resigned, August 15, 1863.

CLASS OF 1831.

NATHANIEL S. WOLLE, Private Pennsylvania State Militia, July, 1863.

CLASS OF 1832.

WILLIAM P. SMITH, First Lieutenant 198th Pennsylvania Volunteers. Wounded at Charles City ⅹ Roads, and at Hatcher's Run. Served four years in Virginia.

WILLIAM H. THOMPSON, Lieutenant-Colonel 38th Pennsylvania State Militia, July 3, 1863.

WILLIAM H. BUTLER, Clerk to Colonel Ingalls. Post Commissary at White House, Virginia, May, June, July, 1861.

BENJAMIN F. GARVIN entered the U. S. Navy, March 29, 1847. Appointed Chief Engineer, ranking with Commander, May 11, 1858. Fleet Engineer Mediterranean Sea Squadron. Fleet Engineer of Admiral Lee's North Carolina Squadron, which captured City Point, Fort Fisher, etc. Was on board the Frigate Colorado (first rate) at the capture of Fort Fisher. Still in the service.

CLASS OF 1833.

WILLIAM KISSAM, Corporal 27th New Jersey Volunteers, September 4, 1862. Served in Virginia. Honorably discharged, July 2, 1864.

CHARLES E. SMITH, Major 11th Michigan Cavalry, August 31, 1863. Colonel, June 12, 1864. Brigadier-General U. S. Vols., March 13, 1865. Served in Virginia, Tennessee, North and South Carolina and Georgia. In the battle of Cynthiana, Ky., had his horse killed under him, and another wounded. Mustered out of service, August, 1865.

GILES B. OVERTON raised a company for the 42d Pennsylvania Volunteers (Bucktails), and before mustered into service appointed Captain 14th U. S. Infantry, June 18, 1861. Served in Virginia on the staff of Major-General Sykes. Brevet Major, March 13, 1865. Wounded at Chancellorsville in the thigh-bone, and still carries the bullet. Resigned July 25, 1865.

CLASS OF 1835.

JOHN J. PETERS, Private 15th New York Cavalry, September 3, 1864. Served in Virginia. Discharged on account of disability induced by typhoid fever, June 12, 1865.

WILLIAM HIGGINS, Private 2d New York Volunteers, April 26, 1861. Served three months.

MATHIAS T. HUEBNER, Private Pennsylvania State Militia, July, 1863.

SAMUEL RICE, Private 46th Pennsylvania Volunteers.

August 8, 1861. Detached as Clerk Quartermaster General's Department to September 17, 1864. Re-enlisted Private 97th Pennsylvania Volunteers. Served in Virginia, North Carolina and Georgia. Mustered out with his regiment, September, 1865.

SAMUEL C. WOLLE, Orderly Sergeant 38th Pennsylvania State Militia, June 30, 1863. Mustered out with his regiment, August 7, 1863.

CLASS OF 1836.

GEORGE P. IHRIE, Brevet Brigadier-General U. S. Army. June 12, 1862, Aide-de-Camp of General U. S. Grant in the siege of Corinth, serving respectively as Acting Inspector General and Commissary of Musters. Distinguished himself in the defence of Trenton, Tenn., December, 1862, saving from capture the railroad trains there. He continued with General Grant until April, 1863. Still in the service.

NATHANIEL MICHLER was graduated at West Point, July 1, 1848, and promoted Brevet Second Lieutenant Topographical Engineers. Second Lieutenant, April 7, 1854. First Lieutenant, May 19, 1856. Captain, September 9. 1861. Major, April 22, 1864. Brevet Lieutenant-Colonel, August 1, 1864. Brevet Colonel, April 2, 1865. Chief of Topographical Engineers Army of the Cumberland, on the Staff of Major-General D. C. Buell; also, under Generals Rosecrans and Sherman, until transferred to the Army of the Potomac. Captured near Rockville, Md., June 28, 1863, and paroled. Constructed defences on the Maryland Heights, at Harper's Ferry. Brevet Brigadier-General U. S. Army, April 2, 1865, for gallant and meritorious conduct during the war. Still in the service.

24 *

CLASS OF 1837.

JOHN BAILLIE McINTOSH, son of Colonel James S. McIntosh, U. S. A., killed in the storming of Molino del Rey, Mexico, September 8, 1847. Colonel Third Pennsylvania Cavalry, September 23, 1862. Brigadier-General, July 21, 1864. Brevet Major-General U. S. Army, March 13, 1865. Served in Virginia. Had a leg shattered by a minie ball while gallantly leading his brigade at the battle of Opequan, Va., September 19, 1864, rendering amputation necessary.

Highly complimented by General Sheridan in his report of the battle of Abram's Creek, Va. General A. T. A. Torbet describes the action as follows:

"On the 13th of September the Second Brigade, 3d Division (Brigadier-General McIntosh commanding), moved up the Berryville and Winchester pike, drove the enemy's cavalry before them three miles, and within two miles of Winchester came upon a regiment of infantry (the 8th South Carolina). By a sudden dash of the 3d New Jersey and 2d Ohio Regiments the 8th South Carolina was broken, completely surrounded, and the entire regiment, officers, men and colors, marched into camp. Too much praise cannot be given General McIntosh for his quick decision and gallantry on the occasion." Still in the service.

WILLIAM FINLAYSON, Private 23d Pennsylvania Volunteers, served in Virginia. In service two years. Deceased.

CLASS OF 1838.

WILLIAM H. MOORE, Captain 12th New Jersey Volunteers, September 8, 1862.

LEBBEUS CHAPMAN, JR., Brigade Quartermaster 11th Brigade New York National Guards, June 23, 1863. Captain on staff of Brigadier-General J. C. Smith.

CLASS OF 1839.

WILLIAM J. DIXON, Surgeon in a Western regiment.

LEWIS R. HUEBNER, Corporal 34th Pennsylvania State Militia, July 3, 1863.

CLASS OF 1840.

OTHNIEL DE FOREST, Colonel 5th New York Cavalry, October 1, 1861. Served in Virginia. Honorably discharged, March 29, 1864. Died in 1867.

THOMAS L. MCKEEN, JR., Major 38th Pennsylvania State Militia, July 3, 1863.

CLASS OF 1841.

ROBERT A. CLEWELL, Private 129th Pennsylvania Volunteers, August 12, 1862, to May 18, 1863. Served in Virginia. First Sergeant 202d Pennsylvania Volunteers, September 2, 1864. Mustered out of service, August 3, 1865. Died June 30, 1867.

CHARLES T. HARRISON served in the army and navy. Dangerously wounded before Petersburg, Virginia.

CLASS OF 1842.

ANDREW A. RIPKA, Captain 119th Pennsylvania Volunteers, September 1, 1862. Served in Virginia. Resigned on account of illness, March 3, 1865.

JOHN M. WINPENNY, Private 19th Pennsylvania Volunteers, April 27, 1861. Served in Maryland. Mustered out with his regiment, August 29, 1861.

HENRY A. TROEGER, Private 10th Illinois Volunteers, August 28, 1861. Served in Tennessee, Alabama and Mississippi. Detached as Chief Surgeon's Clerk at the Nashville Hospitals. Discharged on account of disability, resulting from exposure, December 2, 1863.

EDWIN J. BACHMAN, First Lieutenant 33d Indiana Volunteers, August 22, 1861. Detached Acting Assistant Quartermaster of Colonel John Coburn's Brigade. Chief of Ordnance Army of Kentucky, on the staff of Major-General Gordon Granger. Participated in General Sherman's march. Three years in the service.

CLASS OF 1843.

THOMAS OVERINGTON, Private 6th Pennsylvania State Militia, September, 1862.

WILLIAM R. THOMAS, First Lieutenant 46th Pennsylvania Volunteers, September 4, 1861. Served in Virginia. Resigned in consequence of illness, April 4, 1862.

AMOS C. CLAUDER, Private 34th Pennsylvania State Militia. July 3, 1863. Died October 14, 1868, at Bethlehem, Pa.

CLARENCE MICHLER, Captain 1st Louisiana Cavalry. Appointed Inspector of Cavalry of the Military Division of the West Mississippi, on the staff of General Davidson. Wounded, and served throughout the war.

CLASS OF 1844.

ALFRED B. DAVIS, Acting Master U. S. Navy, for

special duty as Pilot attached to North Atlantic Blockading Squadron. November 5. 1864.

SAMUEL G. SPACKMAN, Hospital Steward 12th New York National Guards Regiment, June 20, 1863.

HENRY T. BACHMAN, Private Captain J. D. Cunning's Ohio Cavalry, July 25, 1863. Volunteered to repel the invasion of General John Morgan.

JOHN J. HESS, Quartermaster 119th Pennsylvania Volunteers, August 5, 1862. Served in Virginia. Honorably discharged. February 27, 1864.

STEPHEN SUTTON, Private 1st Minnesota Volunteers. Served three years.

ISAAC PRINCE, Special Delegate U. S. Christian Commission, June 22, 1864, to minister to the sick and wounded soldiers in the military hospitals and on the battle-fields throughout the country. July, 1865, received a commission from the American Missionary Association to minister to the spiritual welfare of 3d U. S. Colored Cavalry, stationed at Hilton Head, S. C. Served in Virginia and South Carolina.

CLASS OF 1845.

CHARLES GOEPP, First Lieutenant 9th Pennsylvania Volunteers, April 24, 1861. Acting Adjutant, May 15, 1861. Mustered out with his regiment, July 29, 1861.

JOHN J. PERKIN, Private of a battery of artillery. Served in Virginia.

CLASS OF 1846.

GRANVILLE HENRY, Private 34th Pennsylvania State

Militia, June, July, August, 1863. Contracted severe illness during his term of service.

EDWIN HOUSEL, Private 2d New Jersey Volunteers, April 26, 1861. Served in Virginia. Died at Elizabethport, N. J., August 2, 1861.

HENRY K. THOMAE, Private 7th New York Volunteers, April 19, 1861.

JACOB O. BROWN, Fifer 3d New Jersey Volunteers. Served nine months.

GEORGE F. THOMAE, Private 7th New York Volunteers, April 19, 1861.

OLIVER T. BEARD, Private 71st New York State Militia, April 21, 1861. Detached Lieutenant 28th New York S. M., and mustered out as Captain. Major 48th New York Volunteers, August 8, 1861, in General McClellan's Army of the Potomac. Ordered with his regiment to join General W. T. Sherman's expeditionary force to Hilton Head, S. C. After the battle there fought, promoted Lieutenant-Colonel, and Provost Marshal of the Southern Department. Colonel Beard here rendered valuable services in removing obstructions from the inlets below Savannah, in planting batteries on the swampy sea-islands, and by a secret mission into the city, for which he was publicly commended by the commanding general, and also by Admiral Dupont. Promoted Colonel of a negro regiment, and was the first officer to lead colored troops into action. Served in this capacity in Florida.

CHARLES HENRY HUTCHINSON, Private 19th Pennsylvania Volunteers, April 27 to August 29, 1861. Lieutenant of a New York regiment, and afterward appointed Independent Scout of the Army of the Potomac. In service three years.

CLASS OF 1847.

HENRY A. BIGLER, First Lieutenant 209th Pennsylvania Volunteers, September 16, 1864. Captain, May 16, 1865. Served in Virginia. Mustered out, May 31, 1865.

JOHN BARTRAM, Private 95th Pennsylvania Volunteers. Served in Virginia. Severely wounded.

JOHN TRUCKS, JR., Private 32d Pennsylvania State Militia, July, 1863.

WILLIAM H. CRAWFORD, First Lieutenant 153d Pennsylvania Volunteers, October 11, 1862. Served in Virginia. Mustered out with his regiment, July 24, 1863.

RICHARD R. TSCHUDY, First Lieutenant 12th Pennsylvania State Militia, September 16, 1862.

HENRY CREASE, Second Lieutenant 23d Pennsylvania Volunteers (Birney's Zouaves), July 17, 1861. Promoted First Lieutenant for gallantry at Gettysburg. Taken prisoner at White's Ford, September 12, 1862, and confined in Libby Prison twenty-five days, when exchanged. Wounded at Cold Harbor, June 1, 1864. Engaged in fifteen battles in Virginia. Honorably discharged, September 8, 1864. At present a Paymaster in U. S. Navy.

CLASS OF 1848.

FREDERIC A. CLAUDER, Private 1st Regiment Sickles' Excelsior Brigade, May 21, 1861. Served in Virginia. Honorably discharged, July 10, 1864.

OBADIAH T. HUEBNER, Sergeant 38th Pennsylvania State Militia. July, 1863.

JOSEPH BURKE, Private Anderson Cavalry, served in Kentucky, Tennessee, and in Sherman's famous march. In service three years.

PETER D. KEYSER, Captain 91st Pennsylvania Volunteers. September 20, 1861, on staff of Major-General Naglee. Served in Virginia. Wounded at Fair Oaks. Resigned on account of ill health, August 15, 1862. Re-entered the service as Acting Assistant Surgeon U. S. Army, from July, 1864, to March, 1865.

EYRE KEYSER, First Lieutenant 183d Pennsylvania Volunteers. Dangerously wounded in the head by a minie ball in the battle of the Wilderness, and again wounded at Cold Harbor, Va. Brevet Adjutant for gallantry. Mustered out of service, August 9, 1864.

CHARLES J. ANDERSON, New York Volunteers

CLASS OF 1849.

JAMES E. AUDENREID, Captain 2d Pennsylvania Cavalry, September 17, 1861. Served in Virginia. Wounded in the battles of Second Bull Run, of the Wilderness and of Deep Bottom; in the last engagement severely so, having been struck in the arm by a shell. Honorably discharged, October 6, 1864.

OWEN RICE, JR., Captain 153d Pennsylvania Volunteers, October 7, 1862. Wounded in the arm at Chancellorsville, Va. Mustered out of service, July 23, 1863.

CLARENCE E. SIEWERS, Private Battery 112th Pennsylvania Volunteers, December 9, 1861. Served in Virginia. In the service one year. Has never been seen or heard from by his comrades and relatives.

PHILIP S. P. WALTER, Assistant Surgeon 2d Pennsylvania Cavalry, February 12, 1863. Honorably discharged, December, 1863.

FRANK C. STOUT, Sergeant 129th Pennsylvania Volunteers, August 12, 1862, to January 8, 1863. Second Lieutenant 129th Pennsylvania Volunteers, March 28, 1863. Captain 34th Pennsylvania State Militia, June. July, August, 1863.

ABRAHAM C. DAVENPORT, Private 14th New York State Militia. September 6, 1862. Transferred to 5th New York Veteran Volunteers, June 2, 1864. Served in Virginia. In service two years and nine months.

CHARLES B. WAINWRIGHT, Private 17th Pennsylvania Volunteers, April 25, 1861. Mustered out, August 2, 1861. Served in Maryland.

BENJAMIN D. PHILIP, Second Lieutenant 14th New York Volunteers, June 10, 1861, and Aide-de-Camp to Colonel Alfred M. Wood. Served in Virginia. Severely wounded at the first battle of Bull Run. Honorably discharged on account of wounds, January 2, 1862. Deceased.

CLASS OF 1850.

HENRY A. TITZE, Orderly Sergeant 56th Illinois Volunteers, November 30, 1861. Discharged on account of illness, September 8, 1862. Re-enlisted 136th Illinois

25   T

Volunteers. May 13, 1864. Mustered out, October 22, 1864.

WILLIAM C. TITZE, Private 66th Illinois Volunteers, December 30, 1863. Detailed as Orderly at Headquarters Sixteenth Army Corps from May to September 2, 1864. Served in Tennessee. Georgia, South and North Carolina. Mustered out of service, July 15, 1865.

WILLIAM H. FENNER, Private 176th Pennsylvania Volunteers, November 3, 1862. Served in Virginia. Mustered out with his regiment, August 18, 1863.

REUBEN J. STOTZ, Second Lieutenant 153d Pennsylvania Volunteers, October 11, 1862. Served in Virginia. Mustered out with his regiment, July 24, 1863.

HENRY LEIBFRIED, Private 153d Pennsylvania Volunteers, October 7, 1862. Served in Virginia. Mustered out of service, July 23, 1863. Died August, 1867.

CLASS OF 1851.

JOHN FREDERIC R. FRUEAUFF, First Lieutenant 1st Pennsylvania Volunteers, April 20, 1861. Mustered out with regiment, July 27, 1861. Major 153d Pennsylvania Volunteers, October 11, 1862. Detached as Assistant Inspector General on staff of Major-General McLaws. Wounded slightly at Chancellorsville. Served in Maryland and in Virginia. Mustered out of the service, July 24, 1863.

SAMUEL LICHTENTHAELER, Private 5th Pennsylvania Militia, September, 1862.

JOHN PHILIP WENZEL, Lieutenant Pennsylvania Cavalry.

THOMAS EUGENE CUMMINS, Orderly Sergeant 17th New York Volunteers, June 21, 1862. Served in General W. T. Sherman's campaigns. Wounded in the shoulder at the battle of Secessionville, South Carolina, June 16, 1862. In service three years and ten months.

WILLIAM H. LOYD, Second Lieutenant 11th New Jersey Volunteers, August 11, 1862. First Lieutenant, November 17, 1862. Captain, March 9, 1863. Major 7th New Jersey Volunteers, October 17, 1864. Detached Assistant Adjutant General on staff of Major-Generals D. B. Birney and Pierce. Served in Maryland and Virginia. Wounded at Gettysburg and at Boynton Plank Road, Va. In the service two years and six months.

RICHARD HENRY CHAPMAN, Private 19th Pennsylvania Volunteers, April 27, 1861. Served in Maryland. Mustered out with his regiment, August 29, 1861.

CLASS OF 1852.

HENRY T. CLAUDER, Private 67th Indiana Volunteers, August 20, 1862. Served in Kentucky, Tennessee and Mississippi. Taken prisoner at Clumfordsville, Ky., and paroled December, 1862. Mustered out of service, June 20, 1865.

CHARLES V. HENRY, Private 10th New York Volunteers. Quartermaster 91st New York Volunteers, September 18, 1863. Major and Assistant Quartermaster 5th Army Corps, on staff of Major-General Warren, August 29, 1864. Brevet Lieutenant-Colonel, September 3. 1866. Served in Virginia, and in the Gulf Department under General Buell. Honorably discharged, November 19, 1866.

John W. Jordan, Assistant Commissary Starr's Philadelphia Battery, attached to 32d Pennsylvania State Militia, June, July, August, 1863.

Thomas V. Kessler, Private 8th Pennsylvania State Militia. Served in Maryland, July, 1863.

William H. H. Michler, Assistant Surgeon 1st Pennsylvania Volunteers, April 20, to July 27, 1861. Appointed Surgeon Mack's Regular Battery 4th U. S. Artillery. Stationed as Surgeon U. S. A. at Fort Union, New Mexico, January 1, 1869. Still in the service.

J. Theophilus Zorn, Private 38th Pennsylvania State Militia, July, 1863.

George A. Carey, Corporal 51st Pennsylvania Volunteers, August 20, 1861. Served in Virginia and North and South Carolina. Captured at the Weldon Railroad, and confined for seven months in Salisbury, Belle Isle and Libby Prisons. Mustered out of service, July 27, 1865.

William F. Harris, supposed to have been in the Navy, and known to have been washed overboard from a vessel while at sea.

George Williams, Quartermaster Sergeant 6th New York Independent Battery. Served in Virginia. Engaged in twenty-six battles. Declined accepting a commission, although frequently offered him during his three years of service. Drowned in 1864 at La Belle, Michigan.

William B. Persse, First Lieutenant 163d New York Volunteers, August 27, 1862. Served in Virginia. Honorably discharged, January 20, 1863.

CLASS OF 1853.

GEORGE W. SHIELDS, Acting Assistant Surgeon U. S. Navy, Mississippi Squadron, November 24, 1863. Died August 10, 1867, at New Orleans, of yellow fever.

THEODORE A. NIXON, Corporal 16th Indiana Volunteers, April 22, 1861. Mustered out, May 14, 1862. Died January 20, 1867.

GEORGE H. EPLEE, First Lieutenant 203d Pennsylvania Volunteers, September 12, 1864. Acting Adjutant General 2d Brigade, 2d Divison, 10th Army Corps. Served in Virginia and North Carolinia. Mustered out, June 22, 1865.

MARCELIN L. DE COURSEY, Private Commonwealth Artillery, April to August, 1861. Private Anderson Troop, October 5, 1861. Detached First Lieutenant 15th Pennsylvania Cavalry. Captain, March 15, 1863. Mustered out, October 23, 1863. Chief Clerk to Provost Marshal General Fry, at Washington, D. C., until April 1, 1865. Had a narrow escape from death in the battle of Stone River, Tenn., having his horse killed under him, pistol-holsters and spurs shot away, and two balls passing through his coat.

EDWIN LICHTENTHALER, Private 129th Pennsylvania Volunteers, August 15, 1862. Served in Virginia. In service two years.

EDWIN LONGMIRE, Second Lieutenant 2d Pennsylvania Artillery, December 16, 1861. Served in Virginia. Resigned June 29, 1862.

25 *

NATHANIEL C. LONGMIRE, Private 124th Pennsylvania Volunteers, August 18, 1862. Served in Virginia. Mustered out, May 17, 1863.

WILLIAM D. FIECHTNER, Private 195th Pennsylvania Volunteers, July, November, 1864.

HORACE HOMER, Assistant Surgeon Medical Department of the Susquehanna. Appointed Special Relief Agent U. S. Sanitary Commission. Served three years.

CAMILLUS NATHANS, Second Lieutenant New York Volunteers. Wounded in the hand and hip. Served in Virginia.

ANDREW D. HARPER, Private 13th New York State Militia.

EUGENE WALTER, Leader of Regimental Band 47th Pennsylvania Volunteers.

WILLIAM H. BIGLER, Private 34th Pennsylvania State Militia, July, 1863.

EDMUND A. OERTER, Private 38th Pennsylvania State Militia, July, 1863.

JOSEPH JOHN RICKSECKER, Private 5th Pennsylvania State Militia.

FRANCIS JORDAN, JR., Private Miller's Philadelphia Battery, September 11, 1862. Served in Maryland.

CLASS OF 1854.

WALTER BARRETT, Major 84th Pennsylvania Volunteers. August 30, 1861. Lieutenant-Colonel, June 21,

1862. Served in Virginia. Resigned on account of injuries received at Fairfax Court-house, September 10. 1862.

LOVELL PURDY, Major 5th New York Volunteers. Excelsior Brigade, August 27, 1861. Served in Virginia. Wounded in the battles of Williamsburg, Chancellorsville and the Wilderness. Honorably discharged on account of wounds received before Petersburg, June 19, 1864. Promoted Lieutenant-Colonel, September 3, 1866. by the U. S. Government, for gallant services during the war.

N. WALLER HORTON, First Lieutenant 9th Pennsylvania Cavalry, February 13, 1863. Captain, June 16. 1863. Served in Kentucky, Tennessee, North and South Carolina, Georgia and Alabama. Participated in twenty-eight battles. In the last of these, fought at Raleigh. N. C., he was taken prisoner, and after having been confined at Greensboro' for a month, was released. Wounded slightly at Eagleville, Tenn. Mustered out, July 18. 1865. In the service four and a half years.

FREDERIC M. SHOEMAKER, First Lieutenant 36th Pennsylvania Volunteers, February 20, 1862. Resigned July 11, 1862. Adjutant 143d Pennsylvania Volunteers, September 23, 1863. Honorably discharged, September 7, 1864.

BENNEVILLE M. HENRY, Leader 7th Pennsylvania Regimental Band, April 23 to July 29, 1861. Re-enlisted as musician 88th Pennsylvania Volunteers, April, 1863.

JAMES M. R. HARRIS, Private 33d Pennsylvania Volunteers, July 4, 1861. Served in Virginia. Captured before Richmond, and confined in Libby Prison two months, when exchanged. Wounded at Gaines' Mills, and on the second day of Seven Days' Battle. Lost his right eye by a bayonet in a skirmish near Manassas Junction. Honorably discharged from the service, October 27, 1862.

MATTHEW McILROY, Second Lieutenant 49th Pennsylvania State Militia, July 17, 1863. Veterinary Surgeon U. S. Engineer Corps. In the service seven months. Died March 2, 1868.

JOSEPH W. DRINKHOUSE, Private Independent Keystone Battery. Volunteered twice in the three months' service.

ALBERT REMICK, Corporal 40th Pennsylvania State Militia, July 2, 1863.

J. CUMMINGS VAIL, Private Serrell's New York Volunteer Engineers, October 15, 1861. Detached as Clerk of Adjutant General's Department, Port Royal, S. C. Appointed Flag Officer's Clerk on staff of Rear Admiral S. F. Dupont, U. S. Navy, April 24, 1862. Remained with Admiral Dupont until relieved from his command, July 4, 1863. Appointed Captain's Clerk U. S. steamer Iroquois. Honorably discharged from the service on account of illness at Rio de Janeiro, and reached New York January 19, 1865.

FRANK B. WOODALL, Major Illinois Regiment.

EDWIN G. KLOSÈ, Private 34th Pennsylvania State Militia, June 29, 1863.

W. H. THEOPHILUS HAMAN, Private 34th Pennsylvania State Militia, June 29, 1863.

JOHN D. WOLLE, Private 38th Pennsylvania State Militia, July, 1863.

WILLIAM F. BUCK, Private 18th Pennsylvania Volunteers, April 24, 1861. Mustered out, August 6, 1861. Third Assistant Engineer steamer J. E. Bazely, North Carolina Blockading Squadron. This vessel was blown up at the mouth of the Roanoke River by a torpedo. Escaped uninjured.

HENRY A. DAILY, Private 1st Pennsylvania Volunteers, April 18 to July 28, 1861. Private 51st Pennsylvania Volunteers, December 1, 1861. Detached 8th U. S. Infantry, October 28, 1862. Served in Virginia and North Carolina. In active service five years and six months, and never wounded or captured. Honorably discharged, February 22, 1867.

CHARLES A. PLACE, Private 13th New York Volunteers. April 23, 1861. Detached Second Lieutenant 15th Regiment of Engineers. Promoted Adjutant and Captain. Served in Virginia.

CHARLES HENDRICKSON, New York regiment.

CLASS OF 1855.

CORNELIUS A. SIMONSON, Private 9th New York State Militia, April 20, 1861. Detached Second Lieutenant 132d New York Volunteers, July 19, 1862. Promoted First Lieutenant, August 23, 1862, for gallant and meritorious conduct on the field. Served in Virginia. Resigned November 2, 1862.

JEREMIAH V. SIMONSON, Private 18th New York Cavalry. Served in General Banks' Red River Expedition.

Wounded in the foot, and had two horses shot under him. In the service ten months.

WILLIAM R. REMSEN, Volunteer Aide-de-Camp on staff of Major-General Alexander S. Webb, U. S. Army.

JAMES P. HARPER, Private 67th New York Volunteers, June 21, 1861. Served in Virginia. Mustered out of service, July 11, 1863.

ALBERT KAMPMAN, Private 1st Pennsylvania Volunteers, April 20. 1861. Private 46th Pennsylvania Volunteers, November 1, 1862. Served in Virginia. Wounded twice. Taken prisoner at Gettysburg, and confined in Libby Prison. Exchanged, and re-enlisted in 195th Pennsylvania Volunteers.

THOMAS W. ROGERS, Orderly Sergeant 1st Delaware Volunteers. Served in Virginia. In service three years.

CHARLES ERBEN, Second Lieutenant 102d New York Volunteers, February 11, 1862. First Lieutenant, October 5, 1862. Served in Virginia. Wounded in the battle of Antietam, Md. Resigned February 2, 1863.

THOMAS H. SILLIMAN, Private 48th Pennsylvania Volunteers, August 31, 1861. Promoted First Lieutenant. Brevet Captain, April 2, 1865. Served in Virginia. Taken prisoner at Second Bull Run, and escaped. Dangerously wounded in the chest by a minie ball, which he still carries in his body. In service five years.

WASHINGTON YOUNGS, Private 5th New York Volunteers (Duryea's Zouaves). Served in Virginia. In service two years.

Thomas P. Van Buren, Private 46th Pennsylvania Volunteers. Served in Virginia. In service one year.

D. Eugene Bigler, Private 15th Pennsylvania Cavalry. Served in Maryland, Kentucky and Tennessee. Captured at Stone River, Tenn., and paroled. Detached Aide-de-Camp on staff of General J. B. Fry. In service three years.

Bernardus E. Staats, Jr., Private California regiment. Not required to leave the State.

Reuben Oehler, Captain 176th Ohio Volunteers, August 15. 1862. Captured at Chickasaw Bluffs, December 28, 1862. A prisoner at Vicksburg and at Jackson, Miss. Released at New Orleans, March 13, 1863.

Harry S. Gilchrist, Private 30th Pennsylvania State Militia, June 25, 1863.

Thomas M. Gilchrist, Private 3d and 30th Pennsylvania State Militia, 1862 and 1863.

D. Newberry Place, Private 13th New York State Militia, 1862, 1863.

Jacob B. Fisher, Private 22d New York State Militia, June 18, 1863.

George Youngs, Private 22d New York State Militia.

Lawrence H. Forman, Private 5th Pennsylvania State Militia, September 12, 1862.

Peter Tonnele, Private 9th New York Volunteers.

EDWARD J. REGENNAS, Private 5th Pennsylvania State Militia, September, 1862.

J. ALBERT RONDTHALER, Private 5th Pennsylvania State Militia.

CLASS OF 1856.

EDWARD T. HENRY, Private 132d Pennsylvania Volunteers, August 17, 1862. Served in Maryland and Virginia. Discharged on account of illness, January 8, 1863. Third Assistant Engineer U. S. Navy, April 19, 1864, on duty in West Gulf Blockading Squadron. July 28, 1865, detached from steamer J. P. Jackson, and ordered to the Penobscot. Honorably discharged, October 20, 1865.

MARCUS SILVER, Private 91st Pennsylvania Volunteers. Served in Virginia.

EDWARD M. KNOX, Private 8th New York Volunteers, April 20 to July 25, 1861. Second Lieutenant battery of artillery (Irish Brigade), May 14, 1862. Promoted First Lieutenant. Captain 14th New York Independent Battery, January 27, 1864. Served in Virginia. Dangerously wounded in the battle of Gettysburg. Resigned October 23, 1863, on account of his wounds. Has three scars and three commissions.

GEORGE SELLERS, Sergeant 6th Pennsylvania Cavalry, April 20, 1861. Served in Virginia. Honorably discharged, September 6, 1864.

SAMUEL C. BENNERS, Private 15th Pennsylvania Cavalry. Served in Tennessee. In service one year.

THOMAS M. WEAVER, Quartermaster Sergeant 51st Pennsylvania State Militia, June 29, 1863. Private 215th

Pennsylvania Volunteers. Detached Clerk of Military Examining Board at Fort Delaware. Mustered out of service, July 31, 1865.

JOHN F. STADIGER, Private 153d Pennsylvania Volunteers, October 7, 1862. Served in Virginia. Mustered out with his regiment, July 24, 1863.

DANIEL CORELL served in a Western regiment at the siege of Vicksburg.

FRANK V. Moss, Private 2d U. S. Artillery, February 21, 1865.

WILLIAM W. YOHE, Private 1st Pennsylvania Volunteers, April 20, 1861. Second Lieutenant 112th Pennsylvania Volunteers, September 26, 1862.

GEORGE A. YOHE, Private 46th Pennsylvania Volunteers, September 4, 1861. Mustered out of service, December 12, 1861.

JOHN PRICE WETHERILL, Private 43d Pennsylvania State Militia, July, 1863.

RICHARD M. SHOEMAKER, JR., Private 8th Pennsylvania State Militia, September, 1862. Served in Maryland.

HARDING WILLIAMS, Corporal Starr's Philadelphia Battery, September, 1862.

WILLIAM TRAUTWINE, Private 32d Pennsylvania State Militia, July, 1863.

HAYDN H. TSCHUDY, Private 12th Pennsylvania State Militia, September 16, 1862.

26

W. HERMAN T. FRUEAUFF, Private 5th Pennsylvania State Militia, September, 1862.

WILLIAM YOUNGS, Private 22d New York Regiment, July 13, 1863.

SAMUEL W. CALDWELL, Third Sergeant Independent New Jersey State Militia.

ABRAHAM W. THOMAS, Private 18th Pennsylvania Cavalry, August 16, 1862, transferred with his regiment to the Army of the Tennessee, December, 1862. Participated in the battle of Chickamauga. Captured near New Market, Tenn., December 23, 1863, and imprisoned successively near Morristown, Tenn., in Scott Prison, Richmond, on Belle Isle, at Andersonville, Savannah, Millen, Blackshear Station (seventy miles below Savannah), Thomasville, Ga., and a second time at Andersonville, between December 23, 1863, and March 18, 1865. Paroled near Vicksburg, April 23, 1865. Honorably discharged at Harrisburg, June 1st, 1865.

Served in Maryland, Virginia, Tennessee, Kentucky and Alabama.

From Mr. Thomas' narrative of personal experience in Southern prisons and pens, your Recorder extracts the following: While near New Market we were all dismounted and resting, when the picket came in at full speed, reporting that the rebels were coming upon us. Corporal Lyons, who was in charge of the advance, gave the order to mount and come on, and in a moment we were on the road through the woods to meet the foe. As soon as their advance were within reach of our carbines, we let go at them, and as they turned and fled, we drew our pistols and charged. I captured one fellow, and was running him to the rear, when I was met by one of

our advance, who could not keep up with the speed of
our fresh horses. At his suggestion I foolishly handed
my prize over to him for disposal, and advanced a second
time. But this was my misfortune; for the rebels flanked
me, and as I was trying to make my escape, in turning
through the trees, I was knocked off my horse, and so
much hurt by the fall that, of course, I was captured.
One captain, two sergeants and six privates of our regiment shared the same fate. We were run to the rear at
a double quick, after having been stripped of our blank-
ets and of our coats; and when in the hands of what was
called a provost guard, searched from head to foot, and
robbed of everything we had, even of our letters and pho-
tographs of dear ones. That night we were quartered in
an old log cabin, and given some half dozen white potatoes and a pinch of salt. Borrowing a kettle, we boiled
and eat half of the allowance, keeping the rest for next
day's breakfast. But when we came to look for them in
the morning, they were nearly all gone, the rebels having
eaten them themselves. It was Christmas day of 1863,
and I hundreds of miles from home, and in the hands of
a set of thieves. Yet I looked for an early exchange,
and then I would have another chance at them, and this
kept me in good spirits. But this chance was never to
come. We were now marched to Morristown, and after
our number had increased by accessions to fifty, to Rus-
selville, and reported to General Longstreet. He ordered
us part of the way back to Morristown, where we were
quartered in an old coal-shed, or blacksmith shop, built
of rails. This might have been passably agreeable for a
summer residence; but it was about New Year, and the
rails were so far apart as to allow of running one's foot
between them, and the snow blew all over us. Fifty-two
of us were crowded into this pen, which was eleven feet

and four inches by fifteen feet, with a South Carolinian ordered on each side, each with a bayonet and a loaded musket on his shoulder. General Longstreet would pass by almost daily, and refused us permission to collect wood enough to keep ourselves warm. We were also kept on a short allowance of water; for a canteen full of which some of our men, who had been lucky enough to hide their money, would pay a dollar greenback. Our rations were one quart of grits, or very coarse flour, and the shin and shoulder-bones of beef, which the rebels had previously stripped of the meat for their own consumption. Here we remained for two weeks, and were then started on the march for Bristol and the Virginia and Tennessee line. a distance of ninety-four miles. Just before taking the cars at this place for Richmond, I purchased a blanket from one of the citizens, and sharing the treasure with Sergeant W. B. Chase, who had been captured with me, *under it we became very warm friends!*

On the 4th of March, 1864, we left Richmond for the South. On the way from our prison to the cars we were guarded by a lot of young boys, with red caps, sons of the aristocracy of Richmond, who displayed their chivalry by poking their bayonets into us (accompanying the action with an oath large enough to choke them) whenever we happened to be a few inches out of line. These fellows were our escort as far as Gaston, where we fell into the hands of the 24th North Carolina Regiment, a pretty clever set. At Branchville we changed cars and guards. The officer in command packed about a hundred men and six guards into each box-car, which had no windows or means of ventilation excepting the side doors, which were closed all to about six inches, for fear of our jumping out. The captain had us all lie down, and gave his men orders to shoot any one who would raise his head without first asking permission. We arrived at Andersonville on the 10th, about midnight, in a heavy rain. Like so many head of cattle they drove us into the stockade, and in the pitchy darkness we laid ourselves down to rest where best we could. Next morning, Captain Wirz came in, and gave orders about our rations ; told us to make ourselves comfortable for a few days where we were, as he intended to build barracks for us. This was all sham. Prisoners continued to come in every day, until upward of twenty thousand were quartered within the thirteen-acre enclosure. A new stockade near by was now in course of erection, but before it was completed the number had increased to thirty-five thousand. Some time in June they opened the new stockade. On the 2d of July part of the old one gave way. Captain Wirz, when he saw the timbers falling, was very much excited, signaled the citizens by two shots, ordered the guards out, and had them in line all that afternoon and night, while negroes were at work repairing the damages. Our rations consisted of about half a pint of coarse cornmeal and two ounces of bacon.

We left Andersonville on the 8th of September, and arrived at Savannah next day. Our rations here were somewhat better, for we received a cup of meal, a cup of rice and a pretty good-sized piece of meat. In the evening of the 12th of October we reached Millen. Our daily allowance in this home of starvation was one gill of cornmeal, one gill of rice and about an ounce of bacon. This was the only place where, in my experience, the sick were entirely neglected. Suffering from diarrhœa since March, I was so prostrated that I could neither walk nor help myself in the least. I was truly in a pitiful condition ; and had it not been for the kindness of my two friends, Adam Drinkhouse and John Meredock, I suppose I would have been numbered with the dead.

We left Millen on the 21st of November, passed by the outskirts of Savannah, and were landed from the cars about seventy miles below the city, at a place called Blackshear's Station. Here we were treated kindly, and remained for nearly two weeks in a pine forest, with but a chain guard around us. On the 6th of December we were transported to Thomasville, at the terminus of the South-western Railroad, and near the Florida line. On the 18th of December we were marched away some fifty miles, the greater part of the men barefoot. We now first learned the reason of these many moves. Our cavalry were on the track, had cut the railroad at several places, and when we left Millen were only six hours behind. On this fatiguing march we had a brutal set of guards. On leaving the pine forest, they fired the huts we had built, while one of their number on horseback scoured the camp with a pack of hounds to hunt up any Yankees that might have been concealed under the leaves and brush. The consequence of this needless cruelty was the burning to death of some of the feeble and helpless sick. On the march the guards were strung alongside of us, about two paces apart, and artillery was in the rear of both columns. A major, Burk by name, who appeared to be in command, ordered his men, in case there should be any attempt on our part to overpower them, that they should file to the right and left, so that the artillery might make a clean sweep. On arriving at a creek, or a swamp, Burk would place guards on the foot-log, and seated on his horse, with pistol in hand, threaten to shoot any man who would attempt to cross by the log, compelling us to walk through mud and water waist-deep. On the 24th of December we reached a place called Albany, and on the next day Andersonville, a second time. Here we found things looking badly ; the ground within the stockade had been ploughed, nearly all the wells we had dug in the previous summer had been filled up, and there was not a piece of wood to be found convertible into a tent-pole. The tent we were fortunate enough to own, and which could accommodate eight men, was made of meal sacks, which we had stolen or *captured* from the rebel quartermaster during our stay at Thomasville and Blackshear Station. The guards were not as cruel as they had been during our first imprison- ment, for then they would shoot down whoever happened to get near the dead line. Now they even opened trade ; and in the night you might often see a score of men walking around the line with a bag buying up meal, peas and grubbers (peanuts). It was customary for the mer- chants above to throw down a sample of their goods, and for their customers to throw up a sack containing the money for the desired wares ; prepayment being indis- pensable. Some of the fellows—or I should rather say felons—however, would keep the sack and the money too, giving us nothing in exchange but an order to clear the line under penalty of being shot. So we worked the game upon them by making counterfeit money from writ- ing paper, which we would pass at night. At last on the 25th of March, 1865, we left Andersonville for exchange, not, however, without having first been made the victims of unfeeling avarice, the Rebs asking us fifty dollars for a chance to be enrolled on the first list for exchange. As there were but few of us who could pay this sum, they gradually lowered the demand, until finally the pris- oner who would give them the brass buttons from his coat would be released before his neighbor who had none to give. A friend of mine, who had money sewed up in his clothing, bought four of us out for fifteen dollars.

CLASS OF 1857.

J. ARTHUR BENADE, Private 128th Pennsylvania Volunteers, July 28, 1862. Served in Maryland and Virginia. Mustered out with his regiment, May 19, 1863.

P. HENRY BENADE, Private 192d Pennsylvania Volunteers, July 12, 1864. Served in Maryland and Virginia. Mustered out with his regiment, August 24, 1865.

BOWMAN H. McCALLA, Midshipman U. S. Navy, November 30, 1861. Served on board Frigate Susquehannah sent in pursuit of the " Stonewall." Still in the service.

SAMUEL R. COLLADAY, Private 19th Pennsylvania Volunteers, April 27, 1861. Corporal 6th Pennsylvania Cavalry, August 29, 1861. Second Lieutenant, June 30, 1863. First Lieutenant, November 1, 1863. Captain, March 20, 1865. Captured at Brandy Station, Va., June 3, 1863. Confined in Libby Prison over nine months. Rejoined his regiment, April 1, 1864, but was so debilitated, in consequence of his sufferings while a prisoner, that he was unable to endure the rigors of service, and compelled to resign, June, 1864. Re-entered the service January 1, 1865. Served in Virginia, Kentucky and Tennessee. Mustered out August 7, 1865.

THEODORE BERRIEN, Corporal 22d New York Volunteers, June 28, 1863. Hospital Steward 102d New York (National Guards) Regiment, August 1, 1864. Private 56th New York Volunteers, April 1, 1865. Detailed

Chief Order Clerk to General Gilmore at Charleston, S. C. Mustered out November 22d, 1865.

ALBERT DRINKHOUSE, Private 129th Pennsylvania Volunteers, August 14, 1862. Mustered out with his regiment, May 18, 1863.

FREDERIC BARRET, Hospital Steward 84th Pennsylvania Volunteers, 1861. Served in Virginia. Honorably discharged on account of wounds, December, 1862.

CHAMBERS C. DAVIS, Private 19th Pennsylvania State Militia, September 15, 1862.

HENRY BAIN, Color Sergeant Pennsylvania Gray Reserve Regiment, September, 1862.

GEORGE L. SIMONSON, Private Starr's Philadelphia Battery, July, 1863.

WALTER L. Moss, Commissary Sergeant 176th New York Volunteers, February 28, 1865.

JACOB A. Moss, Bugler 5th Pennsylvania Cavalry, July 1, 1861. Entered the U. S. Navy, June, 1863, and afterward transferred to the Regular Army.

A correspondent writes: "Jacob was always in hot water, but displayed great bravery in more than one engagement. In one skirmish he succeeded in running down a 'Johnny Reb,' bringing him back to camp with all his accoutrements. In April, 1865, he shipped from New Bedford in a whaler, and died from cruel treatment off the coast of Greenland in the autumn of the same year."

CLASS OF 1858.

WILLIAM A. DUER, Acting Ensign U. S. Navy, North

Atlantic Squadron, July 24. 1863. Served on board the iron-clad " New Ironsides" in the attack on Fort Fisher, N. C. Still in the service.

EPHRAIM H. MACK, Private 11th New Jersey Volunteers. Served in Virginia. In the service ten months.

PETER SNYDER, Private 196th Pennsylvania Volunteers. July, 1864. Private 2d Pennsylvania Cavalry, January, 1865. Mustered out of service, August, 1865.

JOHN H. SENSEMAN, Corporal 195th Pennsylvania Volunteers. Served in Virginia.

CHARLES D. BISHOP, Private 26th Pennsylvania Volunteers, June 17, 1863. Captured near Gettysburg, Pa., and paroled. General Bushrod W. Johnson ordering the prisoners' shoes and boots from their feet, he was compelled to walk barefoot to Carlisle, Pa.

JOSEPH A. LOUTEY, Private 1st Pennsylvania State Militia, September, 1862.

WILLIAM STILES, JR., Private 14th Pennsylvania State Militia, September, 1862.

P. M. LAFOURCADE, Private Pennsylvania Gray Reserve Regiment, July, 1863.

GEORGE C. LEWIS, Private 3d Pennsylvania State Militia, September 12, 1862. Private 30th Pennsylvania State Militia, June 16, 1863.

CLASS OF 1859.

JOSEPH W. LONGMIRE. Private 31st Pennsylvania Volunteers, June 15, 1861. Second Lieutenant 2d Pennsylvania Heavy Artillery. Captain 17th U. S. (Colored) Infantry. Wounded at battles of Cold Harbor and Chancellorsville, Va. Served in Virginia.

Benjamin P. Whitney, Private 27th Pennsylvania Volunteers, June 19, 1863.

Theodor C. Engel, Private 73d Pennsylvania Volunteers, April 12, 1862.

Joseph Kampman, Private 195th Pennsylvania Volunteers, February 14, 1865. Mustered out of service, January 31, 1866.

David F. Rank, Private 26th Pennsylvania State Militia, July, 1863.

Elias W. E. Whyte, Private 11th U. S. Infantry. February 15, 1865. Mustered out of service, November, 1866.

Class of 1860.

Harry Setley, Private Independent New Jersey regiment.

Adolphus P. Stone, Private New York Volunteers.

Class of 1861.

Samuel H. Love, attached to Marine Guard U. S. steamer Pensacola. Stationed at Mare Island, California, March, 1865.

James G. Prince.

Class of 1862.

Thomas H. B. Hull, Private 15th Regiment U. S.

Army, February 1, 1865.   Transferred to 24th Regiment. Detached as Clerk of Provost Marshal's General Office at Mobile, Ala.   Served in Mississippi, Georgia and Alabama.   Honorably discharged, February 1, 1868.   Fifteen years of age when he enlisted.

WILLIAM C. M. STAATS, Clerk 4th Regiment U. S. Light Artillery.   Served in Tenhessee.   In service the last year of the war.

CLASS OF 1863.

HENRY A. LEE, Private 103d Pennsylvania Volunteers.

CLASS OF 1864.

FRANCIS W. KNAUSS, Private 5th Pennsylvania State Militia, September 12, 1862.

LEWIS P. CLEWELL, Private 34th Pennsylvania State Militia, June, July, August, 1863.

THE MILITARY RECORD

OF

ALUMNI

WHO WERE ENROLLED IN THE SERVICE AGAINST
THE UNITED STATES.

MILITARY RECORD.

ROLL OF ALUMNI WHO SERVED AGAINST THE U. S.,
AND FELL IN BATTLE, OR DIED OF DISEASE CON-
TRACTED IN THE SERVICE.

CLASS OF 1837.

JAMES MCQUEEN MCINTOSH, son of Colonel James
S. McIntosh, U. S. A., who fell in the battle of Molino
del Rey, Mexico, September 8, 1847. The subject of
this brief memoir was graduated at West Point, July 1,
1849. Resigned his position as Captain 1st U. S. Cavalry, May 7, 1861. Joined the service against the United
States, in which he was appointed Brigadier-General, and
lost his life in the battle of Pea Ridge, Ark., March 7,
1862.

The following account is from the pen of an eye-witness: "About ten in the morning came the news of the
charge made by the Mounted Texan Rangers, under
Generals Ben McCulloch and McIntosh, upon the United
States batteries. The carnage had been fearful, and an
officer of distinction was reported killed; no one conjec-
tured who it could be. This was unexpected and start-
ling. Matters began to wear a serious aspect; and just

after nightfall, hearing a wagon from the direction of the battle-ground passing my door, I went out to make some inquiries, and found that it contained the body of General McIntosh, who fell nearly at the same time with McCulloch.

" The body was taken into the house of an acquaintance of mine. I entered, and there he lay, cold and stark, just as he was taken from the spot where he fell, a military overcoat covering his person, and the dead forest leaves still clinging to it. His wound had not been examined ; I aided in opening his vest and under-garments, and soon found that the ball had passed through his body, if not through the heart. Some officers of the 3d Louisiana—some of them wounded—came with the body. Their regiment, the best in Van Dorn's army, had suffered severely. After the fall of McCulloch and McIntosh, and the capture of Colonel Hebert, there was no one to take command of that portion of the army, to which circumstance the loss of the battle of Pea Ridge is attributed."

CLASS OF 1842.

JAMES G. S. BOYD, Lieutenant of the Buckingham Lee Guard, 20th Regiment Virginia Volunteers. Killed at the battle of Rich Mountain, Va., July 11, 1861.

At a session of the court held for Buckingham county, Va., November 11, 1861, "it is ordered that the following resolutions be entered on record :

" *Resolved*, That the members of this Bar deplore the tragical and untimely end of our late friend and associate, J. G. S. Boyd ; and that it affords us melancholy pleasure to declare our high appreciation of his fine talent, his chivalrous bearing, and the many noble and generous qualities that adorned his character.

" *Resolved*, That the dauntless courage and self-sacrificing heroism displayed by Lieutenant Boyd on the fatal field at 'Rich Mountain' were worthy of the best days of chivalry, were honorable alike to himself and to the country that sent him forth to do battle against the invaders of our native soil, and that his services on that occasion should ever be held in grateful remembrance by his countrymen.

"*Resolved*, That we tender to the family of Lieutenant Boyd the assurance of our sympathy, and that the Clerk of this Court be instructed to forward a copy of these proceedings to the Richmond and Lynchburg papers for publication."

CLASS OF 1843.

CHARLES J. CLAUDER, Private 33d North Carolina Volunteers, July 14, 1862. Killed at the battle of Fredericksburg, Va., December 11, 1862. His body has never been recovered by his relatives.

CLASS OF 1847.

THOMAS LEROY NAPIER was graduated at West Point, 1858. Resigned April 21, 1861, and entered the service against the United States. June, 1861, appointed First Lieutenant with the provisional rank of Lieutenant-Colonel. October, 1863, commanded three batteries of Light Artillery at Mobile, Ala. Commanded 7th Georgia Battalion at Chickamauga, where he was wounded. Contracted disease from exposure, and died September 5, 1867. A gallant officer.

CLASS OF 1858.

WILLIAM AUGUSTUS CONRAD, Private 21st North Carolina Volunteers, June 1, 1861. Died of typhoid fever in hospital at Richmond, Va., January 12, 1862. His

27 *

remains were conveyed to his home, and buried in the Moravian burial-ground at Bethania, N. C.

ROLL OF ALUMNI WHO SERVED AGAINST THE U. S.

CLASS OF 1821.

WILLIAM SCHNIERLE, General South Carolina State Militia.   Resides in Charleston.

CLASS OF 1826.

STEPHEN R. MALLORY, Ex-U. S. Senator from Florida. March 23, 1862, confirmed as Secretary of the Navy in Jefferson Davis' Cabinet.   April, 1865, arrested with Alexander H. Stephens by General Upton's command, and confined at Fort Lafayette, in accordance with instructions of W. H. Seward, Secretary of State.

CLASS OF 1834.

ALBERT STEIN, General in the army.   Particulars unknown.

CLASS OF 1827.

FRANCIS L. FRIES, engaged in the manufacture of clothing for the army at Salem, N. C.   His factory was completely sacked by the populace during General Palmer's advance in 1865.   Deceased.

CLASS OF 1836.

BENJAMIN F. SCULL, Private Jefferson Guards, 1st Arkansas Volunteers, April 27, 1861.   Appointed Major and Surgeon of Cleburn's regiment, February 15, 1862, in which capacity he served until ordered to the west side of the Mississippi by the War Department to superintend "supplies in the District of Arkansas."   Paroled at Little Rock, Ark., June 15, 1865.   Died in 1869.

THEODORE F. KEEHLN, a member of the Forsythe Co. (North Carolina) Medical Board.

CLASS OF 1840.

DAVID H. VAN BUREN, Special Messenger of the War Department at Richmond.

CLASS OF 1842.

CHARLES E. SHOBER, Captain 2d North Carolina Battalion, March, 1862. Lieutenant-Colonel, October 1, 1862. Resigned on account of ill health, May, 1863. Entered the service again as Colonel 6th North Carolina Reserves, October, 1864. Compelled a second time by failing health to resign, February, 1865.

THEODORE F. WOLLE, drafted to serve in North Carolina State Militia, October 18, 1864. Released two days afterward, through the efforts of influential friends, by order of Governor Z. B. Vance, and appointed Professor of Music in the State Institution for Deaf and Dumb.

CLASS OF 1847.

NATHAN MUNRO NAPIER, Captain 4th Georgia Cavalry. While commanding an outpost in Kentucky was severely wounded by a musket ball, which entered the left side of the nose, tearing away the right eye and part of the cheek-bone. Taken prisoner.

EDWIN I. ELDRIDGE, Surgeon 16th Georgia Volunteers, June, 1861. Brigade Surgeon Cobb's Georgia Legion, September, 1862. Assigned to General Howell Cobb's staff, and Chief Surgeon Department of Georgia and Tennessee until the surrender.

CLASS OF 1849.

AUGUSTUS F. PFOHL, Hospital Steward 33d North Carolina Volunteers, July 11, 1862. Detached to Forsythe County Medical Department, November 4, 1862.

CLASS OF 1850.

ROBERT SPEARING, 1st Lieutenant Louisiana Artillery. Captured at Gettysburg, July 3, 1863.

CLASS OF 1852.

FREDERICK GOSEVISCH, Private Platte Cavalry Rangers, and transferred to Arkansas Artillery, General Hardee's division. Wounded at Shiloh. On General Beauregard's evacuating Corinth, he assisted in holding the bridge at Tuscumbia Creek for ten hours, protecting his rear. November, 1862, compelled to leave the army in consequence of a difficulty with his captain. He writes : " In 1863 I joined the United States Army, although for the same cause under different colors. Enlisted in 52d Kentucky Mounted Infantry, and became First Sergeant. Being generally garrisoned in companies at country towns throughout Kentucky, and being fortunate enough to have raw officers over me, I found many opportunities of favoring the adherents of the lost cause secretly." December 23, 1864, was captured at Hartford, Ky. (together with the company), by General Lyon, but was paroled, and in 1865 mustered out of service.

CLASS OF 1853.

ELAM W. WITMER, impressed into a cavalry company while residing in Texas. After serving a short time succeeded in escaping, and reached his home at Cincinnati, Ohio.

CLASS OF 1854.

CHARLES W. SEIDEL, Private 15th Georgia Volunteers, July 10, 1861. Elected Captain July 2, 1863. Wounded at Garnett's Farm, near Richmond, Va. Taken prisoner at Gettysburg, July 3, 1863, and sent to Fort Delaware. Remained there until exchanged, March 8, 1865.

CLASS OF 1856.

FRANK RABORG, Private Platte Cavalry Rangers, General Jeff Thompson's army. Served in the swamps of South-east Missouri.

CLASS OF 1858.

HENRY T. BAHNSON, Hospital Steward 2d North Carolina Battalion, January 1, 1863. Taken prisoner at Gettysburg, confined in Baltimore City Jail for three weeks, and then transferred to Fort Delaware. Exchanged December 24, 1863. Re-entered the service, January, 1864. Transferred to 1st North Carolina Sharpshooters. Surrendered with General Lee at Appomattox Court-house, May 9, 1865.

NATHANIEL S. SIEWERS, a member of 1st Battalion North Carolina Regimental Band; enlisted. November, 1863. Mustered out, May, 1865.

ABRAHAM G. JONES, Private 5th North Carolina Cavalry, September 21, 1862. Captured near Newbern, N. C., and wounded afterward in the neck by a pistol ball at Dinwiddie Court-house. Served until General Lee's surrender.

JAMES J. B. JONES, Private 1st Battalion North Carolina Sharpshooters, March 29, 1864. Served until the surrender.

NATHAN C. MUNRO, Captain under special orders of the War Department, July, 1862. Wounded at battles of Decatur, Ala., and Franklin, Tenn. Taken prisoner, and confined for several months at Elmira, N. Y. Exchanged and re-enlisted. April, 1865, surrendered with General Joseph E. Johnson's army.

CLASS OF 1860.

CHARLES B. PFOHL, Second Lieutenant 4th Battalion North Carolina Junior Reserves, May 22, 1864. Captured at Fort Fisher, and a prisoner of war at Fort Delaware, from December 24, 1864, to June 19. 1865.

RECAPITULATION.

Number of pupils who served in the U. S. Army and Navy. 206
  "   killed or died of disease............. 27
  "   missing 1
                  234

Table of Rank of Pupils Attained in the Army.

General.................................... 5
Colonel.................................... 2
Lieutenant-Colonel........................ 4
Major..................................... 6
Adjutant.................................. 5
Brigade and Regimental Quartermaster...... 3
Surgeon................................... 6
Captain 22
First Lieutenant.......................... 13
Second Lieutenant......................... 8
Sergeant.................................. 15
Corporal.................................. 8
Chaplain 1
Judge Advocate............................ 1

Table of Rank of Pupils Attained in the Navy.

Fleet Engineer, ranking with Commander..... 1
Captain 2
Third Assistant Engineer................... 2
Surgeon.................................... 1
Acting Ensign, Midshipman and Captain's Clerk........ 4
   Prisoners captured and confined in Libby and other
   Prisons................................... 16

Number who served *against* the U. S..................... 23
  "   killed or died of disease........................ 5
                  28

General 3
Colonel................................... 1
Lieutenant-Colonel........................ 1
Major..................................... 1
Brigade Surgeon........................... 1
Captain 3
Lieutenant................................ 3
   Prisoners captured and confined in U. S. Forts, etc.. 9

Total...................... 262

THE
CONTRIBUTORS
TO THE
MEMORIAL FUND.

CLASS.

1799—John Beck........................... Litiz, Pa.
1809—Edmund G. Dutilh.................... Philadelphia.
1812—The representatives of Henry J. Boller,
    deceased .... "
1814—Edmund Draper...................... "
    Henry Smith...................... Burlington, N. J.
    Ernest F. Bleck..................... Bethlehem, Pa.
1815—Elihu L. Mix......................... New York.
1816—Theodore R. Sitgreaves.............. Easton, Pa.
    John C. Jacobson.................... Bethlehem, Pa.
1817—The representatives of William H. Jor-
    dan, deceased...................... Philadelphia.
    Edward Minturn..................... New York.
    Henry A. Shultz.................... Nazareth, Pa.
1819—Eugene A. Frueauff.................. Litiz, Pa.
1820—Henry I. Schmidt.................... New York.
1821—James Henry......................... Bolton, Pa.
1822—Andrew A. Humphreys.............. Washington, D. C.
    Sidney A. Clewell................... Philadelphia.
    Thomas J. Albright.................. St. Louis, Mo.
    The representatives of Edward Jordan,
    deceased .... Philadelphia.
1823—Joseph H. Hildeburn................ "

	Seth W. Paine	Troy, Pa.
1825—	Robert Draper	Philadelphia.
	Joseph J. Albright	Scranton, Pa.
	Abraham Bininger	New York.
	Arthur Gillender	"
1826—	John Baker	"
	Levin A. Miksch	Bethlehem, Pa.
1827—	Captain William Man	Philadelphia.
	Francis Jordan	"
	Edward O. Smith	"
1828—	John F. Kohler	"
	George Shober	"
	Thomas Sparks	"
	John B. Dash	New York.
	Aquilla E. Albright	Scranton, Pa.
	Maurice C. Jones	Bethlehem, Pa.
1829—	William J. Albert	Baltimore.
	Lewis F. Kampman	Bethlehem, Pa.
	Francis F. Hagen	Staten Island, N. Y.
1830—	Reuben A. Henry	Scranton, Pa.
	Manuel T. Bolmer	Yonkers, N. Y.
	Nehemiah D. Smith	New York.
	Thomas J. Scott	Philadelphia.
1831—	Sidney J. Solms	"
	Lazarus D. Shoemaker	Wilkesbarre, Pa.
	Nathaniel S. Wolle	Litiz, Pa.
	Andrew G. Bininger	New York.
1832—	William Meyer	"
	James Lee, Jr	Boston.
	Thomas Brodrick	Wilkesbarre, Pa.
	Henry J. Van Vleck	Bethlehem, Pa.
	George A. Kohler	Philadelphia.
	Charles Lafourcade	"
	Robert C. Davis	"
	Benjamin F. Garvin	"
1833—	George M. Wagner	"
	Paul M. Wagner	"
	Philip A. Cregar	"
	John C. Philip	Brooklyn, N. Y.
	Charles E. Smith	Kalamazoo, Mich.

CLASS.

	Samuel Colgate	New York.
	H. J. Brooks	"
	Giles B. Overton	Towanda, Pa.
1834	William C. Reichel	Bethlehem.
	Edmund de Schweinitz	"
1835	William Higgins	New York.
	Edward S. Hall	Philadelphia.
	A. H. Van Vleck, in memory of Arthur L. Van Vleck	Litiz, Pa.
	Matthias T. Huebner	"
	Samuel C. Wolle	Hokendauqua, Pa.
1836	Nathaniel Michler	Washington, D. C.
	James S. Keen	Philadelphia.
	Frederic G. Riter	"
	Calvin G. Beitel	Easton, Pa.
1837	John Baillie McIntosh	Washington, D. C.
	James McNair	Pit Hole City, Pa.
	Eugene T. Henry	Oxford, N. J.
	Joseph Dean Philip	Brooklyn, N. Y.
	William Henry Gunther	New York.
	George W. Day	"
1838	Lebbeus Chapman, Jr.	"
	James H. Wolle	Bethlehem, Pa.
1839	Horatio S. Parke	New York.
	Edward Innes	Easton, Pa.
1840	Samuel Thomas	Catasauqua, Pa.
	Thomas L. McKeen, Jr.	Easton, Pa.
	Washington Fitler,	Philadelphia.
1841	Charles Klosè	"
	Edwin T. Eisenbrey	"
	James N. Beck	"
	Mrs. H. K. Womrath, in memory of George K. Womrath	"
	John Thomas	Hokendauqua, Pa.
	Max Goepp	New York.
1842	Benjamin J. B. Davis	Philadelphia.
	John P. Kluge	Aspinwall, C. A.
1844	Herman A. Brickenstein	Bethlehem, Pa.
	John H. McKinley	New York.
	William A. Lilliendahl, *"for book"*	"

CLASS.

1845—Charles Goepp...................... New York.
    C. Edward Kummer................. Bethlehem, Pa.
    E. H. Walter...................... Scranton, Pa.
    Andrew K. Womrath................ Philadelphia.
1846—Daniel B. Heilig ....   "
    Granville Henry..................... Bolton, Pa.
    Edward T. Kluge.................... Litiz, Pa.
1847—Henry Crease.... .... Annapolis, Md.
    Jacob C. Mixsell.................... Easton, Pa.
    Frederick E. Steinle................. New York.
    Richard R. Tschudy................. Litiz, Pa.
    Frederic K. Womrath............... Philadelphia.
    John Trucks, Jr......................   "
1848—Henderson Gaylord, in memory of Asher
    Gaylord......................... Plymouth, Pa.
    Abraham R. Beck.................. Litiz, Pa.
1849—Henry H. Huntzinger.............. Pottsville, Pa.
    Robert J. McClatchey............... Philadelphia.
    James E. Audenreid.................   "
1850—Francis S. Kent...................   "
1851—Richard Henry Chapman............   "
    William H. Loyd............... .....   "
    Wilson Loyd........................   "
    John Frederick R. Frueauff.......... Hollidaysburg, Pa.
1852—Charles V. Henry................. Albany, N. Y.
    Andrew G. White...................   "
    Henry T. Clauder.................. Bethlehem, Pa.
    Charles B. Shultz..................   "
    John Cennick Harvey............... Brooklyn.
    Henry Widmayer................... New York.
    Robert Laughlin.................... Philadelphia.
    Thomas V. Kessler.. ....   "
    John W. Jordan....................   "
1853—William H. Jordan.................   "
    Francis Jordan, Jr..................   "
    F. Augustus Tilge.................   "
    William H. Nixon...................   "
    Marcelin L. de Coursey.............   "
    Nathaniel C. Longmire.............   "

CLASS.

Henry G. Latimer, in memory of David
    Teford Latimer...................... Plainfield, N. J.
Jacob Culp......................... Mount Bethel, Pa.
Daniel R. Bennett, in memory of Horace
    C. Bennett........................ Jenkintown, Pa.
H. G. Tombler, in memory of Edmund
    A. Shouse......................... Easton, Pa.
Elam W. Witmer.................... Cincinnati.
Herman Uhl........................ New York.
Andrew D. Harper..................   "
William Augustus Street............   "
1854—Lovell Purdy.....................   "
Charles Gilsey.....................   "
Peter Gilsey.......................   "
William E. Bute....................   "
Lucian E. Weimer.................. Lebanon, Pa.
Garret P. Bergen.................. Brooklyn.
Henry A. Daily.................... Easton, Pa.
Joseph R. Kenney.................. Philadelphia.
Joseph W. Drinkhouse..............   "
Samuel Drinkhouse.................   "
1855—Cornelius A. Simonson............ New York.
George Youngs.....................   "
Edwin Coles.......................   "
Charles W. Held...................   "
H. W. Ryerson, in memory of Charles
    Ryerson.........................   "
D. Newberry Place.................   "
Carman E. Anderson................ Brooklyn.
William W. Stearns................ Elizabeth, N. J.
Philip H. Kutzemeyer.............. Jersey City, N. J.
Frank H. Ellis.................... Philadelphia.
Benjamin A. Van Shaick............   "
John Knecht, in memory of John N.
    Knecht.......................... Freemansburg, Pa.
Lawrence H. Forman................ Easton, Pa.
1856—William W. Yohe................. Bethlehem, Pa.
George A. Yohe....................   "
John Fream, in memory of George Lor-
    illard Fream.................... Saugerties, N. Y.

28 *

CLASS.

W. Herman T. Frueauff............. Hollidaysburg, Pa.
Edward T. Henry.................. Bolton, Pa.
Abraham W. Thomas............... Germantown, Pa.
George Sellers.................... Washington, D. C.
Haydn H. Tschudy................ Litiz, Pa.
Edward M. Knox.................. New York.
Jansen H. Anderson............... "
William H. Close................. "
Edward Uhl...................... "
William R. Remsen............... "
Jay Jarvis....................... "
William H. Sneckner............. "
Charles Sigel, Jr................. White's Corners, N. Y.
Harding Williams................. Philadelphia.
Richard M. Shoemaker, Jr......... "
Samuel Price Wetherill........... "
John T. Robbins.................. "
William H. Renshaw.............. "
George A. Landell, in memory of Ben-
    jamin F. Landell............... "
1857—George E. Tilge.............. "
Henry Bain...................... "
Frank S. Rowland................ "
James Day Rowland.............. Cheltenham, Pa.
Albert Drinkhouse............... Easton, Pa.
Peter Schneider, Jr.............. New York.
Phœnix Remsen.. .... "
1858—August H. Grote............. "
Joseph Kuntz.................... "
M. Charles Illig................. Brooklyn.
George C. Lewis................. Wilkesbarre, Pa.
Herman G. Vetterlein............ Philadelphia.
Ewing Jordan.................... "
William Stiles, Jr............... "
Louis T. Tilge.................. "
William A. Meurer............... "
George H. Hibbler............... "
Norman J. Mayer................ New York.
Ferdinand C. Mayer............. "
1859—Bruno F. Mayer............. "

CLASS.

George E. L. Hyatt.................. New York.
Benjamin P. Whitney............... Pottsville, Pa.
David F. Rank..................... Jonestown, Pa.
Arthur E. Hornblower.............. Newark, N. J.
Robert J. Hess.................... Easton, Pa.
Martin Landenberger, Jr........... Philadelphia.
Charles H. Landenberger...........   "
Theodor C. Engel..................   "
Stephen N. Winslow, Jr............   "
1860—Gilbert Jordan....................   "
Benjamin Rowland, in memory of Thad-
    deus Rowland.................... Cheltenham, Pa.
David P. White.................... Norristown, Pa.
1861—Elwood Coggeshall............... New York.
Joseph S. Rowland................. Philadelphia.
1862—George T. Coyne.................. Richmond, S. I., N. Y.
Charles S. Russell................ Philadelphia.
1863—Francis L. Wolle................. Bethlehem, Pa.
Clarence A. Wolle.................   "
James W. Wilson.................. Easton, Pa.
Harlan P. Hess...................   "
Robert P. Rader..................   "
Charles D. Lefevre............... Philadelphia.
Joseph C. Kern...................   "
William P. Kern..................   "
Robert McC. Turner...............   "
Frank C. Phillips................   "
Charles D. Phillips..............   "
Alfred M. Berg...................   "
1864—Louis D. Erben..................   "
Walter Erben.....................   "
Silas L. Early................... Palmyra, Pa.
1866—William A. Himes................ New Oxford, Pa.
———Franklin Stotz.................. Wind Gap, Pa.
———F. E. Huber.................... Bethlehem, Pa.
———J. Drake...................... Easton, Pa.
———Colgate Baker................. Japan.
1818—C. A. Luckenbach (the use of carriage
    on the Memorial Day)............. Bethlehem, Pa.
    Total amount contributed by 246 persons, $4,693.

L'ENVOI.

In presenting the above Report to the Society, its Recorder would beg leave to state that on consulting a majority of the contributors to the Monument Fund as to the disposal of the balance on hand, a universal desire was expressed to appropriate it toward defraying the cost of a new stereotyped edition of Nazareth Hall and its Reunions. To this end he accepted the generous offer of a member to advance what was wanting for the execution of the work in a style of art not incommensurate with the interesting subjects of which it is a repository.

Of his own contributions to its pages, he trusts he will be permitted to say, that the time and labor expended in conducting his researches (mainly through a correspondence which resulted in the accumulation of a large mass of letters) were cheerfully rendered ; and that should his work meet with the approbation of friends of the Institution which is the central object of this volume, his labors will not have been in vain.

All of which is respectfully submitted.

WILLIAM H. JORDAN, *Recorder*,

Appointed at the Reunion of June 3, 1866.

PHILADELPHIA, June 1st, 1869.

74

APPENDIX.

JOHN GILPIN.

Rev. Paul Weiss, born June 22, 1763, at Bethlehem, died October 31, 1840. The John Gilpin was produced while Pastor at Emmaus, circa 1813.

By the courtesy of Mr. Jedediah Weiss, of Bethlehem, we are permitted to insert in this rewriting of Nazareth Hall a literary production of the late Rev. Paul Weiss, tutor in that Institution between 1797 and 1803. Thus we are enabled at the same time to introduce a *German* Gilpin into the world of letters—*German* in person, in idiosyncrasy, in mode of expression; and *German* as a husband, a bon-vivant, a genial fellow well met, a wit and philosopher. *Frau* Gilpin, too, is *German;* and so are Tom Callender, Betty, the post-boy and the six gentlemen on the road. The reader of this picturesque rendition, into which the translator has infused not only the spirit of the original, but his own keen perception of fun and the ridiculous, will almost hesitate to whom to award the greener laurel—to the amiable Cowper, or to the magician whose intellectual legerdemain wrought this wonderful transformation.

3

JOHN GILPIN.

JOHN GILPIN was a citizen
    Of credit and renown;
A train-band captain, eke, was he
    Of famous London town.

John Gilpin's spouse said to her dear:
    " Though wedded we have been
These twice ten tedious years, yet we
    No holiday have seen.

" To-morrow is our wedding-day,
    And we will then repair
Unto the Bell at Edmonton,
    All in a chaise and pair.

" My sister and my sister's child,
    Myself and children three
Will fill the chaise; so you must ride
    On horseback after we."

He soon replied: " I do admire
    Of womankind, but one,
And you are she, my dearest dear;
    Therefore it shall be done.

" I am a linen-draper bold,
    As all the world doth know,
And my good friend Tom Callender
    Will lend his horse to go."

Quoth Mrs. Gilpin: " That 's well said;
    And for that wine is dear,
We will be furnish'd with our own,
    Which is both bright and clear."

JOHN GILPIN.

John Gilpin war ein Bürger, der
 Credit und Ruhm genoss,
Auch Hauptmann einer Schaar war er
 Von *London*, reich und grosz.

"Mein Liebster!" sprach *John Gilpin's* Weib;
 Wiewohl wir sind getraut
Seit zwei Jahrzehnden, haben wir
 Doch nie ein Fest geschaut.

"Auf Morgen fällt der Trauungstag,
 Da stellen wir uns fein
Beim Glockenwirth zu *Edmonton*,
 Mit Kutsch' und Pferden ein.

"Die Schwester und der Schwester-Kind,
 Ich mit drei Kindern werth,
Besetzen dann die Kutsche ganz—
 Du folgst uns nach zu Pferd."

Er sprach gar bald: "Vom Weibervolk
 Find' ich nur eine schön,
Und *die bist du*, mein liebster Schatz!
 Drum soll es auch geschehn.

"Ein Leinenhändler bin ich, kühn,
 Wie alle Welt es weisz,
Und unser Freund, *Tom Callender*,
 Leih't mir sein Pferd zur Reis'."

Frau *Gilpin* spricht: "Dein Wort ist gut,
 Doch Wein ist theure Waar',
Von unserm eignen nehmen wir,
 Er funkelt hell und klar."

John Gilpin kissed his loving wife ;
  O'erjoy'd was he to find
That though on pleasure she was bent,
  She had a frugal mind.

The morning came, the chaise was brought,
  But yet was not allow'd
To drive up to the door, lest all
  Should say that she was proud.

So three doors off the chaise was stay'd,
  Where they did all get in ;
Six precious souls, and all agog
  To dash through thick and thin.

Smack went the whip, round went the wheels,
  Were never folk so glad ;
The stones did rattle underneath,
  As if Cheapside were mad.

John Gilpin at his horse's side
  Seized fast the flowing mane,
And up he got in haste to ride,
  But soon came down again ;

For saddle-tree scarce reach'd had he.
  His journey to begin,
When, turning round his head, he saw
  Three customers come in.

So down he came ; for loss of time,
  Although it grieved him sore,
Yet loss of pence, full well he knew,
  Would trouble him much more.

John Gilpin küsst sein liebes Weib;
   Er fand nun höchst erfreut,
Wiewohl sie nach Vergnügen strebt,
   Liebt sie doch Sparsamkeit.

Der Morgen graut, die Kutsche kam,
   Doch man erlaubte nicht
Vor's Haus zu fahr'n, damit das Volk.
   " Die Frau ist stolz"—nicht spricht.

Drei Thüren weiter hielt sie still,
   Flugs waren alle drin,
Sechs theure Seelen, voller Lust
   Zu fahr'n durch Dick und Dünn.

Die Peitsche knallt, die Räder roll'n—
   Nie freut je Volk sich mehr;
Das Pflaster unten rasselt laut,
   Als ob es rasend wär'.

John Gilpin stand nun bei dem Pferd,
   Die Mähne fasst er schnell,
Dann steigt er auf, will eilends fort,
   Doch bleibt er auf der Stell'.

Den Sattel hat er kaum erreicht,
   Die Reise zu bestehn,
So schaut er um, und siehet stracks
   In's Haus drei Kunden gehn.

Er stieg nun ab; denn Zeitverlust
   Kränkt freilich ihn gar sehr,—
Verlust an Geld, das wuszt' er wohl.
   Kränkt ihn doch noch viel mehr.

'Twas long before the customers
  Were suited to their mind,
When Betty, screaming, came down stairs,
  " The wine is left behind!"

" Good lack!" quoth he—" yet bring it me,
  My leathern belt likewise,
In which I bear my trusty sword
  When I do exercise."

Now Mrs. Gilpin (careful soul!)
  Had two stone bottles found,
To hold the liquor that she loved,
  And keep it safe and sound.

Each bottle had a curling ear,
  Through which the belt he drew,
And hung a bottle on each side,
  To make his balance true.

Then over all, that he might be
  Equipped from top to toe,
His long red cloak, well brush'd and neat,
  He manfully did throw.

Now see him mounted once again
  Upon his nimble steed,
Full slowly pacing o'er the stones
  With caution and good heed.

But finding soon a smoother road
  Beneath his well-shod feet,
The snorting beast began to trot,
  Which gall'd him in his seat.

Die Kunden brauchten viele Zeit,
　　Nach Wunsch bedient zu sein ;—
Indem schreit *Betty* ihm in's Ohr,
　　"Dort steht ja noch der Wein!"

"O weh!" sprach er, "doch bring' ihn her,
　　Auch bring' den Gürtel mir,
Woran ich trag' mein gutes Schwert,
　　So oft ich exercier'."

Frau *Gilpin* (die sorgfält'ge Seel'!),
　　Zwei Krüge fand von Stein,
Zu halten ihren Lieblingstrank,
　　Der wohl verwahrt musz sein.

Zwei Henkel hatte jeder Krug,
　　Er zog den Gurt hinein,
Hängt einen dann auf jede Seit'
　　Ins Gleichgewicht gar fein.

Um nun so ausstaffirt zu sein,
　　Dasz er nichts mehr bedarf,
Den rothen Mantel, nett und rein
　　Er männlich um sich warf.

Nun seht, wie er auf flinkem Rosz
　　Beginnet seinen Ritt,
Gar langsam über Steine ging's
　　Mit wohlbedächt'gem Schritt.

Doch unter wohlbeschlag'nem Huf,
　　Fand es bald eb'ne Strasz,
Und schnaubend gings in vollen **Trab**,
　　So dasz er übel sasz.

29 *

So, " Fair and softly," John he cried,
    But John he cried in vain ;
That trot became a gallop soon,
    In spite of curb and rein.

So stooping down, as needs he must
    Who cannot sit upright,
He grasp'd the mane with both his hands,
    And eke with all his might.

His horse, who never in that sort
    Had handled been before,
What thing upon his back had got
    Did wonder more and more.

Away went Gilpin, neck or naught ;
    Away went hat and wig ;
He little dreamt when he set out
    Of running such a rig.

The wind did blow, the cloak did fly,
    Like streamer long and gay,
Till, loop and button failing both,
    At last it flew away.

Then might all people well discern
    The bottles he had slung—
A bottle swinging at each side,
    As hath been said or sung.

The dogs did bark, the children scream'd,
    Up flew the windows all ;
And every soul cried out, " Well done !"
    As loud as he could bawl.

"Nur sanft und sachte." rief nun *John*,
  Vergeblich rief er dies,
Der Trab ward zum Galopp sehr bald,
  Trotz Zügel und Gebisz.

Er bückte sich, wie jeder musz,
  Der nicht grad' sitzen kann,
Und packt aus aller Macht die Mähn'
  Mit beiden Händen an.

Das Pferd, noch nie behandelt mit
  So wenigem Geschick,
Floh voller Furcht, und liesz im Lauf
  Die ganze Welt zurück.

Fort gings nun, über Hals und Kopf,
  Weg flog Hut und Perrück',
Im Anfang traümte *Gilpin* nicht
  Von solchem Miszgeschick.

Stark blies der Wind, der Mantel schwebt
  Gleich einem Fähnlein schön,
Bis endlich, da kein Knopf mehr hielt,
  Der Wind ihn weg thät wehn.

Jetzt sahe deutlich alles Volk,
  Wie er die Krüge schwang,
Auf beiden Seiten schaukeln sie,
  Wie ich schon sagt' und sang.

Die Hunde bell'n, die Kinder schrei'n,
  Die Fenster öffnet man,
Und alles schreit:—" O das ist brav !"
  So laut als Jedes kann.

Away went Gilpin—who but he?
  His fame soon spread around;
" He carries weight! he rides a race!
  'Tis for a thousand pound!"

And still, as fast as he drew near,
  'Twas wonderful to view,
How in a trice the turnpike-men
  Their gates wide open threw.

And now, as he went bowing down
  His reeking head full low,
The bottles twain behind his back
  Were shatter'd at a blow.

Down ran the wine into the road,
  Most piteous to be seen,
Which made his horse's flanks to smoke
  As they had basted been.

But still he seem'd to carry weight,
  With leathern girdle braced;
For all might see the bottle necks
  Still dangling at his waist.

Thus all through merry Islington
  These gambols he did play,
Until he came unto the Wash
  Of Edmonton so gay;

And there he threw the wash about
  On both sides of the way,
Just like unto a trundling mop,
  Or a wild goose at play.

Weg flog nun *Gilpin*—wer als er!
　　Sein Ruf gar schnell ward kund,
" Er trägt Gewicht!　Ein Wettritt ist's
　　Und zwar um Tausend Pfund?"

Und dann, so bald er nahe kam,
　　War's wundervoll zu sehn,
Wie gleich die Flügel an dem Thor
　　Für ihn weit offen stehn.

Doch als er bückte tief sein Haupt,
　　Wovon der Schweisz ihm flosz,
Zerschmettern beide Krüge sich,
　　Durch einen harten Stosz.

Mit Jammer sah' man, wie der Wein
　　Nun in die Strasze flosz,
Des Pferdes Seiten dampften sehr,
　　Wo sie der Wein begosz.

Er schien, als trüg' er noch Gewicht,
　　Noch hing am Gürtel fest,
Und baumelte auf jeder Seit'
　　Der Krüge Ueberrest.

So setzt' er durch ganz *Islington*
　　Die tollen Sprünge fort,
Bis zu der Wäsch' von *Edmonton*,
　　Dem schönen frohen Ort.

Die Wäsche warf er weit umher,
　　Mit schrecklichem Gewühl,
Als wäre sie ein Hudelwisch,
　　Und wilde Gans im Spiel.

At Edmonton his loving wife
    From balcony espied
Her tender husband, wondering much
    To see how he did ride.

" Stop, stop, John Gilpin !—Here's the house !"
    They all at once did cry ;
" The dinner waits, and we are tired ;"
    Said Gilpin : " So am I !"

But yet his horse was not a whit
    Inclined to tarry there ;
For why?—his owner had a house
    Full ten miles off, at Ware.

So like an arrow swift he flew,
    Shot by an archer strong ;
So did he fly—which brings me to
    The middle of my song.

Away went Gilpin out of breath
    And sore against his will,
Till at his friend Tom Callender's
    His horse at last stood still.

Tom Callender, amazed to see
    His neighbor in such trim,
Laid down his pipe, flew to the gate,
    And thus accosted him :

" What news ? what news? your tidings tell ;
    Tell me you must and shall—
Say why bare-headed you are come,
    Or why you come at all ?"

Sein theures Weib in *Edmonton*
  Erblickte vom Altan
Den lieben Mann, und sah' erstaunt
  Sein tolles Reiten an.

"Halt! halt! *John Gilpin!*—Hier ist's Haus"—
  Schrie'n alle fürchterlich;
"Die Mahlzeit wartet—wir sind müd!"
  Spricht *Gilpin:* "So bin ich!"

Jedoch sein Pferd war nicht geneigt
  Hier zu verweilen sehr;
Warum?—sein Herr besasz ein Haus
  Zehn Meilen ab—zu *Ware.*

Wie je ein Pfeil mit Kraft geschnellt
  Zum fernen Ziele drang,
So flog es—und dies bringet mich,
  Zur mitte vom Gesang.

Ganz athemlos musz *Gilpin* fort,
  Wiewohl er gar nicht will,
Bis an das Haus *Tom Callender's,*
  Dort stand das Pferd erst still.

Erstaunt sieht dieser seinen Freund
  In solchem Aufzug nah'n,
Legt weg die Pfeife, laüft an's Thor,
  Und red't ihn also an:

"Was gibt's? was gibt's—erzähl' es doch,
  Geschwind leg' alles dar!—
Warum kamst du baarhäuptig her?—
  Ja, warum kamst du gar?"—

Now Gilpin had a pleasant wit,
  And loved a timely joke;
And thus unto Tom Callender
  In merry guise he spoke:

" I came because your horse would come;
  And, if I well forebode,
My hat and wig will soon be here,
  They are upon the road."

Tom Callender, right glad to find
  His friend in merry pin,
Return'd him not a single word,
  But to the house went in;

Whence straight he came with hat and wig,
  A wig that flowed behind,
A hat not much the worse for wear,
  Each comely in its kind.

He held them up, and in his turn
  Thus show'd his ready wit:
" My head is twice as big as yours,
  They therefore needs must fit!

" But let me scrape the dirt away
  That hangs about your face;
And stop and eat, for well you may
  Be in a hungry case."

Said John: " It is my wedding-day,
  And all the world would stare,
If wife should dine at Edmonton,
  And I should dine at Ware."

John Gilpin liebte feinen Scherz,
    Auch fehlt's an Witz ihm nicht,
Daher er zu *Tom Callender*
    Gar spaszhaft also spricht:

" Ich kam, weil es dein Pferd gewollt,
    Und hör', mir ahnet was;
Hut und Perrück' sind auch bald hier,
    Denn *sie sind auf der Strass!*"

Tom Callender, froh, dasz sein Freund
    Noch kann so lustig sein,
Erwiedert nicht ein einzig's Wort,
    Und geht ins Haus hinein.

Hut und Perrücke bracht er gleich,—
    Voll Locken die Perrück',
Der Hut war noch in gutem Stand,
    Und zierlich jedes Stück.

Er hielt sie hin, und sprach sodann,
    Gar witzig, schlau, und fein;
" Mein Kopf miszt deinen zweimal auf,
    Drum sind sie nicht zu klein.

" Doch lasz mich nun dein Angesicht
    Vom Unflath auch befrei'n,
Bleib hier und isz,—ich denke wohl,
    Dasz du magst hungrig sein.

Spricht *John*.—" Heut ist mein Trauungstag,
    Die Leut' erstaunten sehr,
Speiszt meine Frau in *Edmonton*
    Und ich spisz hier in *Ware*."

So turning to his horse he said :
    " I am in haste to dine ;
'Twas for your pleasure you came here,
    You shall go back for mine."

Ah luckless speech, and bootless boast !
    For which he paid full dear ;
For, while he spake, a braying ass
    Did sing most loud and clear;

Whereat his horse did snort, as he
    Had heard a lion roar,
And gallop'd off with all his might,
    As he had done before.

Away went Gilpin, and away
    Went Gilpin's hat and wig ;
He lost them sooner than at first,
    For why?—They were too big.

Now Mrs. Gilpin, when she saw
    Her husband posting down
Into the country far away,
    She pull'd out half-a-crown ;

And thus unto the youth she said
    That drove them to the Bell,
" This shall be yours, when you bring back
    My husband safe and well."

The youth did ride, and soon did meet
    John coming back amain :
Whom in a trice he tried to stop,
    By catching at his rein ;

Zum Pferde redend, spricht er dann;
  "Zur Mahlzeit eile ich,
Für dein Vergnügen kam ich her,
  Du gehst zurück für mich—"

O leeres Wort! O eitler Ruhm!
  Er zahlte dafür baar;
Noch red't er, als ein Esel schrie
  Und sang gar laut und klar.

Drob schnaubt das Pferd, als ob ein Leu
  Ihm brüllte in das Ohr
Und galoppirt aus aller Macht
  Wie es gethan zuvor.

Und *Gilpin* ging—Hut und Perrück'
  Flog weg in kurzer Zeit,
Viel früher als das erste mal;
  Warum?—Sie war'n zu weit.

Frau *Gilpin*, als sie sahe, wie
  Ihr Mann gejagt davon
Weit in das Land,—zog sie heraus
  Gleich eine halbe Kron';

Und sprach zum Jüngling der sie fuhr,
  Mit kummervollem Blick,
"Die geb ich dir, bringst du den Mann
  Gesund und wohl zurück.

Der Jüngling ritt,—begegnet' ihm,—
  Und thät gern was er soll;
Er hascht *John Gilpin's* Pferd am Zaum,
  Doch, da ward's erst recht toll.

But not performing what he meant,
　　And gladly would have done,
The frighted steed he frighted more,
　　And made him faster run.

Away went Gilpin, and away
　　Went post-boy at his heels,
The post-boy's horse right glad to miss
　　The lumbering of the wheels.

Six gentlemen upon the road,
　　Thus seeing Gilpin fly
With post-boy scampering in the rear,
　　They raised the hue and cry:

" Stop thief! stop thief!—a highwayman!"
　　Not one of them was mute;
And all and each that pass'd that way
　　Did join in the pursuit.

And now the turnpike gates again
　　Flew open in short space;
The toll-men thinking as before
　　That Gilpin rode a race.

And so he did, and won it too,
　　For he got first to town;
Nor stopp'd till where he had got up,
　　He did again get down.

Now let us sing, " Long live the king.
　　And Gilpin long live he;
And when he next doth ride abroad.
　　May I be there to see."

Denn er vollbrachte nicht, was er
  Sehr gerne wollte thun,
Dadurch erschreckt er *Gilpin's* Pferd,
  Es lief noch stärker nun.

Weg flog nun *Gilpin!* und ihm folgt
  Der Postknecht auf dem Fusz,
Des Postknechts Pferd, froh, dasz es nicl
  Die Kutsche ziehen musz.

Sechs Herren auf der Strasze sah'n
  Wie *Gilpin* jagt vorbei,
Und wie der Postknecht ihn verfolgt,
  Die machten ein Geschrei;

"Halt an den Dieb, den Räuber dort!"
  Es schwieg nicht einer jetzt—
Von allen auf der Strasze ward
  Ihm eilends nachgesetzt.

Doch alle Thore öffnen sich
  Für ihn in kurzer Zeit,—
Man glaubt dasz *Gilpin*, immer noch
  Um eine Wette reit'.

Er that's,—gewann sie—kam zuerst
  Nun in die Stadt mit Sieg,
Und hielt nicht, bis, wo er begann
  Er von dem Pferde stieg.

Nun singt: "Der König lebe lang,
  John Gilpin leb'!—Juchhei!
Und wenn er wieder reiten wird,
  Wär' ich doch dann dabei!"
                        x

MORGETS UND OWETS.

The following elegiac idyl, in Pennsylvania German, is the creation of the late Rev. Emanuel Rondthaler, tutor in the Hall between 1832 and 1839; and we believe one of the first attempts to render that mongrel dialect the vehicle of poetic thought and diction. It is admitted into this repository for a consideration else than its literary merit; the language in which its sentiments are conveyed being that of the neighborhood of Nazareth in part, with whose population students at the Hall in all times were brought into frequent contact. Mr. Rondthaler's lyric is worded in the vernacular of these once so-called "Bushwhackers," between whom and the "Hallers" petty warfare has been waged from time immemorial. Of the origin of the long-cherished difference, history and tradition are silent. Perhaps it was a war of races, accountable only on the assumption of an instinctive antagonism. Perhaps the contest was provoked, for although the "Bushwhackers" were stigmatized as a semi-ferine race, they were a harmless, hard-working people, who gave generously of their orchards and rural stores until the "Hallers" aggravated them beyond endurance by persistent depredations on their choice apples and reserved chestnuts.

The touching appeal which the little poem makes to the finer feelings of our nature, through the medium of external objects most familiar and suggestive to the rustic, loses none of its power, although conveyed in the rude language of his every-day life; while the spirit of Christian faith and hope with which it is imbued reminds us forcibly of what we are apt to forget—that the diviner impulses of our spiritual being are shared alike by all classes of the human family.

MORGETS UND OWETS.

MORGETS scheint die Sunn so schö,
  Owets geht der gehl Mond uf,
Morgets leit der Dau im Glä,
  Owets drett mer drucke druf.

Morgets singe all die Feggle,
  Owets greyscht der Lawb-krott arg,
Morgets gloppt mer mit der Fleggle,
  Owets leit mer sho im Sarg.

Alles dut sich ennere do,
  Nix bleibt immer so wie nau ;
Wos' em Fräd macht, bleibt nett so,
  Werd gar arg bald harrt un rau—

Drowe werd es anners sein,
  Dart wo nau so blo aussickt ;
Dart is Morgets alles fein,
  Dart is Owets alles Lickt.

Morgets is dart Fräd die Fill,
  Owets is es o noch so ;
Morgets is ems Herz so still ;
  Owets is mer o noch fro.

Ach ! wie dut mer doch gelischte,
  Nach der blo'e Woning dart ;
Dart mit alle gute Ghrishte
  Fräd zu have—Roo als fort.

Wann sie mich ins Grab nei drage,
  Greint nett—denn ich habs so schö.—
Wann sie—" Ess is Owet !"—sage—
  Denkt—bei ihm is sell, " all one."

TRANSLATION.

In the morning the sun shines cheerful and bright.
   In the evening the yellow moon's splendor is shed ;
In the morning the clover's with dew all bedight,
   In the evening its blossoms are dry to the tread.

In the morning the birds sing in unison sweet,
   In the evening the frog cries prophetic and loud ;
In the morning we toil to the flail's dull beat,
   In the evening we lie in our coffin and shroud.

Here on earth there is nothing exempt from rude change—
   Nought abiding, continuing always the same ;
What pleases is passing,—is past ! oh how strange !
   And the joy that so mocked us is followed by pain.

But above 'twill be different, I very well know—
   Up yonder, where all is so calm and so blue !
In the morning there objects will be all aglow—
   In the evening aglow, too, with heaven's own hue.

In the morning up yonder our cup will be filled,
   In the evening its draught will not yet have been drain'd ;
In the morning our hearts will divinely be stilled,
   In the evening, ecstatic with bliss here unnamed.

And oh how I long, how I yearn to be there,
   Up yonder, where all is so calm and so blue !
With the spirits of perfected just ones to share
   Through eternity's ages joy and peace ever new.

And when to my grave I shall slowly be borne,
   Oh weep and lament not, for I am so blest !
And when "it is evening" you'll say—or, " 'tis morn"—
   Remember, for me there is nothing but rest !